Deleuze & Fascism

This edited volume deploys Deleuzian thinking to re-theorize fascism as a mutable problem in changing orders of power relations dependent on hitherto misunderstood social and political conditions of formation. The book provides a theoretically distinct approach to the problem of fascism and its relations with liberalism and modernity in both historical and contemporary contexts. It serves as a seminal intervention into the debate over the causes and consequences of contemporary wars and global political conflicts as well as functioning as an accessible guide to the theoretical utilities of Deleuzian thought for International Relations (IR) in a manner that is very much lacking in current debates about IR.

Covering a wide array of topics, this volume will provide a set of original contributions focused in particular upon the contemporary nature of war; the increased priorities afforded to the security imperative; the changing designs of bio-political regimes, fascist aesthetics; nihilistic tendencies and the modernist logic of finitude; the politics of suicide; the specific desires upon which fascism draws; and, of course, the recurring pursuit of power.

An important contribution to the field, this work will be of great interest to students and scholars of international relations, fascism and international relations theory.

Brad Evans is a Senior Lecturer in International Relations at the School of Sociology, Politics and International Studies, the University of Bristol.

Julian Reid is Professor of International Relations at the University of Lapland, Finland.

Interventions

Edited by:
Jenny Edkins, Aberystwyth University and Nick Vaughan-Williams,
University of Warwick

> As Michel Foucault has famously stated, 'knowledge is not made for under-
> standing; it is made for cutting.' In this spirit the Edkins–Vaughan-Williams
> Interventions series solicits cutting edge, critical works that challenge main-
> stream understandings in international relations. It is the best place to
> contribute post disciplinary works that think rather than merely recognize
> and affirm the world recycled in IR's traditional geopolitical imaginary.
>   Michael J. Shapiro, University of Hawai'i at Mãnoa, USA

The series aims to advance understanding of the key areas in which scholars
working within broad critical post-structural and post-colonial traditions have
chosen to make their interventions, and to present innovative analyses of
important topics.

Titles in the series engage with critical thinkers in philosophy, sociology,
politics and other disciplines and provide situated historical, empirical and
textual studies in international politics.

**Critical Theorists and International
Relations**
*Edited by Jenny Edkins and
Nick Vaughan-Williams*

Ethics as Foreign Policy
Britain, the EU and the other
Dan Bulley

**Universality, Ethics and
International Relations**
A grammatical reading
Véronique Pin-Fat

The Time of the City
Politics, philosophy, and genre
Michael J. Shapiro

**Governing Sustainable
Development**
Partnership, protest and power at
the world summit
Carl Death

Insuring Security
Biopolitics, security and risk
Luis Lobo-Guerrero

**Foucault and International
Relations**
New critical engagements
*Edited by Nicholas J. Kiersey and
Doug Stokes*

Deleuze & Fascism

Security: war: aesthetics

Edited by
Brad Evans and Julian Reid

Routledge
Taylor & Francis Group

LONDON AND NEW YORK

First published 2013
by Routledge
2 Park Square, Milton Park, Abingdon, Oxfordshire OX14 4RN

Simultaneously published in the USA and Canada
by Routledge
711 Third Avenue, New York, NY 10017

First issued in paperback 2014

Routledge is an imprint of the Taylor & Francis Group, an informa business

British Library Cataloguing in Publication Data
A catalogue record for this book is available from the British Library

Library of Congress Cataloging in Publication Data
Deleuze & fascism: security, war, aesthetics / edited by Brad Evans & Julian
Reid.
     pages cm. – (Interventions)
   Includes bibliographical references and index.
   1. Deleuze, Gilles, 1925-1995. 2. Fascism. 3. International relations. I.
Evans, Brad (International relations), editor of compilation. II. Reid, Julian
(Julian David McHardy), editor of compilation. III. Title: Deleuze and
fascism.
   JC481.D397 2013
   320.53'3–dc23
                  2012035531

ISBN 978-0-415-58967-3 (hbk)
ISBN 978-1-138-84048-5 (pbk)
ISBN 978-0-203-37470-2 (ebk)

Typeset in Times New Roman
by Taylor & Francis Books

For Michael Dillon

Contents

Contributors

Brad Evans is a Senior Lecturer in International Relations at the Global Insecurities Center, the School of Sociology, Politics and International Studies, the University of Bristol, UK. He has published extensively on the Liberal bio-politics of security, contemporary war and political violence, the politics of catastrophe, along with mediation's on post-liberal political thought. Brad is the author of numerous books and edited volumes, most recently including: *Liberal Terror* (Polity Press: 2013) and *Resilient Life: The Art of Living Dangerously* (forthcoming with Julian Reid, Polity Press: 2014). He is the Founder and Director of the Histories of Violence project (www.historiesofviolence.com) and a member of the Society for the Study of Bio-political Futures.

Julian Reid is Professor of International Relations at the University of Lapland, Finland. He taught previously at King's College London, Sussex University, and SOAS (School of Oriental and African Studies), University of London. He is the author of numerous studies of the liberal biopolitics of war including *The Liberal Way of War: Killing to Make Life Live* (co-authored with Michael Dillon) (New York and London: Routledge, 2009) and *The Biopolitics of the War on Terror: Life Struggles, Liberal Modernity, and the Defence of Logistical Societies* (Manchester and New York: Manchester University Press, 2009, 2007 and 2006).

Leonie Ansems de Vries is Assistant Professor of International Relations at the University of Nottingham Malaysia Campus. She holds a PhD from the Department of War Studies at King's College London. Her doctoral thesis draws upon insights from modern political theory, continental philosophy (especially Deleuze and Foucault) to produce a novel account of political life. At the heart of this research lies a concern with the notion of political life understood as a question of ordering and disordering: the management and disruption of conflicting claims regarding what life may be and become politically. Her current research continues the exploration of the relationship between politics and life from a multidisciplinary perspective. A second research strand interrogates the relationship between governance and resistance. Before joining the Malaysia Campus in 2011, Leonie taught at the Department of Politics and International Relations, Queen Mary University of London.

Ruth Kitchen is a researcher at the University of Leeds. Her work examines the relationships between twentieth- and twenty-first-century French literature and visual culture, critical and cultural theory, and historiography. She has published several articles on guilt in French literature and film concerning the Nazi Occupation of France. Her monograph, *A Legacy of Shame – French Narratives of War and Occupation*, adapted from her thesis, will be published with Peter Lang in 2013.

Erin Manning holds a University Research Chair in Relational Art and Philosophy in the Faculty of Fine Arts at Concordia University (Montreal, Canada). She is also the director of the *Sense Lab* (www.senselab.ca), a laboratory that explores the intersections between art practice and philosophy through the matrix of the sensing body in movement. In her art practice she works between painting, dance, fabric and sculpture (www.erinmovement.com). Current iterations of her artwork explore emergent collectivities through participatory textiles. Her project *Stitching Time* was presented at the 2012 Sydney Biennale and *The Knots of Time* will open the new Flax Museum in Kortrijk, Belgium, in 2014. Her extensive publications address movement, art, experience and the political through the prism of process philosophy, with recent work developing a notion of autistic perception and the more-than human.

Todd May is a Professor of Philosophy at Clemson University. He is the author of 10 books, including The Philosophy of Foucault, Gilles Deleuze, The Political Thought of Jacques Ranciere, Our Practices, Our Selves, and Death, and Friendship in An Age of Economics (2012). Todd's contemporary philosophical writings regularly feature in The New York Times 'The Stone' column.

Nicholas Michelsen was awarded his PhD by the Department of War Studies, King's College London, where he is currently a Teaching Fellow. He holds an MRes in War Studies and an MA in International Conflict Studies from Kings College London, and a BA(Hons) in International Relations and Philosophy from the University of Sussex.

Michael J. Shapiro is a Professor of Political Science at the University of Hawai'i, Mānoa. He has published extensively on areas of political theory and international politics. Among his recent publications are *Studies in Trans-disciplinary Method: After the Aesthetic Turn* (Routledge, 2012).

Geoffrey Whitehall is an Associate Professor of Political Science at Acadia University, NS, Canada. He teaches courses in Contemporary Political Theory, World Politics and Discourses of Cultures and Technology. His research explores Sovereignty and Pre-emptive Governance and the Aesthetics of International Politics. His publications have appeared in the journals *International Studies Perspectives, Theory and Event, Borderlands* and *Millennium*.

Introduction

Fascism in all its forms

Brad Evans and Julian Reid

The post-war Liberal imaginary is predicated on the doubly political and moral claim to have somehow overcome fascism. As Felix Guattari describes, 'we have been led to believe that fascism was just a bad moment we had to go through, a sort of historical error, but also a beautiful page in history for the good heroes ... that there were real antagonistic contradictions between the fascist Axis and the Allies' (Guattari 1995: 239–40). This book is dedicated to challenging the tenets of such a way of comprehending the differences between fascism and its liberal 'conquerors'. Indeed it is concerned not just with reposing the question of what it would mean already to have overcome fascism, nor simply with questioning the belief that we might still be able to overcome fascism in the future, so that even while recognizing our historical failures and present predicaments better, we might yet achieve a more effective overcoming of fascism. In contrast we are concerned with interrogating contemporary power relations as predicated on the *real* and *necessary* existence of fascism. The problem of fascism today cannot simply be addressed as that of the potential or variable return and reconstitution of fascism, as if fascism had ever, or could ever, 'disappear', only to return and be made again, like some spectral figure from the past. The problem of fascism cannot, we believe, be represented or understood as that of an historically constituted regime, particular system of power relations, or incipient ideology. Fascism, we believe, is as diffuse as the phenomenon of power itself. In other words we are here to explore 'not only historical fascism, the fascism of Hitler and Mussolini – which was able to mobilise and use the desire of the masses so effectively – but also the fascism in us all, in our heads, and in our everyday behaviour, the fascism that causes us to love power, to desire the very thing that dominates and exploits us' (Foucault 2000: xiii).

For the same reasons that power itself is an ineradicable condition of possibility not just for social relations, but relations as such, so fascism, also, must be understood as something elementary not just to political life, but life as such. Relations, fundamentally understood, in all their endless variations simply are fascist. Life, as well, is, we believe, fascist. There is always the desire for power underwriting life. For a life to be lived freely, it cannot fully exorcize the impulse towards or desire for power. With these axioms in mind, we have undertaken this book, with a view to shifting the theory of fascism in International Relations and other social scientific disciplines from their prevailing macro-historical moorings, and boorish preoccupation with interwar and Second World War Europe, to focus on the 'micro-fascism' that Michel Foucault alluded to in his short but brilliant preface to *Anti-Oedipus* (Foucault 2000), the book from which we and all the contributors to this volume have taken our leave in developing the approach that we have here (Deleuze and Guattari 2000). This is a formidable challenge, but it is one we embrace.

The authors of *Anti-Oedipus*, Gilles Deleuze and his collaborator Felix Guattari, sought to debunk the prevailing idea of fascism as either simply a political ideology perpetrated by a wicked elite upon the unwitting masses or a totalitarian mode of organization impressed upon an unintelligent and instrumentally subdued population, to understand it, in socially agential terms, as an expression of the desire of the masses; a 'desiring machine' as well as a 'war machine' which mobilizes every element of the desire of a people for its own repression and eventual destruction. As Brian Massumi describes, fascism, as understood by Deleuze and Guattari, 'is a manic attack by the body politic against itself, in the interests of its own salvation ... it is desire turned against itself' (Massumi 1999: 116). The task we and our collaborators have taken on, inspired by *Anti-Oedipus* as well as the larger corpus of work by Deleuze, in the first instance, is approaching the problem of fascism, thus, as a phenomenon of the desire for one's own repression in order that we might track 'down all varieties of fascism, from the enormous ones that surround and crush us to the petty ones that constitute the tyrannical bitterness of our everyday lives' (Foucault 2000: xiv). Fascism, therefore, in *all its forms*. We find insufficient the wide and diffuse range of both traditional representations of relations between fascism and modernity as some kind of aberration of the modern, as well as critical representations of the potential of humanity for some kind of evacuation of the modern, as if we might yet rid ourselves of the potential to be or become-fascist, by understanding modernity better. Neither of these ways of thinking about the problem of fascism will suffice, invested as each of them is in different ways, in an understanding of fascism as a contingent outcome of either modern power relations gone wrong, or modernity itself as a mistake that can yet be made good. We are seeking to break the mould, here then, with our own Deleuze-inspired account; the very first book, ever written on the precise subject of *Deleuze & Fascism*, by understanding fascism as elementary to politics and power relations *per se*.

We do not believe fascism to have been an event that can ever be historicized, reduced to a discrete time period or state, society and culture, but nor do we believe fascism to be somehow beyond representation. Fascism demands representation, naming and diagnoses, but at the same time such modes of representation, naming and diagnoses can only ever be historical, contingent to the form of fascism being addressed, and remembering, always, that fascism is by definition a multiplicitous phenomenon. Fascism is not, in other words, something that we ought ever to have conceived as being capable of conquering, and sticking with an old, tired and worn-out representation of fascism is the largest trap we have been concerned with avoiding. Fascism is a problem for us, but that does not turn it into a problem we believe we can 'solve'. The worst fascisms arise in response to problems that are poorly understood, and on the back of trite if well-meaning solutions. We are not problem-solvers of fascism. Fascism has no ready-made solution, for power and life have no ready-made solutions. We write to reproblematize it so that the ways in which we respond to it can do other forms of work in the world than simply reproduce the old formulae.

In more substantive terms we are focused here in this book on the transformations in the character of fascism created by the liberalization of modern states and societies, and we are committed to demonstrating the inherently fascist character of liberal modernity itself. As such the book has been edited with a view to developing a theoretically distinct approach not just to the problem of fascism, but liberalism. This is a book in a certain sense, then, about what we might call 'liberal fascism'. Our interrogation of the 'failures' of the liberal post-war project is fuelled by an understanding of fascism today not as a contingent outcome of liberalism's development and expansion, but as an expression of the ontological irreducibility of fascism for liberal power relations *per se*. Nazism was notoriously predicated on the belief that by promoting the security of the Aryan race above that of all other races, and indeed by doing away with other racial groups, so the biological life of the species would be improved. Liberalism and Nazism are not the same, but nor was Nazism the exception to liberalism. For the boundaries between such different but incestuously related biopolitical rationalities, concerned as they have been throughout their history, and as they still are today, with governing the human by weeding out and waging war upon 'the inhuman', are not just porous but infectious. In other words liberalism has to be comprehended not as exceptional to but coextensive with the very form of fascism it claims to have 'conquered'. We point this out not simply because we loathe and deplore liberalism. Even if we do. It is not that liberalism has a particular predisposition for becoming fascist. As we've already said, fascism is a phenomenon that has to be addressed, we believe, as a necessary element of all forms of power relations, which means at the very least all politics. Unless one believes in the possibility and desirability of living in a post-political world, fascism is a phenomenon one has to recognize as constitutive of political practice. It is not simply that we undertake a risk, even, of becoming fascist, in order to be and act as political subjects. Or that such a risk demands the development of an *ascesis*, or art of prevention or purification, in order to render the politics we practise less fascist. Our understanding of fascism is one of it being a necessary outcome, and effect, of being political. We say that fascism is in us, in a way to indicate that not only do we make fascism come about every bit as much as fascism makes us come about, nor that we all contain a potential to become fascist or behave fascistically, but that we exist and act politically only through practices that are themselves already fascist, with little potential to be otherwise. Politics demands of us that we not only desire but love power. Such a love cannot be acclaimed non-fascistically.

While our inspiration in developing this approach, and that of the authors of each of the subsequent chapters, stems from the philosophical and political ruminations on fascism of Deleuze, this way of reading Deleuze on the problem and phenomenon of fascism does make significant departures from existing attempts to glean from his texts what the nature of that problem and phenomenon are. A few before us have undertaken well-intended and worthy readings of Deleuze to demonstrate the extent to which the development of the power and expansion of the liberal world post-1945 cannot be disengaged from the fascist regimes they fought against in the mid-twentieth century. If that were the limit of our argument we would be as well to wrap up now and direct the reader to the many different texts in which this argument has already been diffusely made. Anyways, without reading Deleuze, that the boundaries between liberalism and fascism are porous is obvious by now in this era of global war without end, exercise of exceptional powers of internment without end, the utilization of the camp form, and widespread use of torture against innocents on a mass scale by liberal states and their proxies. Indeed, fascist discourses have only grown and become more engrained in tandem with the proliferation of liberal power relations in recent years to the extent that fascism today is fundamentally a banality of liberal biopolitics, nationally and internationally. Hannah Arendt had a great riff in her book on Eichmann on the 'banality of evil' to explain how the Holocaust was made possible not by fanatics committing exceptional acts but ordinary people going about their daily tasks (Arendt 2006). Such is precisely the case of liberal fascism today. Ride a London Tube train, observe the social surveillance, and you are witnessing a lynch mob in its molecular becoming. Indeed it is obvious to us that fascism today is rarely less pronounced and vicious than in the forms it takes not just among the ordinary, but in and among discourses and practices that declare themselves to be avowedly 'anti-fascist'. The consistent identification of the liberal project in the post-war era with the victim and survivor of the Holocaust is one of the key techniques with and through which liberalism has been able to elide its own fascism such that to be divested of the ability to lay claim to an identity of victim or survivor is itself to be at risk of being on the receiving end of liberal fascist violence. Nothing seems to us more degraded, more banal, than the laying claim to being 'anti-fascist' for the same reasons that nothing seems more undignified than the desire to speak on behalf of 'victims'. This book is not, and could not be further from, a work of anti-fascism. We are not anti-fascists because to believe in the integrity of such a moral claim is to be wilfully blind to the fascism that, necessarily, underwrites one's own political subjectivity. There is no political position with less integrity and compromise with that which it seeks to combat than the card-carrying 'anti-fascist'.

It is well documented, of course, how, in the wake of the 9/11 attacks on the World Trade Center in New York on 11 September 2001, President of the United States George W. Bush informed his public that they were now at war with 'Islamic fascists'. Invoking the problem of fascism in the way that he did was one among many crude means by which Bush attempted to secure the conditions for the horrible war and destruction of peoples that the United States and its liberal proxies have conducted over the last ten years, but the same crudity can be identified in discourses on the Left where fascism is still spoken about as if it were some limited position and practice that can be targeted as well as some behaviour or tendency of which the Left itself is capable, at least, of purifying itself. We are not purists for the same reasons we are not anti-fascists. Politics is fundamentally an impure practice. We are not interested, either, in pursuing the possibility of some kind of ascetic approach to politics and subjectivity on account of our impurity. We believe instead in the necessity of accepting impurity as a condition of possibility for political thought and action. That means accepting that we are all, always fascists of multiple kinds.

Nor, however, are we interested in this book in simply following Deleuze on the problem of fascism. Too much of the work that uses Deleuze for political theorization does so in a facile way, simply obeying the Word of the author in a, given the idiom, absurdly Oedipal fashion. In contrast, we are taking this as an opportunity to reassess the fundamentals that Deleuze, especially in his co-authored works with Felix Guattari, insisted on as a basic diagnosis of the roots of the problem of fascism. If we were simply to follow Deleuze we would of course diagnose fascism, in both its micro and macro forms, in all its forms, as an expression not just of the self-repressive body, but of the 'paranoiac body' – paranoia being that which, Deleuze argued, the body becomes when it can no longer tolerate life, and no longer cope with its excess of desire (Deleuze and Guattari 2000). As remedy we would wager on the schiz as the revolutionary figure and saviour of the fascist subject that Deleuze and his many followers have claimed it to be. However, we cannot agree with those who think that the problem of fascism today can be understood in the same ways that it was in the early 1970s when *Anti-Oedipus* was first published. The problem of fascism is bound up, as Michel Foucault also made clear in his preface to that work (Foucault 2000: xiii–xiv), with the problem of revolution and militancy, and these latter questions, of militancy and what a revolutionary politics might today entail, require entirely reproblematizing from our point of view. If we were simply to accept Deleuze's word as to the ways in which fascism circulates in power relations that function on the exclusion of and violence against life and desire then 'the Schiz', defined as it was by him as that peculiar figure that is permanently 'out for a stroll', given over to life, being led by its desire, would be attractive still to us. However, the problem of power relations in our age is different, qualitatively, to that which Deleuze confronted with incisive provocation.

We have never been so saturated in power relations configured by 'life' and so interpellated into the performance of following our 'desire', such that to attempt to refuse life and desire is itself to find oneself staring into the face of a fascist imperative to live more and desire better. Instead we will pose questions such as whether confronting liberal fascism today requires the cultivation of an intolerance of life, of the reduction of the human to a thing that merely lives. Whether or not, for that political project of resistance to liberal fascism, we need, in contrast with the schiz, a new delirium. Perhaps not a Body without Organs but Organs without a Body. Of which paranoia we might wager to be a highest power; what the organs become when they are divested of the body that makes them cling to their life functions. We might ask questions as to what a paranoiac life is and what a paranoiac body can do. The problem of fascism can no longer just be about dismantling binary constructions of insides and outside, getting out and about 'for a stroll', as if political subjectivity would be possible without its inner life, bereft of a discourse on its security. We do not buy the argument that security and the practice of securing equates automatically with fascism, directly translating 'into snuffing out wildly nomadic and disorganizing desires and destroying those who perpetrate them' (as made by Ravetto 2001: 229). Or put it this way: if it does, then we accept that an understanding of fascism as a form that is fundamental to politics as such needs to account for the equally multifarious politics of (in)security as under-stood through the framework of a *dispositif*. For the same reasons that as Deleuze himself argued 'no information could ever have defeated Hitler' (Deleuze 2000: 269), so we believe that no contestation of fascistic power relations is possible without a vernacular discourse on security and will to secure that which is at stake and imperilled by the constitution of a fascist regime of power.

These are our thoughts. Our way of buggering with Deleuze. As he would have wanted it. We find a lot of limitations to the work of Deleuze. Limits are sites of transgression and that's where we do much of our work in this text. We are not 'Deleuzians' or interested in trying to be. The 'fascist ethos' is as alive in Deleuzian critique, the policing of the boundaries of what Deleuze is said to have meant when he said this or that, and the endless exegesis of his Word. We are not writing here in order to make ourselves into Deleuzian fascists. It would be too easy to rattle out a standard Deleuzian take on the problem of fascism and account for a Deleuzian strategy for the delegitimation and struggle against fascism. Not that we necessarily disagree with the need and real exis-tence of such strategies. It is well attested, for example, that liberal states and the vast multiplicity of discursive forms and agents they have relied upon for their legitimacy post-1945 have continued to preserve a 'fascist ethos' by calling on many of the same narratives and calls to arms against 'inhu-man' enemies on which earlier fascist regimes, especially Nazism, relied. Of course they have, we know that, and have been saying that all along. We admire Deleuze-inspired authors such as Kriss Ravetto who have argued for the necessity of a strategy of 'delegitimation of the modernizing process and its narrativizing project', and for an understanding of the sources of fascism as residing in the reduction of multiplicity to unity itself (Ravetto 2001: 233). Indeed, there is lots of evidence and support to be found for such an approach in Deleuze's works. In his two-volume work on *Cinema*, for example, Deleuze argued that the problem of fascism was rooted, at source, in the classically and, prior to 1945, widely perpetrated political belief in the unanimity of 'the people' and its organic capacity to become true unto itself. It was the hideousness and dangers of that belief in the unity of 'the people' that was, he argued, destroyed by the experience of fascism in Europe during the mid-twentieth century, as well as the exposure of the extent of the European colonial legacy and the continued racisms and exclusions on which US sovereignty remained based. That experience in turn generated, he argued, in the cinematic medium, a shift from 'true' to 'false narration', reflecting a relative loss of faith in the potential for unity on which the ideal of 'the people' had classically drawn. The Holocaust, especially, had exposed the violence which a typified people, mystified to the point of assurance in its own coherence, could do to whoever does not meet the criteria of its essential type, and thus cinema was called upon to reinvent itself so that it would no longer perpetrate the myth of a true narration through which the temporality of a people or its individual characters could be represented as synchronized. Ravetto's analysis and that of practically all of the Deleuzian literature on this thematic of cinema and political aesthetics has bought into this understanding of what fascism was and what has to be done, politically and aesthetically, to avoid its 'return'.

There is an irony here, though, not just to the ways in which authors such as Ravetto have followed the Word of Deleuze, but also to the ways in which, by doing so, they have bought into an historicized understanding of the nature of fascism as such. For such a simplistic way of representing fascism, as something that 'happened', in particular spaces and times, and dividing the fascism of past time from that of present time and the question of future time, does an immense injustice to the greater complexities of the theory of fascism suggested by Deleuze's collaborative works with Guattari. It is not that we think the *Cinema* works are of no or even less value for the development of our own Deleuze-inspired take on fascism. Indeed, we have been at pains, in directing our collaborators in this text, to make them engage more fully with that element of Deleuze's theorization. However, there is a desperate need for creative work at the interstices of these different works of Deleuze, in order to produce new work of greater coherence and ambition than any of them produce by themselves. Also, we believe in the necessity of questioning the problematization of fascism as offered by Deleuze in the *Cinema* works on account of its outdatedness. Deleuze's evocation of post-1945 cinema as responding to a call to struggle against the fascistic violence of imposition of false unanimity upon peoples contrasts, at the very least, with the desire to establish some revised account of the terms and conditions for solidarity in struggles with liberal regimes that are as diversifying and life affirming as they are unifying and death instilling (Reid 2010; Reid 2006; Dillon and Reid 2009; Badiou 2003: 11). So our questions become how does the reproblematization of political struggle, consequent upon history and the growth and expansion of liberal power relations, affect our understanding of the politics of Deleuze's account of the problem of fascism in the twenty-first century? Is Deleuze's thesis concerning the paranoiac nature of fascism and the militant and revolutionary potential of the schiz still convincing?

Todd May kicks us off by reproblematizing the differences between Deleuze's understanding of fascism as a phenomenon of desire and the more traditional Marxist account of its roots in ideology and belief. May recognizes the salience while seeking to transcend the limits of both approaches by theorizing the importance of practices to fascism in the context of contemporary America. As he argues, fascism emerges principally in the practices in which we engage. Not because we desire fascism but because what we desire is fascistic, and not because we believe in fascism but because what we believe is fascistic. In essence May argues that Deleuze was only half right. People do not just desire fascism. Instead, they are committed to various practices that they believe to be important for who they are. Anything that interferes with those practices is seen as a threat. In particular contexts those practices can therefore become fascist, as was the case, he argues, in the United States between 2001 and 2008. If it remains the case that having a commitment to those practices is a matter of desire, so it also remains the case that those practices cannot change without people's awareness. Hence, for May, to understand properly the contemporary relevance of Deleuze's provocation we need to supplement his theory of desire with a Foucauldian view of the history of practices in order to understand the fascism of the everyday.

Michael Shapiro continues the analysis of the fascistic dimensions of the United States through an examination of the aesthetic practices that comprise it. As Shapiro argues, forms of fascism pervade post-war America operating in production of aesthetic subjects, but these are not the fascisms of total war. Indeed these are fascisms concerned with the maintenance of liberal peace rather than simply the mobilization for war. Attempts to conserve the historical definition of what constitutes both a fascist and an anti-fascist aesthetics should be seen, therefore, Shapiro argues, as expressions of the new fascism. Shapiro's evident motivation here is to salvage something of the political out of this nihilistic ruination. What we may term a will to counter the progressive nothingness that grows in the face of localized anxiety. Developing his earlier theory of the 'cinematic heterotopia', which effectively reintroduced political agency into the otherwise dormant discipline of film studies, one that simply portrayed the audience as passive subjects, Shapiro detects in the works of Syberberg and Philip K. Dick, especially, 'counters' to the new fascism. As Shapiro explains, countering the new fascism requires rejecting any attempt to diagnosis it as arising out of particular states of mind or expression of concern for deviant subjectivities, to focus instead on how such diagnoses and securitizations of fascist deviancy operate themselves within essentially fascist registers. Only when we recognize the complicity of hackneyed understandings of the problem of fascism with the actualization of the new fascism will we become able to speak of an anti-fascist aesthetic, Shapiro argues.

Brad Evans follows directly on from Shapiro's contribution to pursue further the nature and logics of liberal fascism. Concerned with the links between micro-fascist desires and macro-fields of political formation, Evans attends to the gradual capitalisation of peace witnessed in the age of liberal dominance. Of crucial significance here, Evans argues, is the displacement of geopolitical territorial concerns with global biopolitical logics of survivability and the impact this has upon the microphysics of power. This permits a biopolitical reading of fascism as societies' wider political functions are openly recruited into a planetary war effort in all our names and for all our sakes. It also provides a novel interpretation of Oedipalization as fascism appears to be an emergent problem bound inextricably to the permanent emergency of our radically inter-connected age. While the contemporary operations of power are altogether contingent, Evans is nevertheless troubled by a more prevailing historical remnant – namely the moral entrapments set by Immanuel Kant. Although Kant's legacy is often associated with the planetary virtues of lasting peace, Evans traces the inauguration of the biopolitical imperative to 'make life live' to the Kantian moral revolution in thought. This biopolitical reading of fas-cism proves telling. With life haunted by its own potentiality, the desire for security is effectively undermined by the very ontopolitical commitments a Kantian-inspired liberal account of life holds true. Securitization thus becomes a more important strategic game as we move beyond a Schmittian paradigm for global affairs into an age dominated by an imperative the mask of mastery of which is to render everything potentially endangering. Such is the story, Evans argues, of liberal fascism.

Geoffrey Whitehall explores further the challenges of liberal fascism by critiquing the doctrine of pre-emption that infamously became the hallmark of the George Bush, Jr, regime. At the heart of liberal fascism, Whitehall argues, is the way in which different logistical movements are learning to coor-dinate, communicate and integrate with an increasingly comprehensive degree of optimization and efficiency. No longer torn between war and peace, liberal fascism functions in the logistical assemblages that constitute the war/peace relation in favour of the former. Central to this assemblage is the concept of the 'global triage' which demands a shift away from the logic of politics to the logic of movement. For Whitehall, two key features of the triage are pre-emption, which pushes the decision into a non-political time, and technology, which enacts those decisions as if through habit. Having explained the sig-nificance of this to our understanding of security, war and power, Whitehall concludes by looking at the way in which the cultivated desire for human optimizations and efficiencies also amplifies a kind of self-hatred of humans and humanity. Liberal fascism, as such, is rooted in this logistical habit that constitutes a human desire to be more human. It desires killing machines that save lives in the name of humanity.

Julian Reid examines Deleuze's account of the roles of cinema as a source of resistance to fascism, focusing on his celebration of the post-war 'cinema of the seer' and the 'people of seers' that Deleuze argued populate it. Seers are characters who have lost the power of action only to gain a more worldly power of (in)sight. Characters for whom the disciplinary organization of the senses necessary for participation in collective mobilizations has not simply broken down but has been displaced by an intense power to see the hitherto unseen. Post-war cinema shows us seers and in doing so, Deleuze argues, underlines the potential for resistance to fascistic imperatives to mobilize and collectivize entailed in our own 'becoming visionary or seer' (Deleuze 1989: 21). It encourages in us the power to see the world for what it is in a way denied to us while we remain in the sensori-motorised relation with the world celebrated in fascist aesthetics. While partially convincing as a response to the historical fascism of the mid-twentieth century, Reid argues that Deleuze's understanding of both fascism and the resistance of the seer are outdated and no longer work in the context of the forms of liberal fascism that organize power relations today. Nevertheless, as Reid shows, when we look at cinema today, we can see that it has responded to these new challenges in ways unforeseen and unexamined by Deleuze. Focusing not just on the figure of 'the seer' but its relations with 'the cretin' in the Dogme classic *Festen*, Reid spins the relation between seeing and creineity in a manner that overcomes some of the limits of Deleuze's own analysis as well as making more sense in the context of the particular forms that liberal fascism is taking today.

Erin Manning's intervention opens onto Ari Folman's *Waltz with Bashir*, exploring how the film resists the fascism of liberal humanism. Through a close reading of Deleuze's *Logic of Sense* and his *Cinema* texts, paired with an engagement with a film that traces a complex history (that of the Sabra and Shatila massacre), Manning traces the dangers of fascism as they surface within *Waltz with Bashir*, and proposes a micropolitical reading that opens onto the possibility of a different politics through its deployment of what Deleuze called 'the power of the false'. Fascist aesthetics are, as Deleuze argued, underwritten by a suicidal myth of 'true narration'; the idea of a world in which the contingencies of life will be gradually subject to order so that the transcendental truth of the fascist subject will eventually be secured and the stories of the past will gradually be given their coherence through the completion of action in the present. Fascism prophesizes its end and moves toward it with suicidal certainty. As Manning argues, *Waltz with Bashir* flirts with these tendencies but ultimately resists them. Engaging with while evading them, it works to produce something quite different from the microfascisms that lure it: an uncertain field, a memory that leads nowhere but to its dynamic futurity. Thus is it, as Manning argues compellingly, that *Waltz with Bashir* refuses both fascism as well as any easy solution to it. A film that offers no promise of security from fascism, nor even the certainty that it is not fascism that is present in it, but which nevertheless, in that uncertainty, offers itself as a politics in the making.

Leonie Ansems de Vries exposes the difficulties of committing to a politics that prioritizes lines of flight, given that Deleuze argued fascism itself to operate on such lines. How, she asks, can we resolve the paradox of life's tendency to create, order and destroy on the same line(s)? Can a politics that prioritizes the creative potentials of the line of flight escape the liberal fascism of emergency governance, which operates on a very similar understanding of life's emergent properties? The political *problematique* that de Vries articulates here is challenging. If what holds the most promising creative potential also carries the most serious danger of destruction, and if the course of movement can neither be controlled or predicted, how is it possible to produce a politics of affirmative becoming without also becoming fascist? In order to draw out the stakes of this play – its fascistic dangers as well as its political promise, de Vries engages Deleuze and Guattari's politics of lines by connecting it, first, to their biophilosophy revolving around the notion of the milieu and, second, to the Spinozan ethics of bodies they produce. This leads her to question whether or not Spinozan ethico-politics of bodies understood in terms of relations of movement/rest and powers to affect/to be affected can hold the promise of a life beyond fascism. Through lines, milieux and movements, she argues that while the subject is capable of *becoming* different to fascistic performances, it remains impossible to *be* free from fascism. This leaves us on uncertain lines that demand our continued vigilance or else we become that which we believe to be politically abhorrent.

Nicholas Michelsen demonstrates that the Deleuzoguattarian schema is an effective conceptual tool box for mapping forms of fascism other than Nazism. Providing a novel reading of the cartographical nature of Deleuze and Guattari's account of Fascism, Michelsen addresses the three lines their work proposes to explore its relevance to our understanding of the politics of suicide. Focusing on self-immolation proves significant since it highlights how their theory of deterritorialization reveals qualitative differences. Michelsen therefore responds here to the key critiques levelled at the theory of fascism developed in *Capitalism and Schizophrenia* by emphasizing the inadequate consideration given by scholars, especially Eugene Holland, to the third (suicidal) line in the schema. He argues that only with attention to the suicidal line can the utility of the Deleuzoguattarian account of fascism be understood. That utility is demonstrated for Michelsen through mapping the concrete case of Japanese fascism, and the tokkōtai or 'special-attack' suicide units of the Pacific War, along the more purposeful lines proposed in *A Thousand Plateaus*. The implication being, as Michelsen writes, 'the terrifying cold peace of deterrence has now passed, but this certainly does not mean that the third line has *disappeared* from contemporary politics. It is rather conjugated anew. Deleuze and Guattari's statement that late-capitalist global order is 'post-fascist' is explicitly *not* positing the rise of a non-fascist order', Michelsen makes clear. 'Rather fascism continues directly into the post-fascist assemblage by way of global innovations of the suicidal line of flight.'

Ruth Kitchen completes our volume by examining fascist violence and aesthetics in French cultural memory through the lens of post-war cinema. Exploring the 'four dangers' of fascism identified by Deleuze and Guattari in *A Thousand Plateaus*, she offers a compelling reading of two films, *The Raven* (*Le Corbeau*) and *Hidden* (*Caché*). These films, released in 1943 and 2005, respectively, refer to two conflicts in French history that have left long-lasting scars on cultural memory – namely, the Nazi Occupation of France (1940–44) and the Algerian War (1954–62). The political contexts in which these films were made were different. Nevertheless, through an examination of their digenetic and cinematic techniques, Kitchen reveals meaningful resonances that traverse the temporality of each production. Drawing in particular upon Deleuze and Guattari's attention to the micro-physical techniques of power and their concomitant applicability to the world of representation, her analysis illustrates how micro-fascist trajectories (low-level fascist acts, attitudes and manifestations) blur the spatial and temporal boundaries of inside and outside, abbreviated in her contribution, to 'inside-out'. In doing so, Kitchen traces the connections between past and contemporary fascisms in filmic techniques and French cultural memory to offer a poignant analysis of fascist aesthetics in the twenty-first century.

References

Arendt, H. *Eichmann in Jerusalem* (London: Penguin, 2006)

Badiou, A. *Saint Paul: The Foundation of Universalism* (Stanford: Stanford University Press, 2003)

Deleuze, G. *Cinema 2: The Time-Image* (London: Athlone Press, 1989)

——*Cinema 2: The Time-Image* (London: Athlone Press, 2000)

Deleuze, G. and Guattari, F. *Anti-Oedipus: Capitalism & Schizophrenia* (London: Athlone Press, 2000)

Dillon, M. and Reid, J. *The Liberal Way of War: Killing to Make Life Live* (New York and London: Routledge, 2009)

Foucault, M. 'Preface' to Gilles Deleuze and Felix Guattari, *Anti-Oedipus: Capitalism & Schizophrenia* (London: Athlone Press, 2000)

Guattari, F. *Chaosophy* (New York: Semiotext, 1995)

Massumi, B. *A User's Guide to Capitalism and Schizophrenia: Deviations from Deleuze and Guattari* (Cambridge, Mass. and London: MIT Press, 1999)

Ravetto, K. *The Unmaking of Fascist Aesthetics* (Minneapolis and London: University of Minnesota Press, 2001)

Reid, J. 'Of Nomadic Unities: Gilles Deleuze on the Nature of Sovereignty' (*Journal of International Relations and Development* Vol.13 No.4, 2010)

——*The Biopolitics of the War on Terror: Life Struggles, Liberal Modernity and the Defence of Logistical Societies* (Manchester and New York: Manchester University Press, 2006).

1   Desire and ideology in fascism

Todd May

> Reich is at his profoundest as a thinker when he refuses to accept ignorance or
> illusion on the part of the masses as an explanation of fascism, and demands
> an explanation that will take their desire into account, an explanation for-
> mulated in terms of desire: no, the masses were not innocent dupes; at a cer-
> tain point, under a certain set of conditions, they *wanted* fascism, and it is this
> perversion of the desire of the masses that needs to be accounted for.
>
> (Deleuze and Guattari 1977: 29)

It is the task of this paper to show that the above quote is exactly half right.
Fascism is a matter of desire. However, it is not only that; it is also a matter of
ignorance or illusion. In fact, it arises at the point at which desire and ignorance and/or knowledge arise. In order to show this, we will contrast Deleuze
and Guattari's thought with that of a contemporary journalist who, to my
knowledge, has not been brought into productive discussion with contemporary
French thought. In *What's the Matter with Kansas?* Thomas Frank argues
that it is precisely a matter of ignorance or illusion (and for Frank, specifically, ideology) that is operative in the dominance of conservative thought in
America's heartland. It is because the masses have been duped into believing
an ideology contrary to their interests that Republicans have come to dominate that part of the country. As with Deleuze and Guattari, this paper will
argue that Franks is exactly half right.

In order to place these two halves into a proper whole, we will need to appeal
to a picture of desire and illusion that roots them in human practice. It is
through a conception of practice that we can recognize that, in a sense, people
can, under certain conditions, want fascism. This is true even though people rarely
tell themselves that it is fascism that they want. Again, it is through a conception
of practice that we can understand how people can be duped into endorsing
fascism, even when it is against their interest. The conception of practice to
be developed here will have affinities with the thought of Michel Foucault.
Although Foucault does not offer a theoretical articulation of this conception,
it can be said to be operative particularly in his more genealogical work.

In order to approach these ideas, I will start with a short summary of
Deleuze and Guattari's treatment of desire and then of Franks's treatment of

illusion. The goal is simply to situate the key elements of these discussions as a backdrop for the positive conception of practice to be developed here. Then I will return to these elements in order to show their proper place in that conception and, one hopes, to show the half-rightedness of each of these treatments. My claim for the alternative conception will not come in the form of an argument. I do not try to show that either Deleuze and Guattari or Franks is half-mistaken. Rather, I seek to put in place a conception of human practice that is compelling enough that the way I situate desire and illusion will also seem compelling. That is to say, in keeping with Deleuze's dictum in *Dialogues*, rather than arguing at length against the reduction of fascism either to desire or to illusion, I will mostly 'go on to something else' (Deleuze and Parnet 1987: 1).

For Deleuze and Guattari, fascism, like much else in human commitment, is not a matter of ignorance or mistaken reflection. This is in keeping particularly with Deleuze's Nietzschean orientation toward human consciousness: that it is secondary or even epiphenomenal. For Deleuze, much of what makes us tick is unconscious. Consciousness comes afterwards. The vast majority of human experience and motivation happens outside our reflective awareness. 'Underneath the self which acts are little selves which contemplate and which render possible both the action and the active subject. We speak of our "self" only in virtue of these thousands of little witnesses which contemplate within us: it is always a third party who says "me"' (Deleuze 1994: 75).

This idea finds expression in *Anti-Oedipus'* central claim that 'the social field is immediately invested by desire, that it is the historically determined product of desire, and that libido has no need of any mediation or sublimation, any psychic operation … *There is only desire and the social, and nothing else*' (Deleuze and Guattari 1977: 29). We must be careful in understanding this citation. It could appear to be more Rousseauian than it is. If we take Deleuze and Guattari to mean that there is only desire on the one hand and the social on the other, it would be only a short step to thinking that the social is an evil that represses desire. This would align their thought with Rousseau's idea (at least in some of his moods) that organized society represses the natural goodness of human being.

However, this would be to forget the central idea of *Anti-Oedipus*: that desire is productive. If there is only desire and the social, it is because desire produces the social. Rather than, as with psychoanalytic theory, desire being desire *for* something, desire directly creates its objects. We can recognize here Deleuze's distinction between the virtual and the actual. The actual is a product of the virtual. The virtual is a field of difference from which all actuality arises. The actual, in turn, emerges from the virtual, while still retaining the virtual within it. In the same way, desire produces the social. Now it may be that the social produced by desire in turn represses or transforms or distorts desire, as the authors argue Oedipus does, but this does not mean that the social is exterior to desire, or that it comes from something or somewhere else. As Deleuze insists throughout his career, there is no transcendence, only immanence. Deleuze and Guattari note in *What is Philosophy?* of all the illusions of philosophy, 'First of all there is the illusion of transcendence, which, perhaps, comes before all the others' (Deleuze and Guattari 1994: 49). To say that there is only desire and the social, then, is to say that there is only desire and what it creates, which includes the social.

On this view, if there is a problem of fascism, it is a problem of desire rather than of illusion or ideology. 'It is not a question of ideology. There is an unconscious libidinal investment of the social field that coexists, but does not necessarily coincide, with preconscious investments, or with what preconscious investments "ought to be." That is why, when subjects, individuals, or groups act manifestly counter to their class interests ... it is not enough to say: they were fooled, the masses have been fooled' (Deleuze and Guattari 1977: 104). The picture Deleuze and Guattari are trying to overcome here is a traditional Marxist one. On this picture, the reason the masses do not immediately seek their own interests – which would necessarily be revolutionary ones – is that they have been ideologically deceived. They have been convinced that their interests are aligned with, rather than contrary to, the interests of the ruling class. If this is right, the political task would be to educate the masses, to get them to recognize their true interests. Otherwise put, the first task of political struggle would be to overcome the ideological blinders that have prevented the masses from seeing their true interests.

The problem with this picture is, in Deleuze and Guattari's view, that it sees things the wrong way around. It is not that we come to desire fascism rather than revolution because we mistakenly believe that fascism is good for us. Rather, it is because we become invested in fascism that we come to believe in it. Desire as a form of unconscious creation and investment comes first. In fact, from this perspective it does not even matter whether we believe in fascism. We can be entirely cynical and believe in nothing at all. Politics is not a matter of belief; it is a matter of what we desire. To ask why it is that the masses form beliefs that are against their own interests is to ask the wrong question; it is to ask a question at the wrong level. 'We see the most disadvantaged, the most excluded members of society invest with passion the system that oppresses them, and where they always *find* an interest in it, since it is here that they search for and measure it. Interest always comes after' (Deleuze and Guattari 1977: 346).

Even to ask why we desire fascism is to mistake the political project. The goal instead, which is the project of schizoanalysis, is to recognize the character of libidinal investments and then to see what can be done to make those investments more revolutionary. 'The first positive task consists in discovering in a subject the nature, the formation, or functioning of *his* desiring-machines, independent of any interpretations' (Deleuze and Guattari 1977: 322). The second task is 'to reach the investments of unconscious desire of the social field, insofar as they are differentiated from the preconscious investments of interest, and insofar as they are not merely capable of counteracting them, but also of coexisting with them' (Deleuze and Guattari 1977: 350). Rather than interpreting reality for the masses so they that can come to see what is oppressing them, to recognize the fascism which they have been duped into embracing, schizoanalysis aims to discover the particular investments one makes into the social field and then to counter them with other, more revolutionary, investments.

This, I would argue, is why *Anti-Oedipus* is written in the way that it is. There has, of course, been much commentary on the style of the book: its energy, its use of curse words, its slash-and-burn treatment of Lacan and others. However, if we treat the style as something exterior to its message, we miss the point of that style. If the political goal were one of convincing people to believe otherwise than they do, then there might be something juvenile about the writing, but that is not the political goal. Rather, it is to get people's desire going in another direction. *Anti-Oedipus* seeks to realign our desire more than our belief. It seeks to follow its own message that we ask not what something means but how it works. That is why, when Foucault claims in the preface to *Anti-Oedipus* that it is 'a book of ethics' (Deleuze and Guattari 1977: xiii), he is right on target. It is a book that seeks to get us to live differently, not by convincing us of better ways to live, but by offering desire (as well as philosophy and critical social thought) another way to invest in the social field, which is to say another way to create.

If, for Deleuze and Guattari, 'the concept of ideology is an execrable concept that hides the real problems' (Deleuze and Guattari 1977: 344), for Thomas Frank ideology or illusion is precisely the heart of the matter. In *What's the Matter with Kansas? How Conservatives Won the Heart of America*, Frank seeks to understand the Republican strategy from the Regan years of the 1980s to the Bush years of the early 2000s (the book was published in 2004, prior to the second term of the Bush administration), to win the support particularly of middle America and, for Frank's purposes, of Kansans. What puzzles him, which is not dissimilar to what puzzles Deleuze and Guattari, is how people can be brought to support policies that are directly opposed to their interests. Where Deleuze and Guattari undercut the primacy of the concept interests, however, Franks seeks instead to remain precisely on that terrain. His strategy is to show that by focusing on certain cultural issues, the Republicans have been able to garner support for their economic programs, which is really what motivates them:

> The movement's basic premise is that culture outweighs economics as a matter of public concern ... Over the last three decades they have smashed the welfare state, reduced the tax burden on corporations and the wealthy, and generally facilitated the country's return to a nineteenth-century pattern of wealth distribution ... The leaders of the backlash may talk Christ, but they walk corporate.
>
> (Frank 2004: 6)

Frank's critique can be seen as part of Marxist tradition of ideology critique, although he is not, to my knowledge, a Marxist. His view is that by getting people to focus on what have come to be called 'wedge issues' – abortion, homosexuality, violence and sex in movies and on television, evolution, etc. – they can be enlisted in support of the Republicans, for whom these issues matter less than transferring wealth to the economic elites. In fact, as Frank points out, there has been very little change on the wedge issues over the years. When Republicans assume office, they rarely give more than lip service to those issues. (Abortion may be a bit of an exception here, although it is still fundamentally available to most women, even if it is more difficult to obtain.) On the other hand, there has been a massive transfer of wealth from the poor and middle class to the rich, in accordance with Republican economic policies.

This massive transfer of wealth has been devastating for Kansas. While companies that locate in Kansas receive various economic perks, Kansans find themselves in dire economic circumstances. In Kansas in particular, economic deregulation has led to extraordinary wealth for agribusiness, while leaving most Kansans far worse off economically. 'Indeed, over two-thirds of Kansas communities lost population between 1980 and 2000, some by as much as 25 percent. I am told that there are entire towns in the western part of the state getting by on Social Security; no one is left there but the aged. There are no doctors, no shoe stores. One town out here even sold its public school on eBay' (Frank 2004: 60). What Frank describes has not, of course, been limited to Kansas. David Harvey, for instance, who writes more self-consciously in the Marxist tradition, has detailed a global shift of wealth during the course of the neoliberal period (dating roughly from the 1980s to the present). 'After the implementation of neoliberal policies in the late 1970's, the share of national income of the top 1 per cent of income earners in the US soared, to reach 15 per cent (very close to its pre-Second World War share) by the end of the century ... And when we look further afield we see extraordinary concentrations of wealth and power ... ' (Harvey 2005: 16–17).

How has this transfer of wealth been able to go unopposed by those who have been its donors? What is the role of cultural wedge issues in blunting this opposition? For Franks, the wedge issues help erect a distinction between two kinds of people, those elites and us regular folks. Some of us regular folks may have money, but we've earned it the old-fashioned way. Those other folks are just lucky, and don't deserve what they have. 'Class, conservatives insist, is not really about money or birth or even occupation. It is primarily a matter of authenticity ... In red land both workers and their bosses are supposed to be united in disgust with those affected college boys at the next table, prattling on about French cheese and villas in Tuscany and the big ideas for running things that they read in books' (Frank 2004: 113–14). Wedge issues, then, function as ideology. They do not so much *cover up* the fact that there are disparities of wealth as *contextualize and minimize* it.

For the Republican strategists, wedge issues don't operate simply by getting one to focus attention on cultural issues while the economic disparities are being created. On the contrary, these disparities are being created openly. In order to be able to do so, Republicans operate by creating and/or reinforcing a particular sense of identity among those in what are called the 'red' states. That identity consists in humility as opposed to arrogance, reverence as opposed to atheism, and 'above all, *a red-stater is a regular, down-home working stiff*, whereas a blue-stater is always some sort of pretentious paper shuffler' (Frank 2004: 23). Once this identity is created, wealth can be transferred and people impoverished as long as that transfer is being made to others who are just as 'red' as oneself. Moreover, if there is blame to be assigned for the circumstances in which one finds oneself, it belongs not to those who share one's identity but instead to those who do not. As I write these words in May 2010, the Tea Party stands as exemplary of this element of Franks's analysis, blaming Washington, Wall Street and immigrants for the current economic straits of the United States. While the last of these is not an elite 'blue' group, it is a population that is said to be favored by that group because it doesn't understand the trouble caused to real people by immigrants, who, after all, are not really part of 'us.'

We might pause a moment here to consider the relationship between two terms I have invoked together: illusion and ideology. Frank does not make the distinction, although it is perhaps worth marking. Ideology is a matter of beliefs. However, of course, that doesn't distinguish it from science or the study of ethics or anything else with an epistemological character, including illusion. The unique character of ideology is its way of working with beliefs. It works by getting people to develop certain beliefs that will have the effect of making other things happen, things that are the real goal of those instilling the beliefs (or of those who, while not seeking to instill them, still benefit from them). Ideology, then, does not have to be a matter of illusion. One can believe, for instance, that abortion is wrong and also believe, correctly, that liberals support abortion rights, but if one votes out of these beliefs for someone who, while opposing abortion, is more interested in supporting policies that enrich the wealthy, then one is subject to ideology. Opposition to abortion becomes ideological in character.

Often, however, ideology is aligned with illusion. In Frank's analysis, the creation of 'red state' and 'blue state' identities in order to support conservative policies involves not only correct beliefs but illusory ones as well. For instance, one belief underlying support for Republican policies is that a free market will make life better for 'down-home working stiffs.' Of course, it has not. This is an illusion. As we have seen, it is a persistent illusion, since it remains strong in the face of all evidence to the contrary.

Moreover, there can be something illusory in the ideological use of abortion as well. If the Republican strategy of wedge issues uses abortion and identity in order to press an economic agenda, and if, as Frank seems to imply, their real concern is not at all with the former but only with the latter, then those who vote Republican are under the illusion that those they vote for will press their causes in a serious way. As we have noted, once in office it is the economic rather than the social issues that take precedence. To this extent, illusion and ideology converge in that people are voting against their interests at all levels.

One might object here that Frank's analysis is closer to Deleuze and Guattari's than the summary I have offered here suggests. For instance, one might insist that we read Frank's view not as the creation of an ideology but rather as the creation of a desire from which certain beliefs go. On this view, the Republican strategy is to create a sense of identity that becomes the object of desire, a desire that, in the end, works against the interests of those who succumb to the strategy. Below I will argue that such a view, a view that places desire beneath belief, is misplaced. The two must be intertwined. However, in Frank's case this seems to get matters the wrong way around. To be sure, there is desire. Without the identification with the sense of identity the Republican strategy fails. However, the desire is based upon a certain set of beliefs, beliefs about who 'we' are and who 'they' are. Without these beliefs, the desire does not come into play.

Franks's view of the conservative Republican mode of operation, of ideology that mixes certain (perhaps) correct beliefs with certain illusions, is exactly the kind of analysis that Deleuze and Guattari oppose. It is an inversion of their proposed relationship between desire and illusion. As mentioned at the outset, I want to argue that both Franks and Deleuze and Guattari are half right. Both of them are seeing something, but neither of them grasp the whole picture. Before I turn to my alternative picture, let me pause momentarily over the fact that we have not discussed the question of what fascism is. One might wonder whether Franks is really talking about fascism in the sense that Deleuze and Guattari mean it in their approach. If not, then the contrast I have set up is a bit forced.

Deleuze and Guattari say very little about what they think fascism is. Foucault, in his preface to *Anti-Oedipus*, probably offers the closest definition when he writes that, 'the major enemy, the strategic adversary is fascism ... and not only historical fascism, the fascism of Hitler and Mussolini ... but also the fascism in us all, in our heads and our every day behavior, the fascism that causes us to love power, to desire the very thing that dominates and exploits us' (Deleuze and Guattari 1977: xiii). For Deleuze and Guattari, fascism is not a particular arrangement of the state or a relation of the state to its population, but instead a form of oppression that is often embraced by those who are oppressed. If we remove the libidinal aspects of Foucault's definition (which are precisely what is at issue in this discussion), then it is in keeping with Franks's analysis, one that asks how it is that people can endorse and even embrace what oppresses them, as well as others.

It seems to me difficult to deny that Deleuze and Guattari are right to discover an aspect of desire in fascism so defined. There seems to be something erotic about fascism. We can see this in the passions through which people embrace their own oppression. Even the phenomena Franks discusses, the cultural orientation of recent conservatism, evoke strong vehemence and zeal among those who stake their identity there. On the other hand, to reduce fascism simply to a matter of zeal – to divorce it from belief – seems to render it blind. After all, people do not only embrace fascism; they can always tell a story about why their endorsement of (what they do not call) fascism is justified, and even mandatory. Franks captures this belief-character in his approach.

If we want to concede something to both Deleuze and Guattari's focus on desire and Frank's ideological orientation, we need a picture of ourselves that will integrate both. I would like to sketch this picture here, and then show how it can incorporate both these elements of the analysis of fascism, elements that we might call, a bit loosely, the volitional and the epistemic elements. This integration hinges on the concept of practices, through which these elements can be seen operating in complementary ways. Let me first define the concept of a practice, and then turn to the role practices play generally in our lives and then specifically in supporting and maintaining fascism.

Elsewhere, I have defined a practice as 'a regularity (or regularities) of behavior, usually goal-directed, that is socially normatively governed' (May 2001: 8). Regularities of behavior are doings of the same thing, as long as we understand by 'the same thing' a loose sort of sameness. The practice of bicycle riding, for instance, involves peddling a bike. There are many ways to peddle, but all peddling is the same thing in the sense I mean. It is a regularity of behavior, like prescribing medications in psychiatry or talking with students in teaching or recounting the events of the day in diary writing or running the bases in baseball. Almost all practices, moreover, are goal-directed. Bicycling is a form of transportation, psychiatry seeks to cure people of psychiatric problems, etc. This does not entail that people who engage in a particular practice do so *because of* the goal. I may just enjoy riding a bicycle and not care where it gets me. However, the practice itself is structured around the goals of getting from one place to another. The reason I use the term 'usually' is that there are practices that, it might be argued, are not goal-directed. The obvious example is sitting Zen, whose proponents argue cannot succeed if one has a goal in mind. (Whether the particular goal-lessness of Zen should be called a goal is neither here nor there for our purposes.)

The normative governance of a practice consists in both the rules and the ways of doing things that are constitutive of that particular practice. Practices tend to have rules, without which one is not said to be engaging in that particular practice. To fail to follow a rule is not necessarily to be doing something bad; it is simply not to be engaged in that particular practice. If I bring out a deck of cards and start playing solitaire in my classroom, I am likely no longer engaged in the practice of teaching (unless, of course, I am trying to illustrate a pedagogical point in doing so, in which case I'm not really playing solitaire). More pointedly, if I am supposed to be torturing someone, and I begin to educate them on the fine points of how to endure torture, I may be doing a good thing, but I'm not really engaged in the practice of torture at that moment.

Not all norms of practices are rules. There are ways of doing things, often involving bodily movements, that are 'like so' but cannot really be brought under particular rules. When one is learning to ride a bicycle, and the bike starts to sway, one learns to swing it back, like so, in order to stabilize it. In fact, learning to be expert in a practice often involves mastery of many of its non-rule norms. A good teacher has a sense of when to stay with a particular issue and when to move on to the next one, just as a good hockey player gets a sense of just the right instant to cross the blue line.

Having said this much about the normative governance of practices, however, we should also recognize that, for most practices, normative governance is not static. Norms can evolve over a period of time in response to changing circumstances, and one can challenge the particular norms of a practice (or even the practice itself, as one challenges the practice of torture). To return to the example of playing solitaire in class, if one insisted on solitaire as a particular technique with particular results in pedagogical practice, it might become a norm of the practice. This does not mean that it would be required of all those who participate in a practice. Practices have both norms of requirement (if one doesn't follow this norm, one isn't in the practice) and norms of permissibility (one is allowed to do this or that in the practice but it is not required in order to be engaged in that practice).

Finally, the normative governance of a practice is social. This is a point insisted on by Wittgenstein in his private language argument (Wittgenstein 1953). There is no such thing as a private practice. To be engaged in a practice is to be engaged in something that is socially recognized as a particular kind of practice.

Once we see what a practice is, we can immediately recognize that most of what we do over the course of our lives involves being engaged in practices. Jobs, hobbies, child-rearing, athletics: all of these are practices. In fact, outside relaxation and random activity, almost the entirety of our lives are taken up with participation in practices. That is to say, most of our lives are, in one sense or another, socially normatively governed. We should be neither surprised nor disturbed by this. There is no cause for surprise because people are, for the most part, social animals. We interact with other human beings on a regular basis. Those interactions are regulated in various ways. To say that they are regulated is not to say that they are pre-determined in their patterns, any more than to say that a baseball game is regulated is to say that its outcome can be known in advance. The social normative governance of practices is not *necessarily* a straitjacket; it is, more usually, a framework that allows us to interact meaningfully with one another. It is indeed difficult to see how meaningful interaction could occur in the absence of norms.

When does normative governance become a straitjacket? Otherwise put, when can it take on a more fascistic character? There is no one way for this to happen. It could be that the practice itself is defined by norms that make it fascistic. The practice of torture would be an example of this. The norms of torture combined with one's engagement with it as a practice render it immediately fascistic in the sense defined a moment ago. Alternatively, it could be that the practice itself is benign, but that the introduction of certain norms makes it fascistic. Imagine, for instance, the practice of psychoanalysis being governed by a norm that required all successful analysis to integrate people back into society so that they endorsed the current social arrangements. Or yet again, the norm itself could be benign under certain conditions, but be held so rigidly that it is applied even when it becomes inappropriate to do so. Here one can imagine a society without a military draft that establishes a voting age of twenty-one. Later, it votes for a draft for those between the ages of eighteen and twenty-one, without allowing the affected members a say in the institution of the draft. That would have a fascistic character, at least on the part of those who endorse the vote. The relation between norms and fascism, then, is a complex one, having less to do with the fact of norms and more to do with their particular character and operation in particular circumstances.

The concept of practices, I have argued elsewhere, plays a central role in the thought of Michel Foucault (May 1994: chapter 5). In Foucault's genealogical work, practices are the principal unit of the level of analysis. As he once insisted during a discussion of his history of the prisons, 'the target, the point of analytic attack, is not that of "institutions," nor of "theories" or "ideology," but of "practices" ... practices considered as the site of intertwining of what is said and what is done, of rules that one imposes on oneself and reasons that one gives oneself, of projects and proofs [*evidences*]' (Foucault *et al.* 1980: 42). Practices are where knowledge and power take place. Although I cannot give a full accounting of that claim here, let me point out that, for instance, the disciplinary power discussed in *Discipline and Punish* arises within the intersection of various monastic, military, penal and health practices, just as the power of sexuality in the first volume of the *History of Sexuality* arises through a convergence of religious, architectural and therapeutic practices. These practices, as Foucault insists, involve knowledge, or at least claims to knowledge. They require, and in turn generate, various kinds of claims that are committed to by those engaged in the particular practices. The commitment to these claims is holistic. People do not need to commit themselves to all of the various claims generally held in a practice. Just as with the norms of a practice, its epistemic claims can be questioned. However, to be engaged in a practice requires commitment to the broad epistemic outlook framed by that practice. For instance, to be engaged in psychoanalysis requires that one be committed to some idea of the unconscious, to some concept of the role that language plays in the human mind, etc. As Wilfrid Sellars insists, 'empirical knowledge, like its sophisticated extension, science, is rational, not because it has a *foundation* but because it is a self-correcting enterprise which can put *any* claim in jeopardy, though not *all* at once' (Sellars 1963: 70).

It is precisely here, in the general epistemic commitment that practices require, that we find the epistemic commitment to fascism that Frank discusses. It is because people's lives take place largely in the context of practices, and because practices involve ways of knowing (or claiming to know) that fascism arises as an ideological matter, or, more accurately, as an epistemic matter. In order to see this, let's take an example from contemporary discussion: abortion. As Frank discusses, the anti-abortion movement has been particularly strong in Kansas politics. The roots of this movement lie, of course, in fundamentalist versions of Protestantism as well as in the Catholic Church. It is unsurprising, then, that the anti-abortion movement is not simply about abortion. It reflects a larger overall view, one that has to do with the nature of families, the role of government and the primacy of certain religious values. As Frank points out, Kansas' traditional, moderate Republican candidates 'who had patiently worked their way up the party hierarchy for years were seeing the positions they coveted filled instead by some holy-rolling nobody screeching against big government and interested only in doing away with abortion and taxation' (Frank 2004: 97).

How is this a matter of practices? It is a matter of religious practices, which involve knowledge (or claims to know). Essentially, the picture is this. To be committed to, say, a conservative Protestantism is, among other things, to be committed to a certain set of practices. These practices are not only ritualistic expressions of faith. They involve ways of living: what kinds of things one can do and cannot do, how to raise one's children, how to interact with family and neighbors, etc. Further, these ways of living are inextricable from certain beliefs. These beliefs include the view that abortion is wrong because it takes a fully human life. They also include the wrongness of homosexuality. Positively, they involve beliefs in the moral rightness of the traditional family, hard work and keeping what one has earned. One might be tempted to ask whether these beliefs are matters of knowledge or matters of faith. However, for those involved in these practices, that would be a distinction without a difference. The knowledge arises from the faith; an account of knowledge as something like 'justified, true belief' would be inappropriate here.

It is worth noting that in a work that pre-dates his collaboration with Guattari, Deleuze offers a denunciation of illusion that is compatible with the analysis we are offering here. The introductory chapter of his book *Bergson-ism* sees Bergson as involved in a ceaseless struggle against illusion. Although the details of this struggle are a bit wide of our concerns, what is central to Bergson is to get free from the grip of a picture that oppresses us. That picture (which in Bergson's case primarily concerns the relation of space and time) does not only give illusory solutions to the questions we ask; it sets up false problems. 'The very notion of a false problem indeed implies that we have to struggle not against simple mistakes (false solutions), but against something more profound: an illusion that carries us along, or in which we are immersed, inseparable from our condition' (Deleuze 1988: 20). On this view, the illusion in play in the Republican strategy described by Franks, for instance, would be the identities ascribed to 'blue' and 'red' state residents, from which the false solution of voting Republican would follow.

Seeing these practices as matters of knowledge is not difficult. Neither is seeing them as matters of desire. Practices have both epistemic and volitional elements. The volitional elements exist along two registers, one related to the commitment to the practices themselves and the other in the relation of those practices to one's sense of who one is. The first is internal to the involvement in a practice. To be committed to a practice is not simply to ratify its claims to knowledge or some certain number of those claims. It is to engage oneself in that practice through one's behavior. For most of us, even that is not enough. A teacher, for instance, who does not more than behave according to pedagogical norms and endorse the beliefs required by those norms may well be alienated from the practice of teaching. She may be just going through the motions. One can imagine her saying, 'Yes, I believe in the rightness of teaching, and I'm still doing it, but my heart isn't in it.' A person like this is certainly engaged in the practice of teaching, but in an impoverished way. This impoverishment might not be a bad thing: one who is just going through the motions of torturing people might not be quite so interested in causing pain to another. However, we would say of a person like that that she isn't fully committed to the practice.

Full commitment is a matter of desire, and desire in a sense very close to the one articulated by Deleuze and Guattari. It is not desire as a Lacanian lack; it is desire as creative and productive. If, for Deleuze and Guattari, desire produces, then the desire involved in one's commitment to a practice is also productive. It involves a connection to other beliefs, behaviors, things and others, in ways that are not foreign to many of the descriptions offered in *Anti-Oedipus*. Although not all the connections discussed by Deleuze and Guattari are ones involved in practices (for example the connection of mouth to breast), many of them are. The reason not all of them are is that Deleuze and Guattari are offering a more general ontological view rather than the restricted regional one that focuses specifically on practices.

This leads to the second way in which practices are bound to desire. To be alienated from one's practices is to feel that somehow what one is doing is not deeply tied to who one is. Conversely, to be immersed in practices in a motivated way is to draw a sense of who one is through one's involvement in those practices. The answer to the question of who one is often centrally requires reference to the practices in which one is engaged. One is a mother, a teacher, a swimmer, etc. In this tie between one's practices and one's sense of oneself, desire plays a central role. This is not the type of desire we saw a moment ago; it is not the productive desire of being immersed in a practice. Rather, it is the desire that binds one *to* one's practices, that makes them constitutive of who one is. Some practices, of course, are more significant to one's sense of oneself than others. As we will see momentarily, it is those practices – especially religious and economic ones – that often come into play in the creation and promotion of fascism as Deleuze and Guattari define it.

Practices, then, have both epistemic and volitional elements; they are both matters of knowledge (or, in some cases, ideology) and desire. We have not yet answered the question of the relation of practices to fascism. Given the discussion so far, however, it is only a short step to see that some practices either are fascistic, or promote fascism in combination with other practices. In the case of the conservative ideology discussed by Frank, this is manifest. Neither the conservative Christianity nor the Republican economic program he treats is tolerant of different forms of living and acting. They are both very circumscribed in what they consider to be acceptable forms of behavior. For the former, those forms centrally involve traditional gender and family relations as well as certain relations to one's work. These are what the Republicans have exploited in their attempt to create a sense of 'red state' identity. For the latter, it is a matter of endorsing and allowing the spread of a free, unregulated capitalism that, in Frank's view, benefits those who contribute to the true objects of Republican solicitude: the economic elites.

The intertwining of these two groups – conservative Christians and Republicans – lies in the use the latter makes of the former in order to create the particular sense of red state identity that allows the latter to maintain power, often at the expense of the interests of the former. In that sense, one can say, contra Deleuze and Guattari, both that fascism is often a matter of interests, and that people can be fooled into acting against their own interests. It is a matter of interests in that the interests people have that stem from their practices can be fascistic. We can see this in two places in Frank's discussion. First, the interest the Republicans have in maintaining the domination of economic elites has led to support for fascistic practices of conservative Christianity as well as for linking those practices, via a conception of self-reliance and hard work, to free-market capitalism. Second, the interests conservative Christians have in their religious views, and the importance of those practices to their sense of who they are, has led them to support economic practices that are oppressive to many people.

Among those who have been oppressed by the economic practices supported by conservative Christians are the conservative Christians themselves. This is the third place at which interests can be fascistic, and it is the central point of Frank's book. People have been duped into supporting and participating in economic practices that have been detrimental to their interests. Those practices have been economically destructive to the lives and communities of people in Kansas, and elsewhere. This has been allowed to happen in large part through the support of Kansans for practices that have been linked to the practices that they have come to define as determinative of the kinds of people they are.

However, this is only half the picture. Very little of what I have described in the last few paragraphs has been a matter simply of epistemic mistakes. It has also been a matter of desire. This desire emerges in several ways, perhaps most palpably in the virulence with which conservative Christians treat those they think of as 'blue state' people. The anger against 'pointy headed liberals' and others who do not share in the red state identity Frank analyzes are subject to deep, and at times violent, vituperation. The demonstrations of the current Tea Party movement provide abundant evidence of this. People whose identity comes from its commitment to conservative Christianity react strongly to anything that seems to threaten their sense of who they are. This, of course, is not true only of conservative Christians, but of many of us under conditions in which we feel our sense of self to be threatened – which means that desires linked to fascism may not be far from most of us. If who we are is bound to our practices, then those practices are not matters simply of epistemic ratification but of engagement and motivation. They are objects of desire, or better they involve habits, actions and outlooks through which our desire is channeled. If they are fascistic, then we must say that this is because people desire fascism. If that fascism is oppressive to the people immersed in those practices, we can say, or at least half-say, that 'the masses were not innocent dupes; at a certain point, under a certain set of conditions, they *wanted* fascism.'

In accounting for the kinds of fascism discussed by Deleuze and Guattari, then, we can say that it is not solely a matter of state forms but instead lies within, or potentially within, each of us. In order to understand it, we must look both at its epistemic and the motivational aspects. We must see the fascism both in what we think and in what we want and create. We do not, or at least very few of us, think anything we tell ourselves is fascistic. Rather, it emerges in the practices in which we engage. It arises not because we desire fascism but because what we desire is fascistic; it arises not because we believe in fascism but because what we believe is fascistic. As a result, we must be vigilant about fascism, not only among conservative Christians but among ourselves and our own commitments. What we desire and what we believe have consequences that are often beyond our own reckoning. It is not, then, just *those others* on whom we must keep an eye, although they have given us much reason to do so. We must also keep an eye on ourselves, lest the critique of fascism we employ become a type of fascism that we embrace.

References

Deleuze, G. *Bergsonism* (New York: Zone Books, 1988)
——*Difference and Repetition* (New York: Columbia University Press, 1994)
Deleuze, G. and Guattari, F. *Anti-Oedipus: Capitalism and Schizophrenia* (New York: Viking Press, 1977)
——*What is Philosophy?* (New York: Columbia University Press, 1994)
Deleuze, G. and Parnet, C. *Dialogues* (New York: Columbia University Press, 1987)
Foucault, M. *et al.*, *L'impossible prison* (Paris: Éditions de Seuil, 1980)
Frank, T. *What's the Matter with Kansas? How Conservatives Won the Heart of America* (New York: Metropolitan Books, 2004)
Harvey, D. *A Brief History of Neoliberalism* (Oxford: Oxford University Press, 2005)
May, T. *Our Practices, Our Selves: Or, What it Means to Be Human* (University Park: Penn State Press, 2001)
——*The Political Philosophy of Poststructuralist Anarchism* (University Park: Penn State Press, 1994)
Sellars, W. *Science, Perception, and Reality* (London: Routledge and Kegan Paul-Humanities Press, 1963)
Wittgenstein, L. *Philosophical Investigations* (New York: MacMillan, 1953)

2 Anti-fascist aesthetics

Michael J. Shapiro

> The new fascism is not the politics and the economy of war. It is the global agreement on security, on the maintenance of peace – just as terrifying as war. All our petty fears will be organized in concert, all our petty anxieties will be harnessed to make micro-fascists of us; we will be called upon to stifle every little thing, every suspicious face, every dissonant voice, in our streets, in our neighborhoods, in our local theaters.
>
> (Gilles Deleuze 2006: 138)

Introduction: expanding the meaning of fascism

Doubtless Deleuze's characterization of 'the new fascism' is disturbing to those who are invested in their experience of the fascism associated with 'the politics and economy of war.' For example, Bruno Bettleheim's incessant attacks on anyone who tried to characterize the phenomenon reflect the hostility of many of fascism's war-time victims toward attempts at explaining, re-inflecting, or expanding its meaning (Bettleheim 1986). That hostility toward people who poach on one's experientially cultivated, ideationally entrenched enmities is expressed by one of Don DeLillo's aesthetic subjects, Win Everett, a character in his *Libra*, a novelistic biography of Lee Harvey Oswald, the alleged Kennedy assassin. At one point in the narrative Everett, the fictional commander of the abortive Bay of Pigs invasion, is listening to a radio announcer reporting on Cuba's role in 'Marxist subversion in our hemisphere':

> He didn't need announcers telling him what Cuba had become. This was a silent struggle. He carried a silent rage and determination. He didn't want company. The more people who believed as he did, the less pure his anger. The country was noisy with fools who demeaned his anger.
>
> (DeLillo 1988: 148)

Throughout his *Libra*, DeLillo gives Win Everett a psychological profile, especially a paranoid security mentality. Among other things, Everett checks the door locks and the knobs on the gas stove more than once before retiring every night. However, given the genre within which DeLillo is writing, Everett and the rest of the novel's characters are better thought of as aesthetic rather than as psychological subjects. The implications of such a shift in the approach to subjectivity are explicated in Leo Bersani and Ulysses Dutoit's analysis of Jean-Luc Godard's film *Contempt* (1963), a film in which a couple becomes estranged, as the wife Camille (Bridget Bardot), has her feelings for her husband Paul (Michel Piccoli), turn from love to contempt. Bersani and Dutoit point out how Godard's focus, which is not on 'the psychic origins of contempt' but on 'its effects on the world,' shows 'what contempt does to cinematic space ... how it affect[s] the visual field within which Godard works, and especially the range and kinds of movement allowed for in that space' (Bersani and Dutoit 2004: 21–22).

Similarly, the fascist mentality enacted in DeLillo's *Libra* is expressed not as a psychodynamic development but in the way the novel's moving bodies, driven by their preoccupation with securing the imagined coherence of their identity-allegiance to 'America' and to US hemispheric dominance, reaffirm a Cold War cartography. Thus for example as DeLillo recreates the historical characters, Lee Harvey Oswald and David Ferrie, and mobilizes them for an encounter in the novel at the historical moment just prior to the abortive Bay of Pigs invasion of Cuba, their different mentalities are animated in the ways they give Cuba alternative morphologies. Ferrie complains: 'You can't invade an island that size with fifteen hundred men,' to which Oswald replies, 'Cuba is little.' Ferrie responds, 'Cuba is big,' and Oswald once again says, 'Cuba is little' (DeLillo 1988: 321). As I note elsewhere, the 'polyvocal poetics of Cuba' that the encounter between the characters effects, maps much of the desire-shaped, geopolitically focused ideoscape of the America of the John F. Kennedy presidency (Shapiro 1992: 80).

While *Libra's* gloss on fascism is oblique, another DeLillo novel, *White Noise*, approaches the phenomenon more directly, albeit still from the point of view of invented characters. His main protagonist, Jack Gladney, who is the Chair of the Department of Hitler Studies at 'the College on the Hill,' has an academic calling that fits well with his preoccupation, a fascist-emulating obsession with death (as Susan Sontag has famously observed, the fascist aesthetic includes a deep desire for intimacy with death; Sontag 1975). DeLillo's Gladney enacts another aspect of the fascist aesthetic. He screens a Nazi documentary that is reminiscent of Leni Riefenstahl's regime-sponsored documentary of Hitler's visit to Nuremburg, *The Triumph of the Will* (1934). His department's documentary features mass, militarized rallies with:

> close up shots of thousands of people outside a stadium after a Goebbels speech, people surging, massing, bursting through the traffic, Halls hung with swastika banners, with mortuary wreaths and death's-head insignia. Ranks of thousands of flagbearers arrayed before columns of frozen light, a hundred and thirty aircraft searchlights aimed straight up – a scene that resembled a geometric longing, the formal notation of some powerful mass desire.
>
> (DeLillo 1985: 25–26)

Appeals of fascism

The historic Nazi rally simulated in *White Noise* conveys an aspect of the appeal of Hitler's party at the time it was assuming power. However, although much of the party's mass appeal was orchestrated by its visual displays (its public semiotics), it should also be noted that the party developed its following at a time of national economic deprivation. In a classic explanatory-oriented investigation of the rise of the Nazi party in Germany, Rudolph Heberle describes the economic and related status crises experienced by various social strata in Germany in the 1920s and 1930s and surmises:

> It should not be difficult to understand why, in such circumstances, a party led by fanatic patriots, which denounced radically all existing parties, which claimed to be independent of any particular economic interests, the only champion of the real people and the *avant-garde* of the awaking nation, would exert immense attraction for the uprooted middle class elements, for politically untrained youths, for political adventurers, and for counter-revolutionaries in general.
>
> (Heberle 1945: 6)

Elaborating, Heberle writes, 'When the terrible depression with its mass unemployment cast its shadow on the people's minds, when masses of young voters grew up who had never had a permanent job or any job at all, the Nazi party offered at least activity, an outlet from the doldrums, and also shelter, food, and uniforms, attractions which made it a bitter competitor of the Communists in certain proletarian areas of the metropolitan cities … ' (Heberle 1945: 9).

Heberle conducts a data analysis to validate his economy-focused explanatory model. Focusing on public opinion and party voting patterns of diverse occupational groups in the rural, Schleswig-Holstein region of Germany from 1918 to 1932, he shows how the National Socialists were able to displace other radical parties, not only by playing on economic issues (all the parties were doing that) but also by promoting mass participation. However, there are hints of the other kind of appeal to which DeLillo gestures and to which Heberle refers as well, an aesthetic appeal that is evident in Heberle's remarks on uniforms and mass participation. The appeal of the National Socialist's elaborate and colorful uniforms and regalia was part of their aesthetic strategy. That strategy's effectiveness is registered in a statement attributed to Walter Henisch, a press photographer who served as Josef Goebbels's official war photographer. Henisch, a man wedded to his photographic art and not to the Nazi ideology, is described by his son Peter (in his novelistic biography of his father) as explaining the attraction of the National Socialist party when they marched into Austria: 'Compared to the Socialists and even more to the conservatives, the Nazi's were remarkable. They did something for your senses, especially for your eyes, and therefore for the camera' (Henisch 1990: 50). What Walter Henisch experiences is one small marker of a more pervasive aspect of the appeal of fascist aesthetics, which shows up in popular culture texts, especially films such as *The Night Porter*, *The Damned*, and *Scorpio Rising* in the form of 'the eroticization of Nazi regalia in certain gay cultures' (Schnapp 1996: 236). Such contemporary aesthetic effects of Nazi or more generally fascist aesthetics points to what Kriss Ravetto has observed as the way 'Fascism occupied the unique (if not contradictory) space of a historical past and a political present' (Ravetto 2001: 5).

Of course, as is well known, photography was only one dimension of the Nazi media strategy. Goebbels was particularly struck with the capacity of cinema to create mass appeal and was especially taken with Sergei Eisenstein's cinematic celebration of the Russian revolution. While Eisenstein rebuffed Goebbels after the latter wrote for advice about propaganda films (Eisenstein 1988: 280), the very form of his cinematic art was also recalcitrant to Goebbels's propaganda plans. As Jacques Rancière points out in a gloss on the film-propaganda relation in Eisenstein's films, Eisenstein's films cannot function as propaganda because 'a propaganda film must give us a sense of certainty about what we see, it must choose between the documentary that presents what we see as a palpable reality or the fiction that forwards it as a desirable end [and] ... Eisenstein systematically denies us this sense of certainty (Rancière 2006: 29).

While Rancière sees Eisenstein's films as recalcitrant to a fascist aesthetic, he construes Brechtian theater as positively anti-fascist:

> If Brecht remained as a kind of archetype of political art in the XXTH century, it was due not so much to his enduring communist commitment as to the way he negotiated the relation between the opposites, blending the scholastic forms of political teaching with the enjoyments of the musical or the cabaret, having allegories of Nazi power discuss in verse about matters of cauliflowers, etc. The main procedure of political or critical art consists in setting out the encounter and possibly the clash of heterogeneous elements ... to provoke a break in our perception, to disclose some secret connection of things hidden behind the everyday reality.
>
> (Rancière 2006: 30)

Rancière's gloss on Brechtian theater resonates with Walter Benjamin's discussion of the fascism-aesthetics relationship (in a Brecht-inspired essay). Although Benjamin famously noted the fascist tendency to aestheticize politics, he also saw cinema's potential as an anti-fascist genre because of the way it alerted (shocked) the spectator rather than, as was the case with the Nazi aestheticization, simply encouraging mass allegiance through collective expression (as he put it in his 'Work of Art ... ' essay: Benjamin 1968), or encouraging the displacement of political sensibility through commoditization and mass consumption (as is implied throughout his incomplete *Arcades* project). What accords especially well with Rancière's reference to a 'break in perception' is Benjamin's reference to the shock effect of film. As Benjamin puts it:

The spectator's process of association in view of these images is indeed interrupted by their constant, sudden change. This constitutes the shock effect of the film, which, like all shocks, should be cushioned by heightened presence of mind. By means of its technical structure, the film has taken the physical shock effect out of the wrappers in which Dadaism had, as it were, kept it inside the moral shock effect.

(Benjamin 1968: 238)

In his conclusion on fascist aesthetics as the aestheticizing of politics in 'The Work of Art … ' essay, Benjamin writes, 'All efforts to render politics aesthetic culminate in one thing: war' (Benjamin 1968: 241). However, here I want to focus on a cinematic aesthetic that supplies a critical response to what Deleuze calls the new fascism (to repeat part of the epigraph at the beginning of this essay), which is immanent in the current structure of 'peace': 'All our petty fears will be organized in concert, all our petty anxieties will be harnessed to make micro-fascists of us; we will be called upon to stifle every little thing, every suspicious face, every dissonant voice, in our streets, in our neighborhoods, in our local theaters' (Deleuze 2006: 168).

Heeding Benjamin's optimism that cinema can provide an anti-fascist aesthetic, while bearing in mind Deleuze's take on the manifestation of the contemporary micro fascism, I turn to some artistic texts that produce a Deleuzian antidote to the micro fascism to which he refers. To appreciate the Deleuzian conceptual riposte to micro fascism, we have to understand the primary individual and collective identity fantasies (and their material implementations) that have animated the original fascist aesthetic. Among the most telling was the architectural projects that the Italian fascists undertook in the city of Arezzo. In order to overcode the contingencies associated with a complex, historically assembled ethnoscape that belied attempts to attribute racial homogeneity to an originary Italian nation, they decided to designate the Arentines as the original Italian race. In order to backdate the Arentines' role in creating the basis of the nation, they altered Arezzo's buildings by medievalizing them.

The project 'was simultaneously a tool for civic redefinition and a means for declaring Fascist allegiance' (Lasansky 2004: 107). Specifically, the fascists sought to 'recover Arezzo's idealized medieval past' by changing the façades of buildings to turn back the architectural clock from what was a renaissance architecture to a medieval one (Lasansky 2004: 117). The fascist project was aimed at turning the contingency of presence into fateful organic solidarity, at inventing a coherent and unitary historical people and individual identity coherences (racial among others) that accord with exclusionary membership in the collective. Architecture was one among several of the artistic genres that were pressed into the service of securing identity coherence. Festivals, exhibitions, theatre and film were also used. Like Goebbels, Mussolini saw film as 'the regime's strongest weapon.' Accordingly, the regime produced short documentaries that featured 'shots of individuals outfitted in period costumes and panoramic views of medieval and Renaissance buildings decorated for the occasion with hanging tapestries, banners, and flags' (Lasansky 2004: 99).

Counter-aesthetics: Syberberg

Although cinema was central to the fascist aestheticization of politics, it also lends itself to a politics of aesthetics. While the aestheticization of politics encourages ritual allegiance, a text that enjoins a politics of aesthetics 'suspends the ordinary coordinates of sensory experience and reframes the network of relationships between spaces and times, subjects and objects, the common and the singular' (Rancière 2004: 65). Here I turn first to Hans Jürgen Syberberg's *Hitler: A Film from Germany* (1977), which resembles the anti-fascist aesthetic in DeLillo's *White Noise* as well as comporting with a Brechtian anti-fascist aesthetic (part of Syberberg's explicit intention). The aesthetic is Brechtian in the sense described by Benjamin (already noted) in that its shock effect creates a 'heightened presence of mind' and in the sense described by Rancière in that it creates breaks in perception through its 'clash of heterogeneous elements.' *Hitler* is a seven-hour film the primary heterogeneity of which combines Brechtian and Wagnerian aesthetics to effect what Syberberg refers to as an 'aesthetic scandal: combining Brecht's doctrine of epic theater with Richard Wagner's musical aesthetics, cinematically conjoining the epic system as anti-Aristotelian cinema with the laws of a new myth' (Syberberg 1982: 18). The 'scandal' is heightened as well by Syberberg's combination of cinematic genres, a mixing of 'documentation with subjective interpretation and imagination with historical fact' (Mueller 1980: 60). In Susan Sontag's well-wrought phrases, the film is a 'medley of imaginary discourse' with a 'complex sound track … interspersed between and intermittently overlaid on the speeches of actors,' and with 'a varying stock of emblematic props and images' (Sontag 1973: 143). Moreover, by focusing on minor characters – for example Himmler's masseur Felix Kersten, and Hitler's valet Karl-Wilhelm Kraus – the film encourages the viewer to discover 'horror in the banal' (Syberberg 1982: 13).

One of the film's major analytic assumptions, which Syberberg shares with DeLillo, is that Hitler as an historical subject is fundamentally a cinematic character. In DeLillo's case, that assumption is enacted in his *Running Dog*, a novel the main drama of which is based on a search for rumored pornographic film of Hitler, created during the last days of the war. At the end of the novel, the film turns out to be something else. It shows Hitler as an aesthetic figure, imitating Charlie Chaplin for a bunch of children.

> The figure shuffles toward the camera, his cane swinging. Behind him, in a corner of the screen, one of the small girls looks on.
>   Briefly the main is flooded in light – the bleached and toneless effect of overexposure. With the return of minimal detail and contrast, he is very close to the camera, and his lifeless eyes acquire a trace of flame, the

smallest luster. A professional effect. It's as though the glint originated in a nearby catch light.

He produces an expression finally – a sweet epicene, guilty little smile, Charlie's smile, an accurate reproduction ...

Three quarter view. At first he seems to be speaking to the smallest of the children, a girl about three years old. It is then evident he is only moving his lips – an allusion to silent movies. One of the women can be seen smiling.

(DeLillo 1978: 236–37)

Syberberg also evokes Chaplin; Hitler's valet does 'a burlesque of Chaplin's impersonation of Hitler in *The Great Dictator*' (Sontag 1973: 148). In contrast to DeLillo's treatment, Hitler is a cinematic subject who does not command direct attention. Rather, Syberberg presents the Third Reich as a whole as a cinematic apparatus. Hitler appears through actors who '*re*enact the kitsch fantasies of the Third Reich' (Santner 1990: 143). Thomas Elsaesser puts it well: 'Syberberg wants to rediscover art, this time imitating not the heroic self- and world-denying stances of German idealism, but one that builds on the kitsch-debris of history, the material consequences of such heroism' (Elsaesser 1981: 116).

While a significant aspect of the anti-fascist aesthetic in Syberberg's *Hitler* is in the way the Hitler phenomenon is presented as a bad movie, a kitschy horror show that focuses on the banal and indirect aspects of Hitler's presence – for example, a commentary by Hitler's valet referring to underpants and night shirts and remembrances of breakfasts and film screenings, to appreciate the effects, we have to recall the heroic versions of Hitler and Germany that the film parodies. For example, as Sontag points out, the film 'uses, recycles, parodies of elements of Wagner. Syberberg means his film to be an anti-*Parsifal*, and hostility to Wagner is one of the leitmotifs: the spiritual filiation of Wagner and Hitler' (Sontag 1973: 155).

To conceptualize the significance of such an aesthetic, we can turn to the insights supplied by Deleuze in his analysis of the painting of Francis Bacon. He suggests that Bacon does not begin to paint on a blank canvas. Rather, 'everything he has in his head or around him is already on the canvas, more or less virtually, before he begins his work' (Deleuze 2003: 71). In order to resist the 'psychic clichés' and '*figurative givens*,' the artists must 'transform' or 'deform' what is 'always-already on the canvas.' It is also the case for Syberberg, the Hitler phenomenon is always-already on screen with its 'psychic clichés' and 'figurative givens.' Hence Syberberg's Hitler deforms what is on screen by deforming not only the heroic operatic epics of Wagner but also the pious, hero-making Hitler documentary, Leni Riefenstahl's *Triumph of the Will*. Ultimately, Hitler is erased as Syberberg's aesthetic subject is Germany's reception of the fascist spectacle: 'There will be no other hero, only us' (Syberberg 1978: 81). In addition, Syberberg's film accomplished an important shift, one from Hitler as character to Germany as the domain of his reception. It is a change, as Deleuze points out, 'taking place inside cinema, against Hitler, but also against Hollywood, against business … A true psychodynamics will not be found unless it is based on *new associations*, by reconstituting the great mental automata that he enslaved' (Deleuze 1989: 264).

Philip K. Dick, another counter-fascist aesthetic

If the artistic mechanisms central to the fascist strategy for securing allegiance were aimed at fixing originary and exclusionary national identity by among other things creating a static, exemplary citizen body the unity of which is organic, what would constitute an anti-fascist aesthetic? Rather than a static, historically invested people with enduring and exclusionary characteristics, the anti-fascist body is one – after Deleuze and Guattari's treatment of the body – that is a turbulent assemblage of different rates of being that co-inhabit a body, the becoming of which involves radical contingency. Insofar as such a body achieves a coherent order, it is not the homeostatic equilibrium of the well-run machine but rather the dynamic coherence of Deleuze and Guattari's 'abstract machine' (Deleuze and Guattari 1987). Cinema is a medium that is doubtless best able to convey such a body, and no film better exemplifies such a capacity than Richard Linklater's film version of the Philip Dick novel *A Scanner Darkly* (2006). Taking Benjamin's assertion that a politically progressive cinema can counter the fascist cooptation of cinema to enact an aesthetics of war, but updating the 'war' from the 1930s and 1940s geopolitical version to the contemporary ones involving wars on drugs and 'terror,' I want to identify the way Linklater's film achieves a contemporary anti-fascist politics of aesthetics.

At the level of its plot, *A Scanner Darkly* resonates well with the micro-fascism problematic that Deleuze articulates. The main character/protagonist Bob Arctor leads a double life. In one, he belongs to a household of drug users; in another he is Fred, an undercover police agent assigned to collect damaging evidence on the household's drug culture. The Dick scenario is as follows: The war on drugs has not gone well because a highly addictive, illegal drug, Substance D, which is made from a small blue flower, has spread all over the country. Bob Arctor is the undercover agent assigned to infiltrate the drug culture. In his undercover role, he moves in with drug-using housemates in a poor Anaheim, California neighborhood. When at his police station he is co-named Fred, and he hides his identity from fellow officers by wearing a 'scramble suit' that produces rapid changes in visible identity (in effect a visual realization of the Deleuzian 'turbulence' as 'different rates of being' co-inhabit a single body). Moreover, the Dick story and Linklater film version add a grammatical twist to the Deleuzian version of micro fascism. Rather than a general 'we' who are invited to 'stifle every little thing, every suspicious face, every dissonant voice, in our streets, in our neighborhoods, in our local theaters,' Bob Arctor, as Fred, is called upon to stifle *himself*. As the story progresses, he becomes a divided subject who is both part of the surveillance team and one of its investigative targets. In order to maintain his cover after he becomes part of a drug-using household, Arctor uses substantial amounts of Substance D, which causes the two hemispheres of his brain to work independently and, ultimately, to compete ('Bob' has a dissonant voice within). Although one narrative thread of the film speaks to the damaging effects of drug use, Bob's schizoid condition constitutes an escape from normalized subjectivity. His schizoid body is nomadic in Deleuze and Guattari's sense, for its movements resist the modes of identification that bodies are captured by when they operate in terms of the usual organic functions.

The Surveillance regime, recognizing Bob's/Fred's growing dependence on and seeming disability from Substance D, treats Arctor's developing schizoid tendencies as a psychological issue. They see him as one suffering from a neurocognitive deficit and rename him Bruce, seeking to create a subject they can treat. However, although the Bruce/Fred/Arctor body is psychologized by the policing authorities, in the context of the film that body is better rendered as an aesthetic rather than a psychological subject. Two conceptual assets emerge from such a shift. First, the focus on the body as an aesthetic subject turns us away from psychological phenomena and toward a spatial analytic as I noted in my earlier reference to Bersani and Ulysse Dutoit's reading of a Jean Luc Goddard film *Contempt*. As is the case in Godard's film about an increasingly estranged couple, a focus on aesthetic rather than psychological subjectivity illuminates cinematic space – in this case a space that mimes the micro-fascism of securitization – as the film inter-articulates the life world with the panoptics of drug surveillance. In that process, the scanner is a primary focal point. As a result, one of the film's (like the book's) primary questions, which Fred/Bob asks himself, is 'What does the scanner see?':

> I mean really see? Into the head? Down into the heart? Does a passive infrared scanner like they used to use or a cube-type holo-scanner like they use these days see into myself. I see only murk outside, murk inside. I hope for everyone's sake the scanners do better. Because, he thought, if the scanner sees only darkly, the way I myself do, then we are cursed, cursed again and like we have been continually, and we'll wind up dead this way, knowing very little and getting that little fragment wrong too.
>
> (from *A Scanner Darkly*)

Second, while a primary narrative thread of the film is a story about the dangers of drug use, the Fred/Arctor body is recalcitrant to the narrative. Vincent Amiel's observations on the subversive cinematic body serves well here. Amiel analyzes those films (e.g., those of Robert Bresson, Buster Keaton and John Casavetes) in which what he calls 'the cinematographic body is no longer an object of film knowledge; rather it is a model of knowledge via editing ... [It is] simultaneously that which is filmed and that which (re)organizes the film in the mind/body of the spectator ... [becoming the] source rather than the object of cinema' (Game 2001: 50–51).

While in what Amiel calls 'classic cinema' the moving bodies were simply vehicles for a story, in his terms the tendency was to 'abandon the body's density for the exclusive profit of its functionality,' so that it was merely 'at the service of narrative articulations,' in much of contemporary cinema 'the idea is for the cinema to dis-organ-ize the body ... by means of revealing its fragmented nature, by extracting from it the yoke of unity and consciousness, by giving it back the complexity of its own determinations' (Amiel 1998: 7).

Certainly the protagonist in *Scanner* should be understood aesthetically, even though he develops a psychosis. 'Bruce' (Arctor) discovers the blue flowers that are the source of the drug Substance D. Inasmuch as the blue flower is a symbol of German romanticism, the psychosis-inducing flower is also an aesthetic icon. As such, it assists in recruiting the film into a politics of aesthetics frame rather than moving it toward the simple policy problem of how to treat a drug-induced psychosis. Moreover, *chez* Benjamin, the blue flower motif suggests that the film evokes the pervasiveness of illusion (what Benjamin referred to as phantasmagoria) rather than psychic delusion (where illusion as phantasmagoria is Dick's emphasis in the novel). The cinema version of *Scanner* is ideally suited to such an aesthetic frame, especially because of the way it situates the viewer *vis-à-vis* the couplet of reality versus illusion. As Benjamin suggests in his run up to the blue flower imagery, 'the shooting of a film ... presents a process in which it is impossible to assign to a spectator a viewpoint which would exclude from the scene being enacted such extraneous accessories as camera equipment, lighting, machinery crew, etc. ... Its illusory nature is a nature of the second degree, the result of editing.' Benjamin adds, 'The equipment-free aspect of reality here has become the height of artifice, the site of immediate reality has become the "blue flower" in the land of technology' (Benjamin 1968: 232).

In interpreting Benjamin's meaning here, Miriam Hansen insists that the blue flower imagery helps Benjamin lend a political force to cinema-as-form. For Benjamin, she writes, ' ... if film were to have a critical, [i.e. anti-fascist] cognitive function, it had to disrupt that chain [the mythical chain of mirrors] and assume the task of all politicized art and [quoting Susan Buck-Morss] "not to duplicate the illusion as real, but to interpret reality as itself illusion"' (Hansen 1987: 204). The 'metaphor of the blue flower – the unattainable object of the romantic quest', she adds, suggests the critical role of cinema's 'distortion of distortion.' Most significantly, according to Benjamin, the actor who is able to maintain her/his 'humanity in the face of the apparatus,' frees the mass audience from myth as they 'watch an actor take revenge in their place ... ' (Benjamin quoted in Hansen 1987: 205).

To elaborate the critical anti-fascist aesthetic insights of Benjamin and others that *Scanner* delivers, we can consider the name of Dick's main protagonist, Arctor, likely a reference to the subject-as-actor, and follow his relationship to illusion. Arctor is under cover, acting an identity, performing in effect for the scanners. Moreover, his persona is deployed on both sides of the surveillance process; he is both a subject and object of surveillance and is therefore performing for himself as well. The split in his focus of observation is doubled by the way Substance D has created a split between the hemispheres of his brain. These dual divisions encourage a model of historically fraught subjectivity that is decidedly anti-fascist in more or less the sense in which the Brechtian subject emerges from his theatrical practice. In Brechtian theater, what is in front of the audience, as it is acted out, is conveyed as something that might well be otherwise. The effect is a dualism that points to the possibilities of multiplicity, a sense of not simply what is being done 'but what might just as well have not been done, what might have been something else altogether, or simply have been omitted' (Jameson 1998: 58). As a result, what is presented is a challenge to the fascist desire to reign in contingency in order to establish historical necessity.

A cinematic Philip Dick anti-fascism yet again: *Minority Report*

> Everybody runs; everybody runs.
>
> (John Anderton (Tom Cruise), *Minority Report*)

As Kriss Ravetto (2001: 227) points out, ' ... hundreds of films have been produced on the subject of fascism ... ' However, I want to emphasize that what makes a film anti-fascist is not necessarily a matter of the way it explicitly addresses the historically bounded phenomena that produced a Hitler and Mussolini. Jacques Rancière makes the point well in his reference to the politics of the novel. For example, he suggests that Virginia Woolf's novels are more connected with democratic history than Emile Zola's, not because she wrote 'good social novels but because her way of working on the contraction or distention of temporalities, on their contemporaneousness or their distance, or her way of situating events at a more minute level, all of this establishes a grid that makes it possible to think through the frames of political dissensuality more effectively than the social epic's various forms' (Rancière 2004: 65). Accordingly, one might surmise that Dick's *Man in the High Castle* (1992), which explicitly addressed an America that is organized around the victory of fascism (Germany and Japan have won World War II as the novel begins), is his most anti-fascist story. However, I want to suggest, in accord with Rancière's point, that like his *Scanner*, Dick's *Minority Report*, especially in its cinematic realization, delivers a more effective anti-fascist aesthetic.

The film version of *Minority Report* articulates well the Deleuzian conception of micro fascism and goes beyond *Scanner*'s anti-fascism because it displays a coercive society-wide securitization rather than the more focused assault on one of society's sub-cultures. That securitization is effectively an imposition of a 'peace' that stifles all forms of dissonance. Although the society represented is not explicitly fascist, as it is in Dick's *Man in the High Castle*, it is nevertheless a society of totalizing control, run by a precrime unit that arrests and incarcerates anyone who is interpreted as planning a violent crime. The suborned interpreters are precogs, psychic women who are connected to informational prostheses to form a person-technology assemblage. With its form as well as its content, Steven Spielberg's film version of the story provides the most notable representation of a contemporary politics of surveillance, well captured in Gilles Deleuze's conception of 'societies of control.' Whereas Foucault conceived the disciplinary society, based on enclosures – the school, the factory, the prison and so on – as historically supplanting the old societies of sovereignty, Deleuze argues that the society of control has displaced the disciplinary society. It is not a society of walls and containments but a system of domination that works through modulations and coding procedures: 'In the control societies what are important are no longer numbers and names but codes, a password instead of a watchword' (Deleuze 1992: 5). They are codes that control movements from one function and setting to another and the coding mechanisms are located in dominant centers, centers of capitalism (global incorporations) but also articulated in the control measures of the state.

Although capitalism is disproportionately connected to 'societies of control,' there is also a micro fascism that is state-oriented. With respect to this aspect, Deleuze and Guattari write, 'The administration of a great organized molar security has as its correlate a whole micro-management of petty fears [amounting to] ... a macropolitics of society by and for a micropolitics of insecurity ... ' (Deleuze and Guattari 1987: 215–16). Within this model of securitization, the social order has two opposing modalities: machines of capture in which bodies and spaces are coded, and lines of flight, which are the mechanisms and routes through which people elude the machines of capture. In effect, the lines of flight constitute micropolitical reactions to the mechanisms of capture to resist the society's 'normalizing individualization' (Deleuze and Guattari 1987: 208–31).

Minority Report's enactment of a dynamic opposition between the machines of capture and the micropolitics of escape takes place in Washington, DC, in 2054, where the 'precrime unit,' which has aspirations to become a national program, operates the policing mechanisms through which persons identified as future criminals are arrested and incarcerated. While the eventual escape and return to normal life of one of the precogs, who has been held in a drugged state of suspended animation, is part of the film's drama, the most significant body (the primary aesthetic subject) in the film is that of John Anderton (played by Tom Cruise), who when the film opens is the head arresting officer of the precrime unit. Anderton's moving body, first as part of the mechanisms of capture and subsequently as a fugitive from the unit he formerly led, drives the film's primary narrative. At first he operates as a wholly suborned body, with his movements, for example, gesturally drawing out the information on a future crime from his unit's media technology screen but then, after he is set up and programmed by the unit as a future criminal, as one moving to stymie the machine of capture.

Ultimately, Anderton's exoneration involves a recovery of the precrime unit's suppressed archive of minority reports (submitted by precogs who see the future crime differently). As Philip Dick's version of the story puts it, 'The existence of a majority logically implies a corresponding minority' (Dick 2002: 45). In the film version, the minority reports have been suppressed (because the head of the program, eager to have it implemented nationally, has suppressed them in order to represent future criminal acts as certainties rather than probabilities), and Anderton learns that his only hope is to find the one in his case, if it exists. Ultimately, although the narrative has a positive ending (John Anderton is exonerated, the head of the program is discredited, and the precrime program is eliminated), the film's most significant aspects are non-narrative, anti-fascist and micropolitical.

In the opening scenes, Anderton's body functions as a physical extension of the precrime surveillance and arrest functions, filmed with Anderton's body moving in a musically accompanied ballet that is in harmony with the machinery of prediction; his movements at this stage are wholly modulated and choreographed by the system. Specifically, his swinging arms are shown pulling up the relevant images on a large screen, and subsequently his moving body is shown closing in on the alleged perpetrator. Later, the images of his body and its movements are subversive. As his body challenges the totalizing precrime choreography, he evinces a counter-movement to those of the system's machine of capture, and to do so he has to modify his body to subvert the surveillance system – for example, by having his eyes replaced to subvert the coding system, which reads eyeball patterns.

As a result, Anderton is an exemplary Deleuzian fugitive: 'Everybody runs,' he says when the police first try to apprehend him, and thereafter his running requires him to move in ways that allow him to escape from the coding apparatuses and exemplify Deleuze's suggestion that there are always forms of flow that elude the capturing, binary organizations. Notably, apart from Anderton's movements, which articulate Deleuzian lines of flight by exploiting the gaps in the apparatuses of capture, the subversiveness of his body is also a function of a film form that opposes the body to the narrative. As is the case with the aesthetic subject in *Scanner*, Bob Arctor, John Anderton's body performs as the kind of cinematic body analyzed by Vincent Amiel, a cinematic body that is 'dis-organ-ized' and thus resistant to the functionality of the film narrative (Amiel 1998: 7). As a result, the film uses Anderton's body to realize the Deleuzian political inspiration to resist the apparatuses of capture and thus works not simply through its narrative drama but also through its imagery, as an exemplary anti-fascist aesthetic.

Conclusion: alternative methodological strategies

As I have noted elsewhere, the experience of fascism has had a disproportionate shaping effect on the post-World War II development of the social sciences, especially political psychology. As I put it, 'In the case of political psychology what was enjoined was a search for the fascist personality, understood to be a deviant type susceptible to authoritarian impulses or appeals [and among the inquiries undertaken were] ... the authoritarian personalities studies of Theodore W. Adorno and his associates, Milton Rokeach's work on open versus closed minds, and H.G. Eysenck's addition of a tender-minded versus tough-minded axis of opinion to the study of political ideology' (Shapiro 1996: xix). In sum, for the social sciences in this period, to understand the emergent dangers of fascism, one must inquire into what Adorno *et al.* referred to as the '*potentially fascistic* individual' (Adorno *et al.* 1950: part one, 1). Thus for Adorno *et al.*, as was the case for Eysenck, and Rokeach, the problem of fascism emerges from susceptible mentalities. Those fascism-susceptible mentalities are treated by Eysenck as an ideological complex, a convergence of conservatism with tough-mindedness, articulated as a commitment to capital punishment and other harsh treatments for criminals, among other things (Eysenck 1954: 147). Rokeach (1973) lumped fascist mentality with orthodox Marxism-Leninism and rendered both mentalities as forms of dogmatic cognitive organization, while fascism-susceptible mentalities are treated by Adorno *et al.* as an indication of 'psychological ill-health' (Adorno *et al.* 1950: part two, 891–970).

In contrast, when fascism is interpreted as a *dispositif* – a complex, coercive apparatus – rather than merely as a mentality, we are in a position to appreciate its insidious effects on the social order – its war against difference in the name of social peace – by turning to arts that mobilize aesthetic subjects who both mime and resist fascism's choreography. If we heed familiar social psychology versions of fascism, we license a search for troubled psychodynamic stories and the identification of effective clinical interventions. If we focus on the fascist *dispositif* – where a *dispositif* is 'a thoroughly heterogeneous ensemble consisting of discourses, institutions, architectural forms, regulatory decisions, laws, administrative measures, scientific statements, philosophical, moral and philanthropic propositions ... the said as much as the unsaid ... the elements of the apparatus' (Foucault 1977: 194) – we are encouraged to pursue inventive staging rather than psychological investigation; in short, to turn to the arts as they enact the fascist *dispositif* and thus, for example, to let Hans-Jürgen Syberberg's and Philip K. Dick's imaginations trump Adorno *et al.*'s recapitulation of the quest for dangerous mentalities.

References

Adorno, T.W., Frenke Brunswik, E., Levinson, D.J. and Nevitt Sanford, R. *The Authoritarian Personality* parts one and two (New York: Jon Wiley & Sons, 1950)
Amiel, V. *Le corps au cinema: Keaton, Bresson, Cassavetes* (Paris: Presses Universitaires de France, 1998)
Benjamin, W. 'The Work of Art in the Age of Mechanical Reproduction,' in W. Benjamin *Illuminations* (New York: Schocken, 1968)
Bersani, L. and Dutoit, U. *Forms of Being* (London: BFI, 2004)
Bettleheim, B. 'Interview' (*The New York Times*, Book Review, 5 October 1986, 12)
Deleuze, G. *Cinema 2: The Time-Image* (London: Athlone Press, 1989)
——'Postscript on Societies of Control' (*October* No.59, 1992, 3–7)
——*Two Regimes of Madness* (New York: Semiotext(e), 2006)

——*Francis Bacon: The Logic of Sensation* (Minneapolis: University of Minnesota Press, 2003)

Deleuze, G. and Guattari, F. *A Thousand Plateaus* (Minneapolis: University of Minnesota Press, 1987)

DeLillo, D. *Running Dog* (New York: Vintage, 1978)

——*White Noise* (New York: Viking-Penguin, 1985)

——*Libra* (New York: Viking, 1988)

Dick, P.K. *Man in the High Castle* (New York: Vintage, 1992)

——*Minority Report* (New York: Pantheon, 2002)

——*A Scanner Darkly* (New York: Vintage, 2006)

Eisenstein, S. 'On Fascism, German Cinema and Real Life: Open Letter to the German Minister of Propaganda', in R. Taylor (ed.) *Eisenstein Writings* Vol.1 (Bloomington: Indiana University Press, 1988)

Elsaesser, T. 'Myth as Phantasmagoria of History: H.J. Syberberg, Cinema and Representation' (*New German Critique* 24/25, Winter 1981, 108–54)

Eysenck, H.J. *The Psychology of Politics* (London: Routledge & Kegan Paul, 1954)

Foucault, M. 'The Confession of the Flesh', in C. Gordon (ed.) *Power/Knowledge: Selected Interviews & Other Writings 1972–1977* (New York: Pantheon, 1977)

Game, J. 'Cinematic Bodies' (*Studies in French Cinema* Vol.10, No.1, 2001, 3–9)

Hansen, M. 'Benjamin, Cinema and Experience: The Blue Flower in the Land of Technology' (*New German Critique* No.40, 1987, 179–224)

Heberle, R.B. *From Democracy to Nazism: A Regional Case Study on Political Parties in Germany* (Baton Rouge: Louisiana State University Press, 1945)

Henisch, P. *Negatives of My Father* (Riverside, CA: Ariadne Press, 1990)

Jameson, F. *Brecht and Method* (New York: Verso, 1998)

Lasansky, D.M. *The Renaissance Perfected: Architecture, Spectacle, & Tourism in Fascist Italy* (University Park: Pennsylvania State University Press, 2004)

Mueller, R. 'Hans-Jürgen Syberberg's *Hitler* an Interview-Montage' (*Discourse* No.2, 1980, 60–82)

Rancière, J. *The Politics of Aesthetics* (London: Continuum, 2004)

——*Film Fables* (Oxford: Berg, 2006)

Ravetto, K. *The Unmaking of Fascist Aesthetics* (Minneapolis: University of Minnesota Press, 2001)

Rokeach, M. *The Open and the Closed Mind* (New York: Basic Books, 1973)

Santner, E. *Mourning, Memory and Film in Postwar Germany* (Ithaca, NY: Cornell University Press, 1990)

Schnapp, J.T. 'Fascinating Fascism' (*Journal of Contemporary History* Vol.31, No.2, 1996, 235–44)

Shapiro, M.J. *Reading the Postmodern Polity* (Minneapolis: University of Minnesota Press, 1992)

——'Introduction', in M.J. Shapiro and H. Alker (eds) *Challenging Boundaries* (Minneapolis: University of Minnesota Press, 1996)

Sontag, S. 'Syberberg's Hitler', in *Under the Sign of Saturn* (New York: Farrar Straus Giroux, 1973)

——'Fascinating Fascism' (*New York Review of Books*, 6 February 1975)

Syberberg, H.J. *Hitler, Ein Film aus Deutschland* (Reinbek, 1978)

——*Hitler: A Film from German* (New York: Farrar Straus Giroux, 1982)

3 Fascism and the bio-political

Brad Evans

Reich's warning

Gilles Deleuze's account of fascism owes considerable intellectual debt to the work of Wilhelm Reich. Noting in particular how Reich discredited orthodox wisdom, Deleuze wanted to question how conditions of servitude, humiliation and slavery could actually be embraced given the right conditions:

> Reich is at his profoundest as a thinker when he refuses to accept ignorance or illusion on part of the masses as a explanation of fascism, and demands an explanation that will take their desires into account, an explanation formulated in terms of desire: no the masses were not innocent dupes; at a certain point, under certain conditions, they *wanted* fascism, and it is this perversion of desire of the masses that needs to be accounted for.
>
> (Deleuze and Guattari 2003: 31)

This reading of fascism is undoubtedly provocative. Not only does it bring the emotional (affective) field back into political analysis. It forces us to confront the ways in which any society may actually desire that which ordinarily appears abhorrent: 'Desire stretches that far: desiring one's own annihilation, or the power to annihilate' (Deleuze and Guattari 2003: 183). Importantly, for Deleuze, since fascism is socially invested i.e. *actively produced*, its continued recurrence should alert us to every compromise made with oppressive forms of power. What Foucault identified to be 'Fascism in All its Forms': 'not only historical fascism, the fascism of Hitler and Mussolini – which was able to use the desire of the masses so effectively – but also the fascism in us all, in our heads, and in our everyday behaviour, the fascism that causes us to love power, to desire the very thing that dominates and exploits us' (Deleuze and Guattari 2003: xv).

Deleuze does more than simply cast new light on the nature of fascist power. He moves us beyond the limits of historically specificity. Fascism is quite often mistakenly associated with totalitarian power. This power is embodied in those grotesque projects which, predicated upon the myth of national supremacy, have ethnically cleansed the social body of particular minority groups, i.e. Armenians, Jews, Gypsies and so forth. This reading enables us to identify, rather holistically, highly contingent fascist regimes which have attempted to totalise their grip on power *vis-à-vis* the designated exceptions to the social order. Inevitably, since these regimes are seen to be the outcome of extremely unique conditions/sentiments, attentions are drawn to the perversion of grand modern narratives in order effectively to learn from mistakes in the past, without necessarily abandoning grand political posturing. Fascism, in other words, tends to be explained in terms of its historical departures or pathological aberrations. Those darkened moments that overshadow the otherwise enlightened path towards human progress and emancipation. Whilst this diagnosis has come to dominate political theory, Deleuze noted how it was woefully inadequate and devoid of critical valance. Not only does it fail to account for the intellectual conditions that allows fascism to eventually take hold; it is deaf to Reich's uncomfortable and yet brutally honest cry that individuals actually come to desire the very forms of power that dominate themselves and others alike.

Whilst Deleuze's most pertinent writings on this problematic appeared at the height of the Cold War, the 'capitalisation of peace' he sketched out is arguably even more resonant today. Fully aware that liberal capitalism had the edge over its Cold War rival, he specifically warned against the 'new fascism being prepared for us' (Deleuze 2006: 138). This he believed was a 'global agreement on security' that was 'just as terrifying as war'. A 'vision of peace' tied to 'Terror and Survivability'. Importantly, for Deleuze, since this vision no longer has any respect for territorial integrities, it brings to the fore a new problem of fascism that is tied to a problem of planetary endangerment. More than anticipating the biospherical enclosure of political space, this reading is fully alert to the advent of the post-Clausewitzean security terrain that inverts our understanding or security, power, war and violence:

> Total war itself is surpassed towards a peace more terrifying still. The war machine has taken charge of the aim, worldwide order, and the states are no more than objects or means adapted to that machine. This is the point at which Clausewitz is effectively reversed; to be entitled to say that politics is the continuation of war by other means, it is not simply enough to invert the order of the words so that they can be spoken in either direction: it is necessary to follow the real movement at the conclusion of which the States, having appropriated the war machine, and having adapted it to their aims, reimpart a war machine that takes charge of the aim, appropriates the state, and assumes increasingly wider political functions.
>
> (Deleuze and Guattari 2002: 465)

This chapter will foreground these 'wider political functions'. In doing so, it will argue that any understanding of contemporary fascism needs to move beyond the lure of ideological reification and towards understanding it through the conditioning prism of what Foucault terms the *dispositif* of security if it is to be combated in the twenty-first century.

Bio-political mediations

Deleuze's conception of fascism extends *well beyond* and yet appears *prior to* the tyrannies of a totalitarian state. Bypassing sovereign temporalities, it focuses instead upon those power formations that can appear in many different localised forms whatever the political emblem. These include 'rural fascism and city and neighbourhood fascism, youth fascism and war veteran's fascism, fascism of the Left, and fascism of the Right, fascism of the couple, family, school and office' (Deleuze and Guattari 2002: 214). This brings us to the fundamental distinction Deleuze draws between fascism and the Total State: 'Doubtless, fascism invented the concept of the totalitarian state, but there is no reason to define fascism by a concept of its own devising' (Deleuze and Guattari 2002: 214). Whilst totalitarian regimes are capable of oppressing populations, they result from the actions of a relatively small number of individuals. Fascism, in contrast, works by manipulating what appeals to the general population. It mobilises the masses by drawing attention to political problems of the everyday: 'what makes fascism dangerous is its molecular or micropolitical power, for it is a mass movement: a cancerous body rather than a totalitarian organism ... Only micro-fascism provides an answer to the global question: Why does desire desire its own oppression, how can it desire its own oppression?' (Deleuze and Guattari 2002: 215). This localised focus is significant. Since it is understood 'the masses certainly do not passively submit to power; nor do they "want" to be repressed, in a kind of masochistic hysteria; nor are they tricked by ideological lure', it is the masses' active investment in their own political decay that allows us to challenge all attempts to give fascism ideological determinism.

Deleuze does not, however, seek to diminish the importance of macro-specific fields of formation. His vocal admiration for Primo Levi emphasises this point. Levi's personal testimonies not only explain in the most intimate details the divisive nature of fascistic rule (even amongst the Lager's captors); it was his sophisticated account of the economy behind these relations which obliterated the absurd notion that the phenomena should be consigned to the pages of history: 'Nor is it in the extreme conditions described by Primo Levi that we experience the shame of being human. We experience it in insignificant conditions, before the meanness and vulgarity of existence that haunts democracies, before the propagation of these modes of existence and of thought-for-the-market, and before the values, ideals, and opinions of our times' (Deleuze and Guattari 1994: 107). The argument here is straightforward. Localised or even psychic forms of oppression only make sense once wider fields of political and social formation are taken into account. Or to be more specific, since every regime (dictatorial, monarchical, liberal) has become isomorphous to the politically suffocating dictates of the world market; there is no reason to presuppose that any political project is immune to the active production of determinable inequalities.

So how does desire connect to the wider social field? Deleuze argues that all desire is *assembled*. Desire does not exist in some isolated personal vacuum. It is an integral part of the collective human condition. Desire connects us to the social world, while the social world intercepts individuals with its many complimentary and competing flows. Hence, for Deleuze, 'there is no such thing as social production on the one hand, and a desiring production that is mere fantasy on the other' (Deleuze and Guattari 2003: 29). Social production is 'purely and simply desiring production itself under determinate conditions'. It is nonsense, therefore, to suggest that individuals and society can be empirically separated. They are 'strictly simultaneous and consubstantial' (Massumi 2002: 68). Importantly, however, since it is the assemblage which 'gives desire a fascistic determination' (Deleuze and Guattari 2002: 215), the problem, as Eugene Holland puts it, is to question 'what exactly are the assemblages that produce the "thousand little monomanias [and] self-evident truths ... giving any and everybody the mission of self-appointed judge, dispenser of justice, policeman, neighbourhood SS man"' (Holland 2008: 77–78, quoting Deleuze and Guattari). This is supported by Ian Buchanan (2000), who notes that to understand the relationship between the human and its world, one must take into account both the individual desire to exploit determinate conditions, along with the nature of those assemblages that articulate those desires to the point of their effective normalisation. For it is only through this wider strategic focus which connect localised forms of micro-physical desire with macro-politicised forms of social organisation that the *power over life* can be properly understood.

Deleuze famously re-orientated our understanding of social systems by arguing that 'lines of flight' are primary. One implication of this is to suggest that no social assemblage is ever completely totalising. Life is always potentially greater than the sum of its assembled parts. This brings us to an important distinction Foucault draws between the 'milieu' and the '*dispositif*'. For Foucault, the 'milieu of life' in its original scene is 'the space in which a series of uncertain events unfold' (Foucault 2007: 22). It is a 'problem of circulation' that composes of unmediated natural flows (i.e. weather systems), along with artificially constructed agglomerations (i.e. populations). This space of flows in many senses correlates to what Deleuze termed the 'non-stratified':

> the interior presupposes a beginning and an end, an origin and a destination that can coincide and incorporate everything. But when there are only environments and whatever lies between them, when words and things are opened up without ever coinciding, there is a liberation of forces which come from the outside and exist only in a mixed-up state of agitation, modification and mutilation.
>
> (Deleuze 1999: 72–73)

If the milieu refers to the open field of possibility, for Foucault, the *dispositif* 'works on the basis of this reality, by trying to use it as a support and make it function in relation to each other' (Foucault 2007: 47). It is all about creating a 'specific arrangement' so that life can be made to live: 'no longer that of fixing and demarcating the territory, but of allowing circulations to take place, of controlling them, sifting the good and the bad ... in such a way that the inherent dangers of this circulation are cancelled out' (Foucault 2007: 65). Tasked then with 'modifying something in the biological destiny of the species' (Foucault 2007: 10), the *dispositif* operates by, first, promoting what is 'generally desirable' to the population, and second, seeking to eliminate what is uncertain in any given situation. As Foucault explains:

> By the term apparatus [*dispositif*] I mean a kind of formation, so to speak, that a given historical moment has as its major function the response to urgency. The apparatus therefore has a dominant strategic function ... I said that the nature of an apparatus is essentially strategic, which means that we are speaking about a certain manipulation of relations of forces, of a rational and concrete intervention in the relation of forces, either so as to develop them in a particular direction, or to block them, to stabilize them, and to utilize them. The apparatus is thus always inscribed into a play of power ... The apparatus is precisely this: a set of strategies of the relations of forces supporting, and supported by, certain types of knowledge.
> (Foucault 1980: 194–96)

Whilst Foucault invoked the *dispositif* in the context of the problem of security (*dispositif de la sécurité*), it shares an intimate relationship to the problem of war. Modern societies are 'security conscious' insomuch as our ways of thinking politically have been dominated by the security imperative. Modern societies are equally 'war conscious' insomuch as our ways of acting politically have been profoundly shaped by the battles which have contoured our very existence. There is, however, an important point to clarify here. As both Deleuze and Foucault (following Nietzsche) properly understood, it is a mistake to see war and security as strategically opposite. War is not simply reducible to the absence of peace. Neither does peace necessarily denote a succession of hostilities. Generating the very conditions of political possibility, modern politics in fact resembles *the* extension of war by other means (Foucault 2003). That is to say, since the 'grid of intelligibility' for securitisation continues to extend 'the operational practices and discursive assumptions of the *logos* of war into the *logos* of peace' (Dillon 2008: 176), to reason that peace is the extension of war by other means, surreptitiously implies that those other means are sanctioned, justified, articulated and made real on account of their prevalence within a war/security/life triangulation that mobilises the social body against whatever threatens the *progressive* imaginary of peaceful settlement.

Oedipalisation is fully invested in this entire process. In *Anti-Oedipus*, Deleuze puts aside all previous epistemological and ontological constructions of the subject based on Freudian-inspired structural articulations. Deleuze's main criticism of psychoanalysis (consequently of the Oedipus complex more generally) was that the constitution of human subjectivity is based upon an original moment of negation which consequently entails reliance upon epiphenomena.

Deleuze argued that desire is not, however, based on an essential lack, along with any such binary arrangement which precludes multiple expressions, traversals, possibilities and becomings. More than a problem of sovereign tension/ recovery, the very lacuna of which is premised upon fixed notions of self/Other, it is an ongoing process that re-works kingship by naturalising hierarchies and determinable inequalities in the most micro-political, adaptive and dynamic ways (see Holland 1999). It is therefore the witnessing of Oedipus as a productive (hence economising) over-coding force that concerns the contemporary: 'the child does not wait until he is an adult before grasping – underneath father-mother – the economic, financial, social, and cultural problems that cross through a family; his belonging or desire to belong to a superior or inferior "race"' (Deleuze and Guattari 2003: 278). Oedipus is 'born of an application or reduction [of social dynamics] to personal images, presupposes an investment of a paranoiac type'. Someone who 'engineers the masses, he is the artist of large molar aggregates, the statistical formations or gregariousnesses, the phenomena of organised crowds. He invests everything that falls within the province of large numbers (Deleuze and Guattari 2003: 279).

This brings us directly to the Foucauldian concept of the bio-political. Bio-politics refers to the strategisation of aggregated life for its own productive betterment. It links the 'individual' to the 'population' via a general economy of political rule. Deleuze appreciated the applicability of this concept long before it gained widespread academic currency. In his book *Foucault*, he paid considerable attention to those 'diagrams of power' in which modern systems of production, power and knowledge begin to take into account the 'processes of life', along with the possibility of modifying them: 'administering and controlling life in a particular multiplicity, provided the multiplicity is large (a population) and spread out or open. It is here that "making something probable" takes on its meaning' (Deleuze 1999: 61). This account of power is significant for two key reasons. First, since life becomes the principle referent for political struggles, life's politics either lives up to political expectations or puts the destiny of the entire species into question. As Deleuze says, 'when power in this way takes life as its aim or object, then resistance to power already puts itself on the side of life, and turns life against power: "life as a political object was in a sense taken at face value and turned back against the system so bent on controlling it"' (Deleuze 1999: 76). What resistance therefore extracts is 'the forces of life that is larger, more active, more affirmative and richer in possibilities'. Second, once power is broached bio-politically, it becomes increasingly clear why discourses of (in)security feature heavily in the mobilisation of 'war machines' for the securitisation/betterment of politically (dis)qualified life. For when life becomes the principle object for political strategies, violence so often associated with historical fascism appears less pathological and more reasoned:

> When a diagram of power abandons the model of sovereignty ... when it becomes the 'bio-power' or 'bio-politics' of populations, controlling and

administering life, it is indeed life that emerges as the new object of power. At that point law increasingly renounces the symbol of sovereign privilege, the right to put someone to death, but allows itself to produce all the more hecatombs and genocides: not by returning to the old law of killing, but on the contrary in the name of race, precious space, conditions of life and the survival of a population that believes itself to be better than its enemy, which it now treats not as a juridical enemy of the old sovereign but as a toxic or infectious agent, a sort of 'biological' danger.

(Deleuze 1999: 76)

A bio-political reading of fascism is crucial. Foregrounding notions of 'life necessity', the possibility that oppressive forms of politicisation can take place within legal frameworks becomes clearer. Fascism then is not necessarily a failure of the liberal imagination even if we understand liberalism to be simply a juridical commitment to rights. Neither is there any reason to believe that normative frameworks (especially those tied to universal moral proclamations) can prevent it from appearing within any social assemblage. To the contrary, normative judgements are in fact part of the problem. Essential to the play of power-politics, 'norms' normalise power over by limiting the political field of possibilities. They provide the necessary moral architecture so that a sophisticated assay of life can take place on the grounds of reasonable deliberation. They claim a monopoly over the terms security, rights, justice and peace, so that political judgements on the qualities of life become morally binding. Normative questions are not only therefore central to understanding what qualifies to be politically authentic; it properly disallows life so that its elimination can take place without any crime being committed. Less a problem of legal transgression, normative deliberations allow us positively to enforce *what is necessary for a life to be lived well*. While this entails the promotion of certain qualities so that ways of living thrive, it also entails fundamental decisions about what must be eliminated so that it is possible to overcome those related dangers to the secure sediment of political existence.

The unification of life

Ever since Hobbes wrote his *Leviathan* the concept of sovereignty has been aligned with the unification of life. Wonderfully depicted in the famous illustration which accompanies his manifesto, the body of the sovereign always presumes given unity of the body-politic. Security, then, if there is to be any, insists upon this divine figuration. What confirms political wholeness, the unity of the authentic political subjectivity, infers a completion in the order of things; oneness becoming the natural and intended condition proper to politically qualified life. All else is simply a dangerous impediment to natural togetherness. Whilst this inception of the security imperative into the modern imaginary colonised early modern political thinking to the extent that every political state of mind was ontologically programmed to become a mind of the state, sovereignty alone nevertheless always failed to deliver on its promises. As the supreme source of authority its allegiance has proved incapable of taming the multiplicity of forces in any given social order. This was fully appreciated by Immanuel Kant who, contrary to the neo-Kantian juridical proclamations, insisted that something above and beyond sovereign power was necessary to ensure that *perpetual peace* can be established. So how then is the transcendent field conceived given that sovereign power alone cannot unify the species? Indeed, what is the unifying principle for the human collective given that the human condition is always and already assumed by the limits of its reason to be too dangerously flawed to meet this task alone?

Our answer is actually to be found by paying more considered schematic attention to the wider corpus of Kantian thought. The familiar Kantian narrative suggests that the unifying principle for humanity is located in its juridical commitment rights and justice. Humanity, from this perspective, makes itself real on account of its commitment to those constituted forms of allegiance which reason human togetherness to be the natural order of things. Kant, however, was always dubious that law alone could create the lasting conditions of perpetual peace he so craved. What is more, not only did Kant question our ability to access the universal in any given experience, but he also posed a direct challenge to any universal predilection by introducing into his schematic a highly contingent notion of evil premised on its productive, adaptive and earthly qualities (Anderson-Gold 2001; Michaelson 1990). Kant's project should therefore be less judged against its 'Kingdom of Ends'. His belief in the limits of human reason after-all defied any completed reverence. Neither should he be simply condemned for condemning us to a representational image of thought that ties our political imagination to idealised forms. Why Kant holds such a privileged place in the liberalism tradition is that he introduces with righteous onto-theological quest the bio-political notion that freedom is primarily a societal-wide problem of good versus dangerous circulations. Since the Kantian project in other words merely deploys universal narratives (in all their idealistic representational forms) in order to mask the contingent problem of life necessity (which firmly relating it to 'unnecessary' conditions rendered evil to be something part of this world), what is transcendent is principled through an eschatology of the living – a divine economy of life itself (Evans 2012).

Whilst Kant inaugurated liberalism's bio-political imperative by moralising the productive nature of human activity, the horrors of Nazism justified this imperative's *imperative*. The spectre of the Third Reich both haunts and conditions the liberal imaginary to the extent that its occurrence has subsequently given sure moral purchase to the attempts at strategising planetary life. Nazism could not then be seen to be a tragedy that happened to the European Jewry alone. It has become the model against which all human imperfections (political, economic, social, cultural, or otherwise) could be ultimately judged (Lyotard 1990: 77). This has had a lasting political impact. Not only has the calling 'never again' been used to create protective enclaves for endangered peoples (a policy in itself which reveals the highly contingent application of the liberal responsibility to protect), but it also has been deployed to sanction forms of interventionism that ultimately have led to the collapse of the Westphalia pretence. Whilst the trauma associated with Nazism therefore seemed to destroy the very idea of humanity as a concept the moment it seemed to be gaining widespread political currency, it nevertheless has become the liberal condition of possibility par excellence. That is to say, whilst the holocaust in particular categorically denies any meaningful philosophical intelligibility – especially if one takes the original task of the *philos* to be the order of friendship, every shameful lasting memory it provides resurrects humanistic impulses out of the ashes of its most troubling episode.

Nazi Germany has proved integral to the revival of liberal thought by laying the intellectual foundations for the capitalisation of peace to follow. The work of Friedrich Von Hayek struck a precise chord. In his influential work *The Road to Serfdom* (1944), he managed to offer a damning indictment of state socialism by equating it with the rise of fascist power. Hayek equally managed to rework the theory of the state insomuch as it was recognised to provide a necessary regulatory and policing function essential to the secure functioning of the market economy. Indeed, for Hayek, not only was the free market the best possible model for dealing with the devastating economic problems of the time, but more important still, since it was inextricably bound with individual freedom and liberty, it was equipped with its own moral and political armoury that is necessarily universalistic (Shand 1992). In short, for Hayek, given that the political problems the world faced could be reduced to a matter of economic organisation, questions of economy were by their very nature of moral and political importance:

> The so called economic freedom which the planners promise us means precisely that we are to be relieved of the necessity of solving our own economic problems and the bitter choices which this often involves are to be made for us. Since under modern conditions we are for almost everything dependent on means which our fellow men provide, economic planning would involve direction of almost the whole of our life. There is hardly an aspect of it, from our primary needs to our relations with our family and friends, from the nature of our work to the use of our leisure, over which the planner would not exercise his 'conscious control'.
>
> (Hayek 1944: 69)

The crux of Hayek's argument was straightforward. The false tyrannical promises of 'planning for freedom' meant that societies had abandoned the truly enlightened liberal ideal of man as both a free economic and political animal who was capable of mastering his own moral destiny through reasoned choice. This abandonment had disastrous consequences in the sense that it was the dangerous seduction of socialist-inspired planning that had taken us on an amoral detour which constrained the intellectual and creative potential inherent to a free market society. The liberated subject was in other words being suffocated beneath the bureaucratic and oppressive weight of planned institutionalism. Hayek thus called for a return of key principles of laissez-faire liberalism which, attending specifically to the freeing up of economic activity, led to the emancipation of the political subject on a planetary scale. As Hayek explains, 'in no other field has the world yet paid so dearly for the abandonment of nineteenth century liberalism as in the field where the retreat began: in international relations' (Hayek 1944: 163). Through Hayek, not only then was a conscious call made to challenge the traditional political integrities enshrined in the principles of Westphalia since they actually stood in the way of global emancipation. Replacing juridical unity with a truly effective global political economy, he made it clear that there was an intellectual obligation to settle the political at all costs:

> We must make the building of a free society once more an intellectual adventure, a deed of courage. What we lack is a liberal Utopia, a program which seems neither a mere defence of things as they are nor a diluted kind of socialism, but a truly liberal radicalism ... Unless we can make the philosophic foundations of a free society once more a living intellectual issue, and its implementation a task which challenges the ingenuity and imagination of our liveliest minds, the prospects of freedom are indeed dark. But if we can regain that belief in power of ideas which was the mark of liberalism at its best, the battle is not lost.
>
> (Hayek 1969: 194)

Whilst Hayek equipped the free market with a sure moral purchase, it is nevertheless possible to detect beneath the surface a shameful deceit. Sovereignty for its part has always betrayed unification. As Schmitt (1996) famously proclaimed, what makes the sovereign concept real is the ability to declare upon the exception. It only functions by mapping out distinctions between politically qualified and politically disqualified in a manner in which the latter informs the former (Agamben 1995). Sovereignty's technical mantra is therefore 'inclusive-exclusion'. It relies upon marks of absolute separation in order to define the realm's moral and political registers. Indeed, it is only by pointing to the epiphenomenal that one's place in the world begins to make any phenomenological sense. Without 'them' who are 'we'? Without 'externalities' why the 'internal'? Without 'endangerment' what need for the 'sovereign'? Such markers have undoubtedly dominated what it means to think politically. Moving through the allegiant frames of Queen and Country, Fatherland, Motherland, Homeland, Nation, and even onto the final great binary of 'outright' destruction made possible by the geo-strategic divisions of the Cold War, sovereign unity has been inextricably bound to a regimes of power and violence that are 'marked out' by clear lines of demarcation between self/other, inside/outside, friend/enemy, citizen/soldier, and so forth. Its unity at best bequeaths uneasy alliance, while at worst Total War.

Progressive unification in contrast is made real on account of its modes of '*in*corporation'. While these modalities emanate from humanistic sensibilities, they are nevertheless initially conceived in 'quantitative' terms. This enables relative comparisons. Indeed, what is progressive as a matter of principle only finds meaningful expression once wagered against the 'regressive'. Since progressive notions of unity are therefore premised upon 'statistical' qualities that sub-divide elements into various deviations from the 'standard', progressive imaginaries consists of 'unifying' and 'divisive' tendencies which make judgements premised upon temporally conceived stages of advancement or backwardness. That is not to suggest a uniform teleology. Modern times are multiple times. Each can live on its own sliding scale. While a progressive imaginary thus emanates from a more/less incomplete account of life, the 'identification' of those of 'inferior quality' who are subject to remedy and demanding engagement births the problem of race by means of the need for a sophisticated taxonomical assay. This is the betrayal. Since these taxonomies have never been simply tied to epidermal schematics and distinctions alone, race has always been tied to the wider problem of societal progression/regression that provides judgement on particular 'ways of life'. The outcome of course has been to invoke humanistic narratives in order to accentuate the most acute and violent divisions amongst the human species.

Zygmunt Bauman's mastery of the Holocaust provides an important complimentary here. As Bauman notes:

> The unspoken terror permeating our collective memory of the Holocaust (and more than contingently related to the overwhelming desire not to look the memory in its face) is the gnawing suspicion that the Holocaust could be more than an aberration, more than a deviation from an otherwise straight path of progress, more than a cancerous growth on the otherwise healthy body of the civilised society; that, in short, the Holocaust was not an antithesis of modern civilisation and everything (or so we like to think) it stands for.
>
> (Bauman 1991: 7)

From Bauman's perspective, the Holocaust appears 'normal' in the sense that it is 'fully in keeping with everything we know about civilisation, its guiding spirit, its priorities, its immanent vision of the world – and of the proper way to pursue human happiness together with a perfect society' (Bauman 1991: 8). Society then embraced ideas of racial supremacy while it sought social perfection: 'What may list that possibility to the level of reality is, however, the characteristically modern zeal for order-making, the kind of posture which casts the extant human reality as a perpetually unfinished project, in need of critical scrutiny, constant revision and improvement. When confronted with that stance, nothing has the right to exist because of the fact that it happens to be around' (Bauman 1991: 229). Not then some moment of exceptional crises. It was in fact normal that the Nazis' fascistic appeal managed to mobilise popular support by manipulating desires to terrifying yet normalizing affect.

Bauman's work exposes fascistic violence in a thoroughly modern (i.e. reasoned, rational and calculated) way: 'Jews were to die not because they were resented; they were seen as deserving death (and resented for that reason) because they stood between this one imperfect and tension ridden reality and the hoped-for world of tranquil happiness ... They were killed because they did not fit, for one reason or another, the schema of a perfect society. Their killing was not the work of destruction, but creation' (Bauman 1991: 76, 92). So contrary to Agamben's insinuations, this particular genocide was not a problem that opened up a threshold between legal/illegal exceptionality. Operating within the law, notions of legality were openly recruited into a wider normative framework in order to set out those who deviated. This narrative is undoubtedly challenging. Detecting within modern reason itself a distinct logic of power which sanctions the wholesale slaughter of millions providing it can draw upon the daily security concerns of life necessity/survivability, fascism is firmly embedded within the operative fabric of bio-political modernity. Not only does this force us to come to terms with the enlightenment's racist heritage, but it demands a more considered appreciation of the lessons to be learned so as to move us beyond the narrowly defined remit of sovereign protections/abuses.

The insecuritisation imperative

For every 'great organised molar security', there always exists 'a whole micro-management of petty fears, a permanent molecular insecurity, to the point that the motto of domestic policy makers might be: a macro-politics of society by and for a micro-politics of insecurity' (Deleuze and Guattari 2002: 215, 216). This logic of supplement is telling. Since security at the widest levels is premised upon the securitisation of the local, what happens locally is always directly concerning since it impinges upon the wider frame of reference. Local forms of insecuritisation today are firmly written against all our securities. With the contemporary milieu of planetary life tied to a global problem of life necessity, no longer does one act out of national survivability alone. Total planetary endangerment is now the default setting for a broadened and deepened security agenda that places life centre to its political strategies. Moving then beyond any geo-strategic account of vulnerability, contemporary liberal subjectivity is now made real on account of its need to be resilient to each and every threat which potentially threatens to engulf total species existence. Insecurity as such no longer registers in epiphenomenal terms. What threatens is no longer 'out there'. It is endemic to a liberal will to rule which, denying the outside any rightful distinction (even though life still exists beyond the liberal pale), imagines a political and social world of active incorporation that is already foreclosed.

This is what it means to live in an age of liberal reason. Not that liberalism is universally embraced; more that everything, as a *de facto* given, *ought* to be incorporated. This has had a number of telling implications: first, encouraging a more proactive phase of liberal engagement, the conduct of war has become fully bio-politicised in the sense that war has been inextricably tied to *human-itarian* considerations (Reid 2006; Dillon and Reid 2009); second, with sover-eign integrities bypassed, maladjusted societies have been increasingly brought into a global imaginary of threat (Duffield 2007); third, since this has led to the merger between the military and the developmental, Clausewitz has effectively been inverted on a planetary scale so that liberal politics has become the con-tinuation of global war by other means (Evans and Hardt 2010); fourth, with the very idea of 'the people' considered to be resolved by the global closure of political space, once-familiar distinctions between the inside/outside, military/ developmental, war/peace and soldier/citizen have entered into lasting crises (Evans 2010); and fifth, since what has become known as the development-security nexus (directly tying the dramatic materialisation of life to conditions of social cohesion) has continued to widen its security ambit to include the environment and climate adaptation, liberal bio-political rule has become generalised so that the management of 'active living space' matters for all our sakes on a planetary scale (Evans and Duffield 2011). None of this has made us feel any safer. It does, however, insist that since nothing, no one and nowhere is strategically marginal, nothing, no one and nowhere can be left to chance!

Whilst the desire to 'save strangers' has been presented to be a triumph of liberal reason, it nevertheless conceals a sophisticated racial assay of planetary life through which 'Others' continually appears to be a problem to be solved. Indeed, saving strangers more often than not requires saving them from themselves. While this neo-colonial tendency can be traced back to the early enlightenment period, new impetus has been added in the post 9/11 moment. Building on from the 1990s' Human Security notion that underdevelopment was dangerous, local maladjustment increasingly has appeared to have pla-netary consequences. What happens in the most remote areas is taken to have dire consequences for our metropolitan districts. Afghanistan proving to be the case point. With the local therefore having collapsed into the global, our sense of (in)security has been firmly written alongside the (in)securitisation of who are deemed to be regressive in a world of radical interconnectivity. So not only does the existence of Otherness become the default setting for pla-netary security governance, but it is right to intervene in order to transform any society providing what is *politically necessary* can be linked to *global problems of life necessity.*

This is not a difficult connect. The idea that we need to think of threats in recombinant planetary terms has become the truism of the twenty-first century (see World Economic Forum 2010). Terror itself now appears so parasitical to every form of disaster that it is fast becoming the basis for a new normalcy as the advent of the all hazard threat spectrum increasingly defines the security terrain.[1] With everything potentially connectable, it is now possible to write of the becoming-terror of each and every societal concern that plagues modern lib-eral societies. Despite, then, the discursive respite in the 'war on terror' nar-rative, the strategic effort has actually *multiplied* to the extent that all forms of crises management are increasingly written as part of the counter-terror strategy. Think, for instance, of the becoming-dangerous of trans-border migrations, toxic agents, infectious diseases, shadow economies and even financial catastrophes, to name a few. Not only does this place the capacity for terror into the heart of all possible eventualities (Evans 2010), but it openly recruits us all into the planetary war effort so that the way we go about our daily business can be written against the demise of those who seek to destroy our politically settled way of life (or vice versa). No wonder that universal commitments have become altogether contingent. The fact that we may need to tolerate the proliferation of security technologies, the re-working of legal safeguards, along with the daily militarisation of public space, simply indicates that today's recombinant crises are always greater than the secure epistemic comforts once afforded by ontologically fixed notions of being in the world.

Overwhelmed by its own hyperbolic contingency, contemporary security practices are no longer tied to limit conditions. Neither do they put most of their energies into realising universal laws. Life instead is increasingly governed through the ongoing emergency of its emergent existence (Dillon 2007). This has had a profound impact upon liberal forms of security governance. Learning from past disasters, whilst seeking to pre-empt the next possible event, the art of governing has become a *proflexive* pursuit open to continual adaptation and change. Provoking what is seen to be dangerously lurking in the shadows, it seeks actively to produce the future by forcing that which is yet to be formed into being. It is here that the economising nature of risk-based strategies really comes to the fore. Not only do risk-based strategies render possible crises amenable for public consumption by relating them to personal costs, but they allow for strategic choices to be made based on likely physical and material consequences. Decisions, in other words, can be made based on the relative value of the occurrence. With liberal societies therefore becoming more adept at producing security-based products for those who can afford the safe futurity they promise, danger-aversion strategies quite literally come at a cost. So while this consumerist approach re-affirms that we currently live in the most insecure of times, the security stakes equally appear far from evenly distributed as fundamental questions of protection and disposability are made on the basis of cost-/effect-/risk-based modelling.

Fascistic exposure

Dangers require exposure to the fact. Manipulated desire also requires exposure to the fact in order to force the body to act upon the present in order to thwart certain possible outcomes. Invariably, the manner in which desires are to be mobilised in the face of certain dangers largely depends upon the political strategies recruiting insomuch as the nature of threat is always rationality-specific. Every threat occasions a rational underpinning which foregrounds its primary specificity in the collective political imaginary. Liberal regimes for their part operate in a particularly novel way. Unlike totalitarian systems which rely upon secrecy, liberalism brings everything into the open. It continually exposes us to that which threatens the fabric of the everyday. Even our own violent excesses are subject to the same treatment. Since the sources of our anxieties do not therefore rest upon the fear of the unknown, i.e. the advent of *disappearance*, fears are generated through a communicative assault which overloads the senses by heightening the stakes of all *appearances*. Indeed, since visual representations of threat so integral to future imaginaries have become globally networked – hence effectively rendering localised drama greater affective power than ordinarily afforded – the visualization of all dangerous encounters becomes the power of the image combined in its affects. Everything in this visually internalised world is connectable – our fears included.

We are reminded by Paul Virilio's (2007) two regimes of fear. Mapping out the distinctions between totalitarian and liberal regimes, Virilio reveals some disturbing connections. While the former invokes paranoia by working in the shadows, the latter strikes at the same senses through *overexposure*. The former, in other words, stifles reality through repression and censorship, while the latter overloads the imaginary in a frenzied assault so that we are anxiously synchronised yet blinded to the attempted mastery of social space. The relationship to violence is particularly telling. While the embodiment of totalitarian regimes is pre-figured in the 'disappeared' – those missing lives who offer no empirical verification of the encounter – liberal violence is virtuously declared. It takes place as an 'open event'. It actively shapes the world anew by '*making* the world safer'. Importantly, for Virilio, these affective relations are never simply articulated in a linear, top-down fashion. Like a networked system they endlessly feed back: 'the synchronisation of sensations that are likely to affect our decisions' (Virilio 2010: 6). While the problem of terror has therefore become connectable with all manner of everyday threats, liberalism produces a different regime of fear that replaces the neat tensions of sovereign (dis)order with the paradox of a bio-political potentiality in which life itself always registers to be greater than the sum of its epistemic parts. This will have a profound impact upon both the spatial and the subject account of living systems.

Once notions of space are fully enclosed, nothing is epiphenomenal to the order of things. What terrifies actually *emerges* from within the afflicted community. It is integral to the modalities which sustain life. It is therefore no coincidence to find that contemporary accounts of terror demand environmental frames of reference (Sloterdijk 2009). Within a global imaginary of threat, we fear what we actually *produce*. That is to say, since what endangers arises from within our living systems, what threatens is integral to that existence (Virilio 2010). Not only does this imply that terror is necessarily indiscriminate. It is also indiscriminable and indistinguishable from the general environment (Massumi 2009). It precludes any prior elimination of the fact on the basis that its sheer possibility inaugurates its simulated occurrence. No longer then a conventionally singular problem, contemporary terrors register in the multiple. Anything can become the material source of our physical undoing. With sequential notions of catastrophe as such firmly displaced by an unending continuum of endemic crises, selective auto-immunity is replaced by the demands for an auto-responsive logic that strategically connects all things liveable. Since this invariably lends itself to pre-emptive forms of governance in which all manner of threats blur into one strategic framework for counter-affection, the political is effectively overwritten as the normalisation of threat foregrounds an account of life already assumed to be settled.

Faced with these conditions, geo-strategic tensions appear to be mere aberrations. Arcane remnants of an outdated past! Not only does this mean that our sense of political community transcends traditional state-centric demarcations, but enmity itself is radically transformed. As Michael Dillon and Julian Reid note, 'Here, there is no Schmittean existential enemy defined, in advance or by what Schmitt calls the miracle of decision, by its radical otherness ... instead, only a continuously open and changing field of formation and intervention: the very continuous and contingent emergency of emergence of life as being-in-formation; becoming-dangerous' (Dillon and Reid 2009: 44). This again is altogether Kantian. While Kant proposed a life of infinite potentiality, life in the process appeared infinitely problematic. The Kantian subject therefore not only finds its proper expression in our complex, adaptive and emergent times, but the paradoxical nature of its potentiality has redefined the security terrain so that *in*disirimination becomes the default setting. This is perhaps what Deleuze had in mind when he previously argued that a 'global agreement on security' was 'just as terrifying as war', for when our very life processes become the source of our bio-political concerns, what Kenneth Galbreith once termed the 'contented society' is displaced by an 'Anxious Mass' who fear the infinitely dangerous: 'All our petty fears will be organized in concert, all our petty anxieties will be harnessed to make micro-fascists of us; we will be called upon to stifle every little thing, every suspicious face, every dissonant voice.'

Whilst it is common to suggest that this dismantling of traditional sovereign allegiance has resulted in a crisis of subjectivity – to say that the subject is in crisis misses the point. Liberal subjectivity is made real on account of its ability to live through the ongoing emergency of its own emergence. Eschewing fixed modes of being, it is forever in the making. The liberal subject is therefore *the* subject of crises (Evans 2012). It lives and breathes through the continual disruption to its own static modes of recovery. None of this is incidental. It is central to paranoiac underpinnings of contemporary forms of fascism. While security has become the main criteria of political legitimacy (Agamben 2001), still we hold onto the belief that subjects of crises are *desirable*. Freed from the boundary-drawing constraints of the past, it is the risk-embracing subject who is enriched beyond their forbear's wildest dreams. This reveals the fateful paradox of our times. Encoded with an altogether more powerful bodily trope, contemporary liberal subjectivity is assumed to be exponentially more powerful and dangerous because of it. It, too, registers the same dynamic, decentralised and recombinant presumptions which give risk societies their very meaning. If its allegiance, then, can no longer be taken for granted, neither can its actions be anticipated with absolute precision. It, too, operates beyond the epistemic pale. While planetary life is therefore seen to be the proper embodiment of liberated political existence, life's emergent globality renders it globally dangerous unto itself because of this potentiality. We must in short learn to embrace and yet fear what we have become.

Life as bio-technology

Late liberalism shares certain features with Deleuzian ontology. Like Deleuze, it eschews fixed notions of being. Undermining traditional forms of sovereign allegiance, it seeks to create political communities anew. Like Deleuze, it also warns against the potential for political endangerment to reside in the most localised of levels. The post-Industrial individual's capacity to inflict a micro-apocalyptic attack is the case point. However, this is where the similarities end. Not only does Deleuze's preference for the micro-political stand in marked contrast to the universal orientations of liberal advocates, but Deleuze's allegiance to the affirmation of difference puts him in direct conflict with the liberal tendency to see the political as a problem to be solved. Hence, whilst Deleuze puts forward a concept of the political that is predicated upon one's affirmative becoming – thereby side-stepping dialectical notions of enmity (Evans 2010a) – liberalism seeks to 'control-becoming' in order to manufacture consent by over-coding the flows of life. If Deleuze, therefore, can be said to have a distinct 'politics of the event' that is open to a future-anterior, the liberal problematic of security takes this anteriority to be its point of departure so that all possible events (which if true to the creative philosophical understanding of the term 'event' necessarily has an inherent political element of becoming-different at its point of emergence) can be inserted into the strategic calculus of the security *dispositif*.

Here we arrive at the problem of 'life as technology'. This problematic has a considerable genealogy in the continental tradition. Beginning with Nietzsche, it would subsequently resonate throughout the critical works of Max Weber, Martin Heidegger and Hannah Arendt, to name a few. While Heidegger in particular is widely regarded to be the most influential theorist of technology, it was in fact Carl Schmitt who offered a purposeful critique that was fully aware of the political, cultural and philosophical stakes (McCormick 1997). Schmitt's contribution is significant for a number of reasons. In particular, for our concerns, it was Schmitt who: first, understood how technologically driven forms of oppression are latent within liberal regimes of power; second, related liberal oppression to the problem of the securitisation of life so that the political gets infiltrated by technologised vision of being; third, understood that technology referred to an entire ontological framework through which notions of political authentication take place; fourth, appreciated how technological processes of authentication are of an entirely different nomos to that of law, so that juridical safeguards tell us nothing and offer no protections from those technologies that fixate on the qualitative and the particular; fifth, paved the way for an understanding of technology that moves beyond mere scientism, so that the bio-affective dimensions to political manipulations are appreciated; and sixth, set out a framework so that juridical 'states of exception' appear markedly different from economising 'states of emergency' that denote a more normal (though no less oppressive) state of political affairs.

Despite Schmitt's revival in the post-9/11 moment, very few have sought to resurrect these particular concerns. Instead, his turn in fortunes in part emanates from liberal engagements that have sought to deploy Schmitt against himself in order to provide liberals with a way of distancing themselves from the perceived geo-strategic excesses of the global war on terror. With exceptionality therefore forming the basis on which a truly internationalist order of things is said to depend, Schmitt has been summoned to reveal the truth of a world in which power operates beyond the law. Leaving aside the fact that these accounts categorically fail to see liberalism as a contemporary regime of power, not only do they maintain the 'friend/enemy' decision in order to draw out their own 'concept of the political' (hence openly adopting Schmitt's methodology as they attempt to criticise him), but by pursuing some pure theory of the exception that does not grasp the ongoing exceptionality of every single law-making process (i.e. every law is made in response to some perceived exceptional moment of crises to prevailing order), there is a complete failure to deal with his wider corpus of which exceptional politics is merely a temporal ordering principle. Hence, while these attempts invariably fall into the precise dialectical trap that Schmitt set (so that enmity is subsequently tied to a vision of (in)humanity complete), no attempt whatsoever is made to deal with the links between Kantian positivism and technological determinism which he believed to be the basis of liberal oppression.

Despite our concerns with Schmitt, there is an evident danger here. Like Heidegger, we cannot get away from the fact that his personal intellectual journey proved to be politically disastrous. His personal affinities with Nazism, in particular, make it extremely difficult to engage his ideas especially in the context of fascism without invoking certain moral outrage. One possible way of navigating through these troubled waters is to expose the fateful paradox of his particular thought process. While Schmitt sought to rework the ideas of Hobbes in order to antidote liberal formalism with the myth of National Socialism, he actually ended up supporting a regime that became the master of the types of technologisation against which his work was so keen to warn. This was certainly anticipated by Walter Benjamin. Warning against the Schmittean 'myth of the nation' which was presented to be the antidote to the liberal age of technology, fascism as Benjamin explained was nevertheless consummate to the aestheticisation of political forms of domination to ideal mythical forms more violent than traditional forms of rule long since overcome:

> The logical result of Fascism is the introduction of aesthetics into political life. The violation of the masses, whom Fascism, with its Fuhrer cult,

forces to its knees, has its counterpart in the violence of an apparatus which is pressed into the production of ritual values … All efforts to render politics aesthetic culminate in one thing: war … 'Fiat ars – pereat mundus' says Fascism, and … expects war to supply the artistic gratification of a sense of perception that has been changed by technology.

(Benjamin 1968: 241)

Despite the violence and failures of Schmitt's thought, he does unwittingly force us to confront the dangers of political theology – whether the myth of unity is to be located in the 'Nation' or indeed the universal predilection to 'Humanity' complete. He also forces us to confront how the politics of technology can close down the fields of political possibility. Liberals, for the most part, have failed to come to terms with these particular debates. One struggles to find any reference whatsoever to issues of technology in the thought of recent luminaries like John Rawls for instance. When the concept is introduced (like bio-politics), a familiar Weberian move is adopted by introducing human agency so as to argue that the liberal subject cannot simply be reduced to some mechanical instrument capable of being prodded into action. Such critiques, however, rest upon particularly bad readings of technology/bio-politics, which tend to follow directly on from earlier counter-criticisms of continental philosophy by arguing against the reduction of life to the level of pure technology. A return to Deleuze is again necessary. Not only did he offer a more considered reflection on the politics of technology which frees us from these purely technical accounts, but his introduction of desire into the social field allows us firmly to cast aside any attempts to link bio-political concerns with the abandonment of political subjectivities.

Deleuze argued that technicity is not simply 'machine-like' or purely 'technical'. Neither do machinic forms of enslavement precede social assemblages: 'machines are social before being technical. Or, rather, there is human technology which exists before a material technology. No doubt the latter develops its effects within the whole social field; but in order for it to be even possible, the tools or material machines have to be chosen first of all by a diagram and taken up by the assemblages' (Deleuze 1999: 34). While some technologies may therefore be completely indifferent to the politics of life, we nevertheless still produce what we desire. Since technologies are not therefore enslaving *per se*, we need to analyse the intimate relationships between social assemblages and the instruments they positively deploy in the daily functioning of their systems of power, knowledge and rule. Appreciating this reversal, Deleuze does more than simply nuance our understanding of the politics of technology by introducing human desire into the frame. By foregrounding the desiring subject, he offers an account of bio-political fascism that is all about *the active liberation of certain political subjectivities/agencies at the expense of others*. Inverting then any account of technologically driven de-politicisation which stands accused of leading to the evacuation of all politics – more seductive still, following Deleuze, bio-politicised fascism refers to the active politicisation of desires to the point of their unmediated technical delivery.

Deleuze exposes the mistaken link between bio-politics and the abandonment of political agency thesis. He also allows us to see that our problem is not one of de-politicisation if one understands this process to be the full reduction of life to some purely instrumental vision of species being. Hence, moving beyond the soulless and emotionless narratives of techno-pursuing instrumentalisation, his critique of affective bio-machinic assemblages reconciles bio-logical capacities with the governance of life in a machine-like manner. With machinic assemblages seconded by social relations, what matters are the socially invested power relations which lead to the (self)-deprecation of life. Whilst historical readings of fascism therefore continue to separate passions from progressive rationalities, our task remains to understand how desire can be manipulated in order to permit the wilful subjectification of ourselves and others. So in spite of the fact that the broadening and deepening of the security agenda is premised on countering any abuse of political power, unless the political is privileged in these encounters there is no guarantee that lives won't be politically suffocated, so that once again Spinoza's tragic question echoes to reason 'why is it that the masses stubbornly fight for their servitude as though it were their liberation?'

Notes

1 This is clearly articulated in the British government's National Security Strategy (2008), which explains: 'the overall objective of this National Security Strategy is to anticipate and address a diverse range of threats and risks to our security, in order to protect the United Kingdom and its interests, enabling its people to go about their daily lives freely and with confidence, in a more secure, stable, just, and prosperous world ... [Threats and risks] are real, and also more diverse, complex, and interdependent than in the past. The policy responses outlined ... , therefore, [are] not only individually vital to our future security and prosperity, but also wide-ranging, complex, and, crucially, interdependent. They reflect an integrated approach to developing policy and building capability, intended to deliver results against a number of linked objectives.'

References

Agamben, G. *Homo Sacer: Sovereign Power and Bare Life* (Stanford: Stanford University Press, 1995)
——'Security & Terror' (*Theory & Event* Vol. 5, No.4, 2001)
——*State of Exception* (Chicago: University of Chicago Press, 2005)
Anderson-Gold, S. *Unnecessary Evil: History & Moral Progress in the Philosophy of Immanuel Kant* (New York: State University Press, 2001)
Arendt, H. *A Report on the Banality of Evil: Eichmann in Jerusalem* (New York: Penguin, 1963)
Bauman, Z. *Modernity & the Holocaust* (Cambridge: Polity Press, 1991)
Benjamin, W. *Illuminations* (New York: Schocken, 1968)
Buchanan, I. *Deleuzism: A MetaCommentary* (Edinburgh: Edinburgh University Press, 2000)
Deleuze, G. *Foucault* (London : Continuum, 1999)

——*Two Regimes of Madness: Texts and Interviews 1975–1995* (New York: Semiotext(e), 2006)

Deleuze, G. and Guattari, F. *What is Philosophy?* (London: Verso, 1994)

——*A Thousand Plateaus: Capitalism and Schizophrenia* (London: Continuum, 2002)

——*Anti-Oedipus: Capitalism and Schizophrenia* (London: Continuum, 2003)

Dillon, M. 'Governing Terror. The State of Emergency of Biopolitical Emergence' (*International Political Sociology* Vol.1, No.1, 2007)

——'Security, Race, War', in Michael Dillon and Andrew Neal (eds) *Foucault on Politics, Security and War* (London: Palgrave, 2008), 166–96.

Dillon, M. and Reid, J. *The Liberal Way of War: Killing to Make Life Live* (London: Routledge, 2009)

Duffield, M. *Development, Security & Unending War: Governing the World of Peoples* (Cambridge: Polity Press, 2007)

Evans, B. 'Terror in All Eventuality' (*Theory & Event*, Vol.13, No.1, 2010)

——'Life Resistance: Towards a Different Concept of the Political' (*Deleuze Studies* Vol.4, No.3, 2010a)

——'The Liberal War Theses: Introducing the Ten Key Principles of 21st Century Bio-Political Warfare' (*The South Atlantic Quarterly* Vol.110, No.3, 2011)

——*Liberal Terror: Global Security, Divine Power & Emergency Rule* (London: Routledge, forthcoming 2012)

Evans, B. and Duffield, M. 'Biospheric Security: How the Merger Between Development, Security & the Environment [Desenex] is Retrenching Fortress Europe', in Peter Burgess and Serge Gutwirth (eds) *A Threat Against Europe? Security, Migration and Integration* (Brussels: VUB Press, 2011)

Evans, B. and Hardt, M. 'Barbarians to Savages: Liberal War Inside and Out' (*Theory & Event* Vol.13, No.1, 2010)

Foucault, M. *Power/Knowledge: Selected Interviews & Other Writings, 1972–1977* (New York: Pantheon, 1980)

——*Society Must be Defended: Lectures at the College de France 1975–1976* (New York: Picador, 2003)

——*Security, Territory & Population: Lectures at the College de France 1977–1978* (New York: Palgrave Macmillan, 2007)

Hayek, F.V. *The Road to Serfdom* (London: Routledge, 1944)

——Studies in Philosophy, Politics and Economics (London: Touchstone, 1969)

Holland, E. *Deleuze & Guattari's 'Anti-Oedipus': Introduction to Schizoanalysis* (London: Routledge, 1999)

——'Schizoanalysis, Nomadology, Fascism', in Ian Buchanan and Nicholas Thoburn (eds) *Deleuze and Politics* (Edinburgh: Edinburgh University Press, 2008), 74–97.

Lyotard, J.-F. *Heidegger & 'the Jews'* (Minneapolis: University of Minnesota Press, 1990)

McCormick, J. *Carl Schmitt's Critique of Liberalism: Against Politics as Technology* (Cambridge: Cambridge University Press, 1997)

Massumi, B. *Parables for the Virtual: Movement, Affect, Sensation* (Durham: Duke University Press, 2002)

——'National Enterprise Emergency: Steps Towards an Ecology of Powers' (*Theory, Culture & Society* Vol.26, No.6, 2009), 153–85.

Michaelson, G.E. *Fallen Freedom: Kant on Radical Evil & Moral Regeneration* (Cambridge: Cambridge University Press, 1990)

Schmitt, C. *The Concept of the Political* (Chicago: University of Chicago Press, 1996)

——*Political Theology: Four Chapters on the Concept of Sovereignty* (Chicago: University of Chicago Press, 2006)

Shand, A. *Free Market Morality: The Political Economy of the Austrian School* (London: Routledge, 1992)

Sloterdijk, P. *Terror from the Air* (Los Angeles, CA: Semiotext(e), 2009)

Virilio, P. *The Original Accident* (Cambridge: Polity, 2007)

——*The University of Disaster* (Cambridge: Polity, 2010)

World Economic Forum, *Global Risks 2010: A Global Risk Network Report* (Geneva: WEF, 2010)

4   Movement and human logistics

Pre-emption, technology and fascism

Geoffrey Whitehall

The likelihood that someone in a Western leadership position (i.e. George W. Bush, Barack Obama, Stephen Harper, Nicolas Sarkozy or Silvio Berlusconi) will be called a fascist today has increased (and perhaps for good reason). Underlying this trend is an abandonment of the exceptionalism of historical fascism and Nazism and, first, the generalization of fascism as if it were a logic of politics, and/or second, the mobilization of fascism as an axiological marker. In this chapter, I am uninterested in the second (but also likely) explanation and am more sympathetic to the possibility of the former. After all, the desire to find *another* way to call someone or something evil, alien or fascist seems to lie within the domain of an ever-proliferating fascist logic of politics.

A similar argument can be made about the often twinned term genocide. Although there has been a proliferating use of the term as an axiological marker of immanent fascism (and strategy for securing global action), there has also been a parallel move away from linking genocide with the Holocaust and Nazism. There are many more examples of genocidal violence that are linked, not with historical fascism, but with colonialism, totalitarianism and imperialism. Aimé Césaire (1972) identified the fascination with the European genocide, for instance, with a discourse of colonialism that treated these horrific events as exceptional instead of as exemplary of something that was practised and perfected on non-Europeans. Similarly, Hanna Arendt (1951) tied the European genocide to scientific racism and bureaucratic efficiencies developed in South Africa. Contemporaneously, Mahmood Mamdani (2001) traces the origins of the populist Rwandan genocide to the production of political (not cultural) identities through direct rule (native/settler) and indirect rule (divide ethnicities and rule) during the colonial project. Mamdani also points to the recent desire to mobilize the term as a tool (or ideological crutch) of Western humanitarian intervention in the Sudan (2009). 'If genocide is indeed', as Michel Foucault argues, 'the dream of modern powers, this is not because of a recent return to the ancient right to kill; it is because power is situated and exercised at the level of life, the species, the race and the large scale phenomena of the population' (Foucault 1978: 137). Perhaps neither genocide nor fascism is entirely exceptional.

In this vein, a logic of politics that replaces lived complexity with epistemological categorizations of self/other, settler/native, civilized/barbarian and friend/enemy is shared by *modern* colonialism, totalitarianism, imperialism, fascism and liberalism. Exploration of this logic of politics has proliferated with the celebration of Giorgio Agamben's work on *the life that can be extinguished without violation to the internal codes of civility* in Homo Sacer (1998). Attention to refuges, enemy combatants, infected lives and the global dispossessed is a meaningful expansion of those earlier efforts to link fascism to broader political logics. However, this singular attention to this logic of politics (sovereignty, security and community) could benefit from some conceptual flexibility (if not liquidity). Privileging the political logic of sovereignty through perpetual critique is undesirable if the objective is renewing the political itself.

In this chapter, I turn away from this logic of politics and instead emphasize a logic of movement. A new political imaginary (both in terms of diagnosis and directive) is needed that does not set up questions of movement in order to celebrate their opposites in security, peace, justice and reason. As such, I begin within movement, war and logistics. An attention to movement, in general, and kinds of movement, in particular, is required to become politically adequate to the challenges of contemporary fascism.

From nomadology to Clausewitz and back again

Deleuze and Guattari's essay *Nomadology* (1986) remains one of the most impressive works upon the political imaginary because it treats movement as a creative force and not as a condition to be solved. From a kind of encounter between the state, as an apparatus of capture, and the nomad, as a line of flight, Deleuze and Guattari introduce an appropriated war machine that is housed in the name of State Security. While the state operates with the assumption that it has captured the war machine in the service of its limited wars, those tendencies towards total war remain ever-present. The war machine retains its deterritorializing nomadism. That the state never had a war machine of its own is, in itself, a kind of warning; the state should not be presumed to be in control of war.

Deleuze and Guattari's acknowledgement of the possibility that the war machine takes itself as its object runs contrary to the Clausewitzian claim that the state may use war as a mechanism to achieve its *limited* political objects (i.e. establish political peace). They warn, 'when total war becomes the object of the appropriated war machine [it] can reach the point of contradiction ... [and become] unlimited' (Deleuze and Guattari 1986: 118). However, 'total war is not only a war of annihilation, but arises when annihilation takes as its "center" not only the enemy army, or the enemy state, but the entire population and its economy' (Deleuze and Guattari 1986: 118). Here, Deleuze and Guattari are not making a claim about the scope and scale of war; instead, nothing escapes total war's unlimited gaze because the appropriated war machine, with itself as its object, exists as a self-actualizing movement. In this event, even the *end* of unlimited war fails to provide a *limit* to this self-actualizing movement. War is without end. Clausewitz's peace becomes a point of transduction as this new automatic logic of movement is born.

Given that Deleuze and Guattari's writings on war in *Nomadology* are directed, in part, towards the problem of fascism, it is worthwhile to ask: did fascism, as a logic of movement, survive World War II? Although they do not exactly give a clear answer to the question in one of their most stunning statements, Deleuze and Guattari do establish the stakes of the question. They assert 'this worldwide war machine, which in a way "reissues" from the State, displays two successive figures: first, that of fascism which makes war an unlimited movement with no other aim than itself; but fascism is only a rough sketch, and the second, post-fascist figure is that of a war machine that takes peace as its object directly as the peace of terror or survival. The war machine reforms a smooth space which now claims to control, to surround the entire earth' (Deleuze and Guattari 1986: 118–19). We are left to wonder, nonetheless, did post-World War II peace become a point of transduction when a new kind of 'post-fascism' was born? Has the whole earth fallen to a kind of generalized war called peace? In response, Deleuze and Guattari's indebtedness to Clausewitz remains instructive.

Clausewitz's optimism about politics limiting the drives of war (i.e. hatred, animosity, the play of probabilities and chance) is revised by Deleuze and Guattari. They reverse his maxim 'war as the continuation of politics through an admixture of other means', to read 'politics is the continuation of war by other means' (Deleuze and Guattari 1986: 118–19). In this spirit, war itself is the driving force. Clausewitz's theory of limited war, as such, is read against his optimistic dismissal of the likelihood of total war. Instead of limiting war, the complexity of hatred and animosity, the reciprocal nature of war and the play of probabilities and chance, in the end, redefine, reenergize and transform war. War, in this sense, might become total (or even absolute). The three reciprocal actions of war that Clausewitz identifies are critical here: first, war leads to the extreme; second, as long as the enemy is not defeated, he could defeat me; and third, a mutual enhancement of fear creates a new extreme (Clausewitz 1982: 103–5). Through these three reciprocal actions, war reveals itself to be its own engine and, irrespective of state policy, its own end. Because Deleuze and Guattari do not give origin or ownership of war to the state, wars need not be restricted to finding their end or limit in political peace. Limited wars may find further fulfilment in one or more continuous wars and become what Clausewitz initially rejected: war is its own object (Clausewitz 1982. 106).

At least two post-World War II horizons are available. First, total war becomes politics (as Benjamin, Foucault and Agamben have suggested). In this instance, the suspensions of habeas corpus, extraordinary rendition are extreme examples of a total war (or total peace) that seeks total domination as its political object. To this end, we are right identifying every form of pastoral power and petty fascism as the real emergency of our times. From humanitarian organizations, to management consultants and community policing, governmentalized war is everywhere! Or (and this 'or' need not be exclusionary), war develops through one of its other constituent parts, retains its own potentialities and becomes a different kind of movement. Specifically, if Clausewitz's war is less about the 'who, what and where' of politics than the exceptional choice of *object*, then the broad underbelly of the war/politics synthesis might be that objective channel of war called 'logistics'.

Treating logistics as the heart, and not the sideshow of war, would require further distortion of Clausewitz's theory of war and would invite developing the position of Clausewitz's critic, Baron de Jomini. For Clausewitz, logistics are not tactical (i.e. use of military force in combat), strategic (i.e. use of combat for the object of war), nor political (i.e. deciding the object of war) (Clausewitz 1982: 173). As such, logistics are only 'conditions' and 'extraneous activities' that are used for the 'maintenance of troops' (Clausewitz 1982: 176). They do include war-like activities (i.e. building infrastructure in the presence of an enemy), but they also include peace-like activities (i.e. maintaining camps, providing subsistence for the troops, caring for the sick and wounded, active management and administration and preparing for war). Jomini warns against underplaying the significance of these components of war. He states 'Logistics comprises the means and arrangements that work out the plans of strategy and tactics' (Jomini 1972: 69). Without proper attention to logistics, as such, the plan (strategy) and its execution (tactics) could not take place.

Jomini's insistence on logistics 'forming one of the most essential parts of the art of war' (Jomini 1972: 252) is not necessarily what makes his contribution interesting. Instead, Jomini's chapter on logistics reveals an ever-expanding logistical horizon. He laments the inapplicability of old definitions of logistics (i.e. the movement of troops) to more modern situations. Instead, an expanded definition risks becoming 'nothing more nor less than the science of applying all possible military knowledge' (Jomini 1972: 253). The importance of harmony of action is so great in war, he concluded, that the subject of logistics expands: it is 'not only the duties of ordinary staff officers, but of generals-in-chief' (Jomini 1972: 254). It should not be surprising, therefore, that the expansion of the military-industrial complex has been a concern since (at least) Eisenhower, and the expanding military-industrial-media-entertainment complexes electrify those interested in contemporary warfare (Der Derian 2001; Singer 2009). No longer can the developments in civil, economic, scientific and technological domains be held separate from the theatre of war. If war were to be waged through peace, as is proposed, it would necessarily pass through the logistics of caring, feeding, training, entertaining and working the population.

I want to suggest that this logistical emphasis can be pushed further than what Jomini allows. There is an even more insidious expansion of logistics in Clausewitz's *own* treatment of affect. Remember, the purpose of war for Clausewitz is to break the will of enemy so that the full force of their battle readiness cannot be mobilized. Clausewitz warns that 'if war is an act of force, it belongs *necessarily* also to the feelings. It does not originate in the feelings, it reacts, more or less, upon them … ' (Clausewitz 1982: 103, my emphasis). Hatred, anger, fear and courage, for instance, are all emotional and moral attributes that we easily identify with a theory of warlike conduct. These attributes could be considered as motivational parallels to tactics, strategy and combat in war. This consideration, in itself, would suggest that the affective register constitutes a general infrastructural milieu in which war occurs. Getting soldiers to fight requires mobilizing this emotional logistics.

Developing this logistical element further, Clausewitz's theory of will does not solely rest with these specific emotional attributes (hatred, anger, courage) but draws from a more fundamental affective register. This is the key point. This affective register is the logistical creation and management of the self. For Clausewitz, what aides in the management of the self is not higher or transcendent qualities like wisdom (Thucydides), situational awareness (Sun Tzu) or judgement (Machiavelli). Instead, he offers a logistical solution: habit. 'Habit', Clausewitz argues, 'gives strength to the body in great exertion, to the mind in danger, to the judgement against first impressions' (Clausewitz 1982: 167). Habit is burned into the very condition of being and becoming different. In war, we have habits of being. 'Habit soon blunts impressions' allowing instantaneous decisions in 'the sphere of activity' (Clausewitz 1982: 160). Habit conditions the decision and it manages the self logistically. In war we are reduced, before we are killed, to the logistical element, the habit of living.

The complete reversal of Clausewitz, therefore, would treat the capture of politics by war as a cursory moment in a much broader capture of politics, war *and* life by an ever-expanding and all-encompassing domain of logistics. Ignoring the centrality of logistics leads to the false difference between contemporary peace and war. Whereas present day neo-Clausewitzians see the revolution in military affairs and the push to full spectrum dominance as reflections of a fundamental transformation of the nature of strategy in contemporary warfare (Rasmussen 2006: 56), a complete reversal would push beyond relations of war and peace into the day-to-day life-habit or management of life itself. Instead of contemporary warfare's new strategy being the management of multiple risks (i.e. terrorism, pandemics, bank failures, resource shocks and mass migration) and its political object being reducing them to zero through total domination or peace (Rasmussen 2006: 65), a complete reversal would identify Deleuze and Guattari's post-fascism within an affective logistics of human being.

Global logisticity as global triage

The war-peace that Deleuze and Guattari identify would be located and would take its time in the logistical systems of systems that function to make eruptions of war possible while managing an ever-present life-habit of quotidian peace. To Clausewitz's chagrin, absolute war would be a singular, self-referential, generalized grinding of peace that consumes the lives of 18 million a year while waiting patiently for the surrender of the next 2.7 billion who live in extreme poverty (Pogge 2008). Habits in war become normalized in peace. This war-peace would be reflected in an automatic functioning, an operating system, a reciprocal cycle fulfilling a kind of permanent pre-emptive global logistical life. Logistical life, Julian Reid explains, 'is lived under the duress of the command to be efficient, to communicate one's purpose transparently in relation to others, to be positioned where one is required, to use time economically, to be able to move when and where one is told, and crucially, to be able to extol these capacities as the values which one would willingly, if called upon, kill and die for' (Reid 2006: 13). However, as Clausewitz warns, 'the noiseless harmony of the whole action ... only makes itself known in the total result' (Clausewitz 1982: 242). We have yet to name this total result.

What we are witnessing today is the actualization of a global triage (Whitehall 2009, 2010). It is a global killing machine designed to save lives. It saves some lives at the cost of others. However, the decision between saving this life or that life is not political (i.e. deciding between friend and enemy; Schmitt 1996); it is logistical. If it were political, then all that would be required to *limit* contemporary fascism, for instance, would be to, as Clausewitz suggests, change the political object through already established political fields (i.e. the state, government, democracy, social movements or the markets). Granted it is political that some lives are deemed to be worth less, that others are treated as if they are worth more, and that these onto-political decisions – about the status of being – are derivative of a prior politicization of life itself and the production of a population to be managed. However, these decisions are consistent with the thesis that war is being continued through politics. A global triage operates in excess of these very politicizations. These decisions constitute cursory moments within the automatic functioning of a global logisticity that is indifferent to the logic of politics and displaces the sovereign decision into habit.

Obvious faces of the global triage have been witnessed in the H1N1 pandemic, the avian flu emergency preparedness plan, the US policy of full spectrum dominance and the global 'war on terror'. Often aspects of international development policy, humanitarian intervention and human rights policy are similarly problematized. Less obvious faces of the global triage, however, operate in normal functioning global trade, finance and industry, at one level, and the production of desire, culture and fashion, at the other. The triage includes global-local collaborators from government, military, industry, media, agriculture, health, education, advocacy and entertainment. At the heart of contemporary fascism is the way in which these different triages are learning to coordinate, communicate and integrate into seamless optimizations and efficiencies. The global triage has two key components: pre-emption, and technology. Pre-emption pushes the decision into a non-political time and technology enacts those decisions as if through habit.

Although the legitimacy of pre-emption is usually debated in military terms (i.e. the US war in Iraq in 2003 or the Israeli attack on Egypt in 1967), the function of pre-emption is more closely associated with legitimacy derived from the precautionary principle and the promise of good governance. Central to these ideals is the creation of a temporal zone intended to buffer the shocks of immediate events. As such, the threat assessment that legitimizes all pre-emptive planning for pandemics, for example, requires the catch phrase: *it is not if, but when*. Tough decisions about life and death, allocation of resources, organizational structures are set in advance so as to offer legitimacy and defer the sense of immediacy. A kind of governing the future from the standpoint of the present seems normal; however, what actually occurs is a *governing of the present from the standpoint of an imaginary future*. Pre-emptive policy makers are, in effect, time travellers in a kind of science fiction. This temporal reversal has significant implications for how decisions are made and politics enabled.

Specifically, within the temporal buffer of pre-emption the boundary between friends and enemies disappears. While the distinction *may* be deployed in the public relations campaigns of such programmes and thereby putting the issues back into a kind of language that the public ironically finds non-threatening, within pre-emptive logistics the boundary disappears entirely. As such, it becomes possible to build momentum by harnessing and amplifying the threat of the enemy (i.e. cinema, video games). When the chimera of legitimacy drop (i.e. democracy, civil liberty, habeas corpus), a well-oiled war machine is revealed. Central to the function of this machine, as Brian Massumi (2007) explains, is to become like the enemy in order to destroy the 'enemy' (i.e. in counter-insurgency exercises and risk management), and further, the enemy may actually be employed and/or enriched in order to make strategic advances (i.e. vaccine programmes, research plans or investment portfolios). Finally, the objectives of the enemy become interchangeable with the promises of good governance (i.e. justice, equilibrium and adaption). Mitigation, as such, has no friends or enemies.

What is crucial for pre-emption to function, moreover, is the change in the nature of the decision. Whereas within a logic that defines politics by the friend/enemy decision (i.e. a privileged function of the logic of sovereignty; Schmitt 1985), pre-emption allows excessive-binary, extra-representational, and in-different distinctions to be made. In other words, pre-emption does not require the choice between this or that (or that …); it *allows* for everything. It operates within an infinite linking of connections. When nothing is denied or affirmed, *whatever works*[1] becomes a kind of operating system. If an alternative definition to the friend/enemy distinction is offered and politics requires *taking or making the time, when you have no time* (Rancière 2009), then not only can the 'political' nature of pre-emption be more fully appreciated, but it also becomes possible to imagine the unexpected kinds of political horizons operating *in and through* a global logisticity. Pre emption makes time by occupying, exploiting and mortgaging the future. It works by sucking up time in which political beings breathe. To politicize logistics would, therefore, be exponentially more difficult. As will be explored later, it would require that *new time be made for a time that never 'is'*.

The technological component of the global triage further depoliticizes and displaces the decision. The further the act of deciding is pushed into the automatic functioning of ever-emerging networks of networks, the more insignificant the action becomes and the more difficult it is to politicize. The decision, as such, is no longer an exception awaiting the sovereign prerogative. Instead it has become a slipstream automatically operating behind the movement. No longer a bottleneck, roadblock or gatekeeper, the decision becomes part of the general logistical flow. Coupled with the normalization of pre-emption, the decision unfolds long after the action has already taken place.

This development has been anticipated. Manuel De Landa (1991) identifies World War II as a logistical (not strategic or tactical) war because it pressed into service the entire resources of the state (De Landa 1991: 108). However, the emergence of cybernetic systems that are automatic, adaptive and self-correcting has further changed the way and the kinds of wars that can be fought. De Landa charts the disappearance of the boundary between advisory and executive capabilities (De Landa 1991: 1) in a process that 'would see humans as no more than pieces of a larger military-industrial machine' (De Landa 1991: 3). This development would allow a system to maintain its shape as it takes 'energy from its surroundings, channelling and dissipating in through [its other] system of nested eddies' (De Landa 1991: 8). The beginning and ending of a manoeuvre, battle and even war becomes insignificant since the movement as a whole strengthens the logistical systems that further energize adoptions and self-corrections.

'The problem', Paul Virilio (2008: 92) emphasizes, 'is not to use technology but to realize that one is used by it'. Not only is it impossible to differentiate the present from the future or the past, who is friend or enemy, but also what is collaborating in the overall pre-emptive movement. The technological component not only pushed the decision into insignificance, but it also makes the pre-emptive movement of networks automatic, habituated and self-correcting. 'The thing about collaborators', he continues, 'is that you do not know you are one ... ' (Virilio 2008: 203). The global triage is like pure war. 'Pure war no longer needs (humans) and that's why it is pure' (Virilio 2008: 180). The purity of the global triage operates in advance of the event in so far as it is the event. It no longer takes humanity as its object because it is not concerned with human well-being.

The technological developments of information networks and everyday machines have far exceeded De Landa or Virilio's projections. As the boundary between military, industrial and civilian logistics collapses, what has emerged is something Deleuze (1992) called the 'societies of control'. In the societies of control, Deleuze explains,

> what is important is no longer either a signature or a number, but a code: the code is a password, while on the other hand disciplinary societies are regulated by *watchwords* (as much as from the point of view of integration as from that of resistance). The numerical language of control is made of codes that mark access to information, or reject it. We no longer find ourselves dealing with the mass/individual pair. Individuals have

become '*dividuals*,' and masses, samples, data, markets, or '*banks*' ... The disciplinary man was a discontinuous producer of energy, but the man of control is undulatory, in orbit, in a continuous network.

(Deleuze 1992: 6)

Alexander Galloway (2004) develops these insights into what he calls 'protocol'. Similar to a society of control, Galloway defines protocol as the 'techniques for achieving voluntary regulation within a contingent environment' (Galloway 2004: 7). This technique takes the shape of a 'distributed network' (Galloway 2004: 11) (which has replaced centralized and decentralized networks) and functions through a logic of *whatever works*. It simply includes, quoting Eric Hall, 'intelligent end-point systems that are self-deterministic, each end-point system to communicate with any host it chooses' (Hall quoted in Galloway 2004: 11). Logistical in nature, protocol is not organized around centres or even objects; instead, they move to the extreme in order to make *things* work.

Such a rhizomatic circuit appears to be contingent and unstable, but ironically, its contingent perpetual emergence *is* its form. This is precisely what makes the global triage capable of operating in total contingency. Mapping the influence of Stephen Wolfram, Kathleen Hayles (2005) calls the aspiration of total knowledge in contingency 'the Regime of Computation' (Hayles 2005: 23). It can operate within contingency because the regime requires no foundation (i.e. god, sovereignty, geometry) to establish truth other than absolute minimalist requirements of differentiating between something and nothing (i.e. one/zero) (Hayles 2005: 22). Proponents of the regime make the strong claim that 'computation does not just simulate the behaviour of complex systems; it is envisioned as the process that actually generates behaviour in everything from biological organisms to human social systems' (Hayles 2005: 19). Not only has the boundary between friend/enemy, military/civilian and social/biological collapsed but so have the boundaries between human, animal and viral. In the midst of the global triage everything is infected life and part of a complex, evolving organism.

Deleuze's comments on cinema's 'automatic and psychomechanical qualities' are instructive in reconnecting pre-emption and technology back to the affective management and creation of the logistical self in the global triage. For Deleuze, the pre-linguistic images and signs specific to cinema's spiritual automation, while retaining open war-like potentialities akin to the highest exercise of thought, also invite a kind of 'somnambulism' in certain movements. Somnambulism denotes a different kind of time in which decisions are mediated through dream-like states of being. Like Clausewitz's habituated soldier, the viewer 'is dispossessed of his own thought, and obeys only internal impressions which develop solely in visions or rudimentary actions' (Deleuze 1989: 263). Here Deleuze's interest is in how German cinema, under fascism, realized how 'the art of automatic movement ... was to coincide with the automization of the masses' (Deleuze 1989: 263). Superseded by the automata of computation and cybernetics, however, the configuration of power no longer rests with a Hitleresque commander. Common to the global triage, societies of control, protocol and computation power are 'diluted in an information network where "decision makers" manage control, processing and stock across intersections of insomniacs and seers' (Deleuze 1989: 265). They converge in a perpetual 'somnambulism' which constitutes a kind of habit of being human. This habit of being transfers logistical information necessary for the global triage to function in theatre. Simply put, the very forces that have become the habit of being human collaborate with the logisticity of the global triage. They collaborate within the affective register of human desire.

Human desire as logistics

That the very forces that define the logisticity of the global triage have come to define what it means to be a desiring human being is certainly troubling. Equally troubling is that to desire otherwise would be to invite suspicion or be disqualified. If the logistical element would optimize the human element, then why would better be rejected? In this sense, Clausewitz's summation, 'all war supposes human weakness, and against that it is directed', is particularly relevant. The desire for optimization is used to defeat human weakness but to do so requires that humanity become the object of war. Humanity is set to war with itself, not consciously, but habitually. The human desire to develop a global triage, as a kind of logistical care of the self, is therefore what is most troubling: we've come to love to hate ourselves.

The problem of contemporary fascism has obviously become more complicated than rehashing the political fascism of the twentieth century. Although it is difficult to make out fascism without recourse to allegorical fictions, Michel Foucault identified a more resilient kind of *comprehensive fascism*. This fascism is a desire within us: 'the fascism in us all, in our heads and in our everyday behaviour, the fascism that causes us to love power, to desire the very things that dominates and exploits us' (Foucault quoted in Deleuze and Guattari 1983: xiii). Ashis Nandy similarly queried the desire within colonialism (i.e. the intimate enemy) that encourages colonized peoples to release forces that alter cultural priorities to fit and even celebrate the logic of colonialism (Nandy 1998). Nandy explains, 'as a state of mind, colonialism is an indigenous process release by external forces. Its sources lie deep in the minds of the rulers and the ruled' (Nandy 1998: 3). One of the fundamental problems, as such, is one that Wilhelm Reich rediscovers in the question 'why do men fight *for* their servitude as stubbornly as though it were their salvation?' (Deleuze and Guattari 1983: 29). Reaffirming Reich's sentiment further, Deleuze and Guattari assert, 'what is astonishing is not that some people steal or that others occasionally go out on strike, but rather that all those who are starving do not steal as a regular practice, and all those who are exploited are not continually out on strike: after centuries of exploitation, why do people still tolerate being humiliated and enslaved, to such a point, indeed that they *actually want* humiliation and slavery not for others but for themselves?' (Deleuze and

Guattari 1983: 29). Guattari explains that within this desire is 'the rise of comprehensive fascism' (Deleuze 1995: 18).

It is not so easy to use human desire or, to evoke a parallel discourse, human will to oppose comprehensive fascism. On the contrary, it is under the banner of freedom that humanity's masses seem to desire more triage, development and security. The little fascist wants more regularity, peace and quiet, compliance, predictability and continuity. These habits are desired and desirable. Moreover, the habit of desiring these habits has grown into a kind of global ethic of care. Care, it seems, has become an instrument of governmentality and a means of securitization (Duffield 2007). While the global triage is now championed as an extreme form of caring for others, this caring is predicated upon an extreme disposability of embodied lives (even our own). Collateral damage in humanitarian wars, planned casualties in global human health, disposable peoples in the name of development, and tradable bodies in economic growth remain indelible images of the global triage. Mitigation, computation, regularity, peace and quiet, compliance, predictability and continuity require that embodied life be despised before 'it' can be cared for logistically. Life must be made a problem before it can be solved. The development of the global triage requires a desiring machine that *loves to hate to love to hate to love* ...

It should be remembered that Deleuze and Guattari introduce the concept of a desiring machine to explain how a subject is produced, not in isolation from the world, but in the midst of a social formation. Desire, they argue, is not a natural impulse. Instead desire is always assembled (Deleuze and Guattari 1986: 399). Desire is an assemblage of 'machines driving other machines, [and] machines being driven by other machines' (Deleuze and Guattari 1983: 1). Desiring machines themselves, as such, 'represent nothing, signify nothing, mean nothing and are exactly what one makes of them, what is made with them, what they make themselves' (Deleuze and Guattari 1986: 288). To be sure, this is not a question of how a desiring machine is *to be* used; the point is that desire itself is always already *using*. Desire becomes a useful habit. 'Desire', Guattari reflects, 'is part of the infrastructure' (Deleuze 1995: 19).

As such, it is not insignificant that Deleuze and Guattari argue that 'people's interest will never turn in favour of revolution until the lines of desire reach the point where desire and machine become indistinguishable, where desire and contrivance are the same thing' (Deleuze 1995: 20). Perhaps in just such a time a new people, not a new humanity, can emerge to take a revolutionary cause as their point of unification. However, this is likely too optimistic. The difficulty is whether or not the social field that Deleuze and Guattari emphasize (capitalism as an undifferentiated abstract machine) neglects the logistical field. In this light, comprehensive fascism need not be an attack by the body politic on itself, or upon its parts. Comprehensive fascism makes 'things' work. It constitutes a kind of global efficacy. It is habitual. As such, it is an order that operates beyond politics and is indifferent to normalized political fields (i.e. the state, government, democracy, social movements or the markets).

Comprehensive fascism makes the world go round, not by targeting the body politic, but by making human habit that desires more habit.

It is no longer clear that we live in a world where it is *only* the state and corporations that want to kill us (or some). There never was any recourse to humanity's multitude in the struggle against fascism. As Deleuze and Guattari remember, 'No, the masses were not innocent dupes; at a certain point, under a certain set of conditions, they wanted *fascism*, and it is this perversion of desire of the masses that needs to be accounted for' (Deleuze and Guattari 1983: 29). The problem is greater. Our habits, our desires are collaborators. We live in a world where eating, drinking, breathing, touching, loving conspires against the integrity of life. Our life systems, our biology, cells, nervous system and chemical balances have become ticking time bombs. Again, human being is not an object in this war; this killing is incidental. Just like the planned casualties of the global triage, it is not so much that the environment wants to kill us, but it will. Just like it is not so much that cancer, for example, wants to kill us, but it will. Involuntary killing, as such, is the marker of our age. We no longer face the dilemma of kill *or* be killed; instead, we now live in a condition in which we expect to kill *and* expect to be killed.

How is it that we live so calmly? While these are processes that humans have created, they have also become motors that are indifferent to those soft bodies that they now shape. In the midst of these global-local, social-biological, war-peace feedback loops, human life has fallen below the threshold of necessity. In this fall we experience a kind of freedom and this freedom constitutes a kind of desire. Seeking favour, relevance and inclusion, it became strategic for humanity to court favour on the logistical side of the auto-correcting curve of total war and contemporary fascism. However, as the desire for promises of life, progress and freedom (for some) has grown stronger, the human being has taken itself as its object. As humans fall below the threshold of necessity, logistics continually presses into the fatty future.

Back to a future which has no future

In sum, the answer to our introductory muse should not be 'can fascism happen again?', but instead remains 'can it be defeated?' (Stannard 1992: xiii). This chapter clearly imagines a future that will be more difficult than the past. I have argued that questions concerning logistics are now more important than past distinctions between war and peace. I have argued that contemporary logistics need to be understood as a kind of global triage that is organized around optimizing human life. However, I have also suggested that this optimization occurs through practices of mitigation and auto-correction that require becoming indifferent to specific human lives and populations. In order for humanity to thrive some other humans must die. While this should seem troubling, it isn't. It isn't because the triage has become a habitual compromise that operates pre-emptively and technologically beyond politics. The habitualization of this compromise, moreover, is not an isolated event. On the contrary, habitualization is the component of logistics that desires mitigation and auto-correction. Habit and logistics are part of the same movement that makes 'things' work. Given the indifference to specific human lives, it would be foolish to assume we (individually) are exempt from humanity's total war on itself. On the contrary, the logistical habit constitutes a human desire to be more human. Humans desire killing machines that save lives in the name of humanity.

At the heart of contemporary fascism is the way in which different triages are learning to coordinate, communicate and integrate into seamless optimizations. This logistical desire to make 'things' work is difficult to politicize. Yet, I remain optimistic that different bodies will endure. There is no escape. As the Invisible Committee writes in their manifesto, *The Coming Insurrection*, 'to go on waiting is madness. The catastrophe is not coming; it is here. We are already situated *within* the collapse of civilization' (Comité Invisible 2009: 96). They joyfully proclaim, 'the future has no future' (Comité Invisible 2009: 23), and here we sit. Perhaps some consolation can be taken in the following Heideggerian strategy: the de-politicization of logistics and the banality of life (systems) will constitute an opportunistic movement. 'The closer we come to the danger', Heidegger asserted, 'the more brightly do the ways into the saving power begin to shine and the more questioning we become' (Heidegger 1977: 317). A kind of tactical solidarity can be re-established and a broader war might be re-engaged that disrupts the habitual supply chain of the global triage and enacts a kind of movement of creative forces beyond universalist strategies that claim human rights, cosmopolitan justice, democratic procedure and international law.

Notes

1 Thanks to my student Stephanie Redden for this phrase.

References

Agamben, G. *Homo sacer: Sovereign Power and Bare Life* (Stanford, Calif.: Stanford University Press, 1998)

Arendt, H. *The Origins of Totalitarianism* (New York: Schocken Books, 1951)

Césaire, A. *Discourse on Colonialism* (New York: Monthly Review Press, 1972)

Clausewitz, C. *On war* (Harmondsworth: Penguin Books, 1982)

Comité Invisible. *The Coming Insurrection* (Cambridge, Mass.: Semiotext(e), 2009)

De Landa, M. *War in the Age of Intelligent Machines* (New York: Zone Books, 1991)

Deleuze, G. *Cinema 2* (Minneapolis: University of Minnesota Press, 1989)

——'Postscript on the Societies of Control' (*October* Vol. 59, Winter 1992: 3–7)

——*Negotiations, 1972–1990* (New York: Columbia University Press, 1995)

Deleuze, G. and Guattari, F. *Anti-oedipus: Capitalism and Schizophrenia* (Minneapolis: University of Minnesota Press, 1983)

——*Nomadology: The War Machine* (New York, NY: Semiotext(e), 1986)

——*A Thousand Plateaus: Capitalism and Schizophrenia* (Minneapolis: University of Minnesota Press, 1987)

Der Derian, J. *Virtuous War: Mapping the Military-industrial-media-entertainment Network* (Boulder, Colo.: Westview Press, 2001)

Duffield, M. *Development, Security and Unending War: Governing the World of Peoples* (Cambridge: Polity Press, 2007)

Foucault, M. *The History of Sexuality* (New York: Pantheon Books, 1978)

Galloway, A.R. *Protocol: How Control Exists After Decentralization* (Cambridge, Mass.: MIT Press, 2004)

Hayles, K.N. *My Mother was a Computer: Digital Subjects and Literary Texts* (Chicago: University of Chicago Press, 2005)

Heidegger, M. 'The Question Concerning Technology', in *Basic Writings* (New York: Harper Collins, 1977)

Jomini, H. *The Art of War* (Westport, Connecticut: Greenwood Press, 1972)

Mamdani, M. *When Victims Become Killers: Colonialism, Nativism, and the Genocide in Rwanda* (Princeton, NJ: Princeton University Press, 2001)

——*Saviors and Survivors: Darfur, Politics and the War on Terror* (New York: Doubleday, 2009)

Massumi, B. 'Potential Politics and the Primacy of Preemption' (*Theory & Event*, Vol.10, No.2, 2007)

Nandy, A. *Exiled at Home: Comprising, at the Edge of Psychology, the Intimate Enemy, Creating a Nationality* (Delhi: Oxford University Press, 1998)

Pogge, T.W. *World Poverty and Human Rights: Cosmopolitan Responsibilities and Reforms* (Cambridge: Polity Press, 2008)

Rancière, J. *Aesthetics and its Discontents* (Cambridge: Polity Press, 2009)

Rasmussen, M.V. *The Risk Society at War: Terror, Technology and Strategy in the Twenty-first Century* (Cambridge: Cambridge University Press, 2006)

Reid, J. *The Biopolitics of the War on Terror: Life Struggles, Liberal Modernity, and the Defence of Logistical Societies* (Manchester: Manchester University Press, 2006)

Schmitt, C. *The Concept of the Political* (Chicago: University of Chicago Press, 1996)

——*Political Theology: Four Chapters on the Concept of Sovereignty* (Cambridge, Mass.: MIT Press, 1985)

Singer, P. *Wired for War* (New York: Penguin Press, 2009)

Stannard, D.E. *American Holocaust: Columbus and the Conquest of the New World* (New York: Oxford University Press, 1992)

Virilio, P. *Pure War: Twenty Five Years Later* (Los Angeles, CA: Semiotext(e), 2008)

Whitehall, G. 'The Aesthetic Emergency of the Avian Flu Affect', in Francois Debrix and Mark Lacy (ed.) *Geopolitics of American Insecurity: Terror, Power, and Foreign Policy* (New York: Routledge, 2009)

——'Preemptive Sovereignty and Avian States of Emergency' (*Theory and Event* Vol.13, No.2, 2010)

5 A people of seers

The political aesthetics of post-war cinema revisited

Julian Reid

What, if any, is the political function of cinema? Gilles Deleuze once argued that the 'classical cinema' of the pre-World War II era participated in perpetrating one of the great myths of political modernity: that of the unanimity of 'the people' as collective subject. Not simply fascist cinema, but Soviet and American cinema of the pre-war era, as well as classical theories of early cinema, assumed the possibility of raising the consciousness of 'the people' through the cinematic medium; of revealing to the masses the shared truths presumed to be their essence, and which given faith and perseverance would serve to convert them from disparate mass into a unified people, thus constituting them as political subjects (Deleuze 1989: 216). For these reasons cinema's role was to serve in the process of typifying the people, of guiding it in its historical process of sorting out its collective identity. The destructions authorized on account of that myth by the Nazis as well as by other regimes elsewhere in and outside of Europe during the twentieth century served, as Deleuze argued, to alter profoundly the course of cinematic modernity. Auteurs of the post-war period took a much more jaded view of 'the people' and deployed cinema in antagonism with the state-apparatus and its myth. Classical political cinema persisted but it was countered by numerous directors working for the 'soul' of cinema. Consequently it was only after World War II that a truly 'modern cinema' emerged distinguished by its perception of the reality that 'the people' as such can never exist. That there is no 'the people,' only 'always several peoples, an infinity of peoples' who cannot and should not be made one (ibid.: 220). Modern political cinema is, then according to Deleuze, a cinema of resistance to fascism, in which the idea of the people as a unified collectivity is itself an intolerable ideal; a political miasma that requires constantly warding off (ibid.: 221).

In Deleuze's time political critique of a radical kind was indeed defined largely by a preoccupation with resistance to the mythologies of national unanimity on which the institutions of European state sovereignty still rested. Here and now, however, the nostalgia for a political subject equipped with some collective locus of identity is equally definitive. The continuing saga of struggles against the state's imposition of false unanimity upon peoples contrasts, at the very least, with the desire to establish some minimal source of unity in struggles with regimes that are as diversifying as they are unifying. How does this reproblematization of political struggle and the politics of resistance affect our understanding of the political function of cinema? Is Deleuze's thesis concerning the modernity of political cinema still convincing? This paper reconsiders his account of the shift from classical to modern cinema for politics in the twenty-first century by focusing on his account of the post-war emergence of a new type of 'people to come,' its 'cinema of the seer,' and the power to perceive 'the intolerable' that distinguishes it. We will see that while not a unity in the classical sense of the term, the people to whom the cinema of the seer addresses itself may nevertheless be thought about as a typology on which a new kind of political community is imagined. In addition, however, this typology, while not of a classical kind, is troubling for a politics of resistance to fascism. It is not entirely clear that Deleuze's 'people to come' succeeds in averting itself from becoming-fascist. This chapter demonstrates this through a reading of key films focused on by Deleuze, and then proceeds to show how cinema of more recent times has moved beyond the naïve account of the politics of seeing that underwrote Deleuze's claims for the people to come in his seminal two-volume study.

From classical to modern cinema

To understand how classical cinema underwrote the myth of the unanimity of 'the people' we have to grasp the function of the model of 'true narration' underpinning both classical cinema and wider political imaginaries of the pre-war era. Classical cinema, dating roughly until around the early 1940s, favored a form of 'true narration' that develops 'organically, according to legal connections in space and chronological relations in time' (Deleuze 1989: 133). Such a cinema portrayed and celebrated a world in which actions generate situations, which in turn generate new actions that link up in a progressive and emancipatory series. A world in which consciousness is gradually raised as things make better sense and justice is gradually done; in which the contingencies of life are subject to order so that a higher truth may be secured; and in which peoples, both individually and collectively, become increasingly coherent. Characters and societies encounter misfortunes in these films but only in the form of challenges which are overcome in their journey to a more complete state. In this sense classical cinema popularized the myth of a 'true narration' on which the major political projects of its period depended; the myth that the many different temporalities of lives can be synthesized in a time that erases their differences and conflicts. Soviet directors such as Eisenstein, Vertov and Dovzhenko all attempted to portray the progressive and linear temporality of 'the people' struggling to overcome historical trials and tribulations in the process of their becoming full subjects (Deleuze 1989: 216). The very purpose of film, for Eisenstein especially, was to inspire the action of the masses-as-people by increasing their sense of themselves as a collective subject possessed of a 'revolutionary consciousness' (Bogue 2003: 169). In Hollywood film of the pre-war era, likewise, directors such as D.W. Griffith mythologized the historical processes and events through which the diversity and conflicts of the American people were overcome in restoration of their essential unity (Deleuze 2005: 30–32; Martin-Jones 2006: 125–27; Iampolski 1998: 49–82).

During the mid-twentieth century, Deleuze argues, a cinematographic muta-tion took place serving to undermine this belief in the unanimity of the people and its narrative time. In explaining its preconditions he makes reference, among other things, to the trauma of World War II and its consequences, the 'unsteadiness of the "American Dream," and the 'new consciousness of minorities' (Deleuze 2005: 210). As he argues, the crisis in cinema precipitated a shift from 'true' to 'false narration,' reflecting a more fundamental collapse in faith in the powers of typification on which the ideal of the nation-state, especially, had historically drawn and which came to grief, quite literally and on a massive scale, in the killing factories of Auschwitz and Buchenwald. The Holocaust exposed the violence which a typified people, mystified to the point of assurance in its own coherence, could do to whoever does not meet the criteria of its essential type. It was as if amid the destructions of the war, and following the acute exposure of the neces-sary links between the myth of *das Volk* and the exterminatory violence of the Holocaust, cinema could no longer believe in the myth of a true narration through which the temporality of a people or its individual characters could be synchro-nized. Thus a new form of 'false' rather than 'true' narration became more influ-ential and a properly 'modern cinema' emerged. In place of chronological time cinema became characterized by a 'chronic non-chronological time' (Deleuze 1989: 129). Whereas true narration functioned to instill coherence in the world and the characters that populate it, false narration functions by tearing it apart. The actions of the characters depicted become aberrant, dysfunctional, generating an aim-less wandering and series of chance, loose connections. The world depicted became one where contingency reigns, where the discernment of differences between what is true and false becomes difficult, and characters are thrown haplessly from situation to situation, without possibility of redemption.

Rather than being a sorry story of disenchantment, however, Deleuze argued that the predominance of 'false narration' in post-war cinema testified to an improvement in its story-telling function. For what cinema did was not to mourn the loss of, or attempt to restore, the possibility of true narration, but to reject it in a positive fashion on account of its failure to approximate what is most real of the world, which is precisely the 'power of the false' (Deleuze 1989: 126–55). The truth is, Deleuze argues, that in its actuality the world does not add up, and as subjects in the world we are necessarily destined always to fail to achieve coherence, only ever constituting false unities forever prey to the decomposing affects generated by the world. To believe and practice otherwise is to resist the *true falsity* of the world. In modern cinema, by way of contrast, we are shown the reality that indeed we never cohere, neither individually or collectively; that the political concept of 'the people' is always bound to fail, that 'the people' will always go AWOL regardless of the attempts of regimes to unify them (Deleuze 1989: 215–24).

Classical cinema's attachment to the ideal of the people as a collective subject was underwritten by a faith in the powers of human agency; of belief in the human capacity to act in the world in order to improve its condition. Modern cinema in contrast, Deleuze argues, shows us the difficulties entailed in seeking a better world, the necessity indeed of believing not in a different world, but in reconciling ourselves with the realities of this world (Deleuze 1989: 170). For the promise of modern cinema is that it enables us to confront the world as it really is rather than seeing it as we might want it to be. Doing so requires that it shifts our attention from the problem of how to act to the problem of how to see. Modern cinema is fundamentally 'a cinema of the seer and no longer the agent' (ibid.: 126). It is concerned with characters who in losing the power of action have gained a more worldly power of (in)sight. Characters for whom the disciplinary organization of the senses necessary for effective action has not simply broken down but has been displaced by an intense power to see the hitherto unseen. Modern cinema shows us seers and in doing so, Deleuze argues, underlines the political potential entailed in our own 'becoming visionary or seer' (ibid.: 21). It encourages in us the power to see the world for what it is in a way denied to us while we remain in the sensori-motorized relation with the world celebrated in classical cinema.

Deleuze's Bergsonism

Deleuze's account of the 'cinema of the seer' can only be understood as an extension of Henri Bergson's account of the politics of perception. Bergson argued that the failure to perceive that which is most real of the world is a constitutive practice in the everyday business of being human (Bergson 1991). In order to make use of the world we literally have to practice evading the reality of the world; distorting and reducing it to perceptions that are unreal but which enable our smooth functioning in the world. Within the political register of experience this involves us, crucially, in distorting the reality of the oppression and deprivation to which we are subject in the world as well as the oppression and deprivation of others on which our own lives are predicated, perceiving the world such that our identities go undisturbed. While we may sense oppression and deprivation on a daily basis, our intellect intervenes within the course of experience to organize our perceptions such that we tolerate what would otherwise seem intolerable. In spite of this fundamentally human quality of illusion it remains conceivable, Bergson argued, for us to develop aesthetic practices with which to unmake our own illusions and 'recover contact with the real' (ibid.: 185). Such practices may well serve to harm us, making us sick with the reality of our own existence, but they will nevertheless bring us closer to those real conditions which Bergson believed to exist at the source of experience. Thus might we, if we choose to follow Bergson, believe in the possibility of developing aesthetic practices to relieve ourselves of the 'necessary poverty of our conscious perception' (ibid.: 38) to see the real poverty and oppressions of a world which otherwise passes us by.

Bergson himself deplored cinema, arguing that it merely recuperates the mechanisms of the ordinary forms of perception on which the sensori-motor systems of humans depend for efficient action (Bergson 1928: 322–23). Deleuze's claims as to the potential of cinema to increase our capacity for (in)sight only would have served to rile him, but the political potential of the arts to enable societies to see beneath the conditions of their own illusions was a phenomenon that he held dear. He argued that the processes by which the limits of our political sensibilities are redrawn are akin to the process by which artists transform public perceptions with creative works (Deleuze 2005: 976). This modern power of art is akin, he also argued, to the ancient powers of seers and prophets in guiding communities (ibid.: 978–79). The celebration of the power of the seer is not, of course, particular to philosophy or cinema. The Greek tragedians and poets celebrated the power of the seer while, in a similar fashion to modern cinema, deploying him or her to warn against the dangers of sensori-motorized action, the classic example being the seer Tiresias who in order to guide Homer's Odysseus home has to intervene and rearrange his senses so that he does not fall victim to the same fate as his unseeing crew (Barnouw 2004: 11); who, when deployed by Sophocles, resists his conscription to the city of Thebes on account of the unseen corruption of its king Oedipus (Gooding 2003). Nor is the dramaturgy of the disruption of the sensori-motor system distinct to cinema. It is the condition of Shakespeare's Hamlet, who faced with the rotten state of Denmark discovers that 'time is out of joint.' Nevertheless, Deleuze argues that modern cinema embodies Bergson's commitment to a politics of perception to new effect. In arguing his case he provided a wide variety of examples across a range of different genres, too vast to detail in total here, and some of which, as I will explain, are less sustainable than others.

A cinema of the seer

The films of Alfred Hitchcock, for example, are richly populated by characters who have developed a profound power to see 'something intolerable and unbearable' (Deleuze 1989: 18), usually precipitated by a physical accident or trauma. Activity and narrative continues in these films, but in ways irredeemably inflected by the vision of the characters depicted. However, in many cases the capacity to see the intolerable is provocative of an action which merely aims at and succeeds in restoring order to the world. Deleuze cites L.B. Jefferies, the hero of *Rear Window*, who by virtue of a car accident is reduced to the 'pure optical situation' of gazing from his apartment window into the homes of his neighbors, on account of which he perceives the evidence of a murder committed by a traveling salesman (Deleuze 2005: 209). Jefferies, however, demonstrates little evidence of a political consciousness as such. Indeed he is an ally of the state seeking only to restore social order with his seeing power. In other cases the power to see is provocative of an action motivated by a desire to undo social order but stopping short of producing political change. A good example is Uncle Charlie in Hitchcock's earlier *Shadow of a Doubt*, whose childhood accident conjures in him the power to see the invisible layer of social and economic corruption underpinning American society, but on account of which he is provoked to commit a series of murders targeting the obscenely rich. In this case the capacity to see is provocative of a political consciousness which produce a series of killings for private profit, which in their turn produce a counter police action through which social order is also restored. A more overtly political case is Martin Scorsese's 1970s classic *Taxi Driver*, in which Travis Bickle returns from the trauma of the war in Vietnam able to see the intolerable character of social relations that permeate everyday life in the city of New York. Provoked but prevented from carrying out a political assassination, Bickle ultimately acts to save a child prostitute from her pimp (Deleuze 2005: 212–13). In this case the power to see the intolerable is provocative of an action, which is itself the product of a desired but ultimately frustrated political action, producing another private act which serves ultimately to restore social bonds.

Both of these latter characters are possessed of a political consciousness shaped by their capacity to see the intolerable, which is in turn constitutive of a desire for action, but for whom the possibility of a political resolution of the intolerable is foreclosed by the organization of the society in which they live. Both Uncle Charlie and Travis Bickle are trapped within a society content with being mere drones in the machinery of a state apparatus which itself is banalized to the point of corruption. Each of these films, and if we follow Deleuze, the 'soul' of modern cinema considered as a whole, depicts the Bergsonian moment at which a character sees the intolerable and the dramaturgy of a call to action that follows. Each of them, however, is distinctive in its attentions to the conditions that frustrate that call and which thus hinder action, inducing either paralysis or, at best, wrong or botched moves. If we assume these films, as Deleuze argues we must, to be representative of the soul of modern cinema, then we must conclude that this is a cinema of political incapacity. A cinema that provides little hope or investment in the possibility of a political resolution of the intolerable conditions of post-war societies.

In a recent work Alain Badiou laments the power of cinema and the dramaturgy of political incapacity to which it has led. Our problem contemporarily, he argues, is not that of how we might see better but precisely how we might rediscover the affirmative courage with which to act better. Speaking up for the residual potential of theatre, which in contrast with cinema, he continues to believe in, Badiou argues that our time requires 'an invention that would communicate, through theater ideas, everything of which a people's science is capable. We want a theater of capacity, not of incapacity' (Badiou 2005: 75). Badiou's position is indicative of the nostalgia for an art and politics of the collective subject; the representation of its essences, the unification of its temporality and the dramatization of its actions. Indeed, Badiou states in very clear terms the need to return to such a model. 'Consensual democracy is horrified', he argues, 'by every typology of the subjective categories that compose it … the duty of the theater is to recompose upon the stage a few living situations, articulated on the basis of some essential types. To offer our own time the equivalent of the slaves and domestics of ancient theater – excluded and invisible people who all of a sudden, by the effect of the theater-idea, embody upon the stage intelligence and force, desire and mastery' (Badiou 2005: 76).

The power that Badiou identifies with theater is superficially similar to that which Deleuze accords to cinema: the power to make seen the otherwise unseen. Theater, when it functions well, deploys the power of seeing in its identification of those invisible parts of a people that a given regime of power would rather went unseen, but the process by which it makes seen the unseen is that of 'typification.' Typification proceeds by eliminating doubt as to the vagueness of the subjective categories that compose a hitherto invisible people in production of some kind of 'essential type' (Badiou 2005: 76; Miller 2006; Natanson 1986). It seeks to reverse the Bergsonian moment of insight whereupon the invisible is seen by mystifying the unseen; its rendering into an illusory typology. Theater operates in the political register by mystifying its public as to the composite nature of the subjects it depicts. It is only by composing rather than decomposing collective subjects, Badiou argues, that the arts can contribute to political struggles, thus clarifying and simplifying public understandings of who the invisible are, vivifying the public perception of them so that they are credited with an intelligence and capacity otherwise denied them, and lending them 'affirmative courage' in their struggles for political power (Badiou 2005: 72–77).

Badiou attempts to restore to the arts a power to build a politics on the sensori-motor function of individuals and peoples. In this venture it is not only the responsibility of arts such as theater to see that which a given regime of power refuses to disclose, but to give fictive unity to the unseen so that they might better comport themselves as collective subjects on the political stage. None of the cinematic characters that Deleuze celebrates as distinguishing modern cinema would appear to meet the criteria that Badiou specifies as necessary for them to be worthy subjects of a political cinema. This is a cinema of incapacity, of paralyzed and traumatized characters who, living in the margins, struggle to muster the courage to fulfill their own convictions. Of characters who, overwhelmed by what they have seen, fail to extricate themselves from the abyss with which they are then faced.

Does this mean, then, that we ought to shelve Deleuze's analysis of modern cinema and leave behind the argument he makes for a 'cinema of the seer'? Ought we to return to an aesthetics of the sensori-motor mechanism to restore a political subject fit for the twenty-first century? There are severe problems with Badiou's account of the politics of aesthetics which would have to be addressed for us to think so. In essence Badiou's argument rests upon a highly elitist understanding of the relation between the arts, its subject matter, and the audience or public. On his account the power to see what would otherwise go unseen is an exceptional practice confined to the arts themselves. It takes the vision of an artist to see, but the representation of the unseen is an art based on techniques for the construction of its illusionary coherence. The subjects depicted in Badiou's account of political theater are not seers but agents issuing and taking orders, possessed of a pragmatic intelligence and will to master the conditions of their own existence. Thus there is a founding elitism and partitioning of roles necessary for such a politics to take place. Badiou imagines a theatre that shows the public its unseen, but which in rendering the unseen visible exercises sovereignty over its public by mystifying it as to its complexities and ambiguities.

Classically, within theater, the seer was conceived and portrayed in his or her exceptionality. Like Badiou's conception of theater, a highly particular power to which a people turned at moments of crisis, giving them directions with which to recover their bearings, in order to resume the journey on which they would eventually secure their truths. What modern cinema does, however, is to democratize the seer by depicting him or her in everyday life while also laying stress on the quotidian and fugitive experience of 'seeing' within post-war societies. It is not that post-war society lacks its seers – it is awash with them – but it lacks the moral and political resources to heed their call. This in effect is the story that modern cinema tells via its depiction of seers and their everyday but fugitive perceptions of the intolerable conditions in which they live and which make their lives possible.

Ought we not then, still, to entertain the possibility of a people of seers? A people distinguished as a collectivity not only by its precise power to see at the expense of acting but also to share and circulate its perceptions of the intolerable? Could the perception of the intolerable be construed, even, as the missing source of a new form of unity among struggles in the twenty-first century? Deleuze himself was convinced that each of these characters – L.B. Jefferies, Uncle Charlie and Travis Bickle – was an expression of a 'new type of character' (Deleuze 1989: 19); even a 'new race' (ibid.: xi). In other words, they each constituted a typology; shared common features, a particular disposition to the world, irrespective of their differences. Could we not conceive of a people constituted by the radical equality with which it perceives the intolerable? More recently, Jacques Rancière has reconceptualized democracy as a capacity for the 'sharing of the perceptible' and the 'redistribution of its sites' (Rancière 2004: 104). Do we not witness here in the modern cinema the celebration of such a democratic practice circulating among the characters it depicts? A new race of character distinguished by the capacity to see that which a regime of power relations would otherwise seek to make invisible; in other words, the seer conceived as an 'essential type.' The idea of a community, which while still 'to come' is nevertheless testified to by art and by cinema especially?

At first glance Deleuze's own discussion of the politics of modern cinema would warn us against such an argument. He differentiates between what he calls 'political' from non-political cinema of the modern era. The concept of political cinema is reserved in his works for cinema mainly of the non-Western world, allowing for a further distinction between European versus American cinema. In spite of his obvious admiration for much American cinema of the post-World War II era, the genre as a whole was hamstrung, he argues, by the absence of a concrete political project to which it could contribute, its critique only serving to correct the misuse of power, in striving to save the remains of the American Dream (Deleuze 2005: 215). One could argue that this is precisely the political function that films such as *Shadow of a Doubt* and *Taxi Driver* fulfilled, in that they depict the futility of becoming politically conscious; the state literally always wins, it would seem, in American film. The European traditions – neo-realism in Italy and the French new wave – were more significant, Deleuze argued, politically, but truly political cinema is to be found in what he quaintly names the 'third world' (Deleuze 1989: 217).

There we encounter a cinema which while concerned with the formation of a collective subject, works on different principles of people-production to classical political cinema which was so beholden of 'the people.' For this cinema is not attempting to address a people presupposed as already there but one that 'is missing' and which therefore requires inventing. However, the post-colonial cinema that Deleuze discusses as exemplary of a political cinema is itself defined by the same perception of the intolerable which he argues distinguishes the soul of American cinema. Modern political cinema is not interested, he argues, in furthering the evolution or revolution of 'the people,' like the classical cinema, but with seeding a 'people to come' which sees 'the intolerable' (Deleuze 1989: 215–17). This 'people to come' has a political conscience possessed of depth at the expense of heights; a depth testified to in its perception of the reality that 'the people' as such can never exist; that there is no 'the people,' only 'always several peoples, an infinity of peoples' who cannot and should not be made one (ibid.: 220). Modern political cinema is specifically a cinema of crisis, in which the idea of a coherent collectivity is itself something intolerable; a condition that requires warding off, and in which marginality is a kind of virtue in itself (ibid.: 221). It is a cinema that responds directly to Vilém Flusser's equally deterritorializing demand for a people which will take upon itself 'the profession and calling' (Deleuze 2003: 15) to reject the 'mystification of customs and habits' (ibid.: 11) on which each and every heimat depends and be 'a vanguard of the future' (ibid.: 15).

There is at the very least, then, a tension here between Deleuze's insistence on a distinction between political versus non-political cinema and the common ground established between these different cinemas on account of their shared typology of a people to come; a people of seers distinguished by its sharing in the perception of the intolerable. This is a tension that runs throughout his work. On the one hand an insistence that the artist alone is quite incapable of creating a people, and that 'a people can only be created in abominable suffering' oblivious to the concerns of art (Deleuze and Guattari 1999: 110). On this reading the cinema of the people to come is conditioned entirely by a political world extraneous to the world of cinema itself (Deleuze 1989: 215–24). In what particular community a filmmaker is located and in what social conditions he or she works will determine whether or not the work obtains a political potential. On the other hand, a Bergsonian belief in the potential emergence of a global subjectivity; the idea of an aesthetic power inherent in the sensible modes of experience that undoes the boundaries of any and every political subjectivity, American or European, Western or non-Western, in constitution of a people to come which is without territorial specificity.

In any case it is questionable whether the comparative framework that Deleuze brings to bear on post-war cinema is sustainable. The distinctions he draws between European, American and non-Western genres of cinema are exercises in the creation of a series of what he himself called 'badly analysed composites' (Deleuze 1991: 28), failing as they do to apprehend the rhizomatic development of post-war cinema, especially its motifs of the intolerable and its character of the seer. There is an only insufficient attempt in Deleuze's analysis to think about the ways in which concepts such as the intolerable were developed across the boundaries of national cinemas, between Western and non-Western worlds, and between cinema and other aesthetic regimes, such as literature, for example. The postwar production of this new typology of a people to come distinguished by its power to see the intolerable was itself a much more complex affair than Deleuze allows for, born out of a series of cross-fertilizations from Western to non-Western worlds and vice versa.

An example that elaborates the point is that of the cross-fertilization that occurred between post-war Japanese literature and post-war American cinema. More particularly between the novels of Yukio Mishima and the films of Paul Schrader, of which *Taxi Driver* itself is a prime example (Schrader scripted the film). Throughout Mishima's novels, from early works such as *Confessions of a Mask* to his classic *Temple of the Golden Pavilion*, through to the final *Sea of Fertility* tetralogy, we encounter characters who bear all the hallmarks of the cinematic seer. Characters confronted with images too intolerable for them to bear; images that produce stuttering enunciations, failed political gestures, acts of violence or self-sacrifice. In every case there is an overt political context to these encounters with the intolerable. For Mishima's characters are always vanquished subjects attempting to deal with the trauma of the defeat and subjection of Japan in the wake of the end of World War II and amid the American-imposed constitution that followed. In one integral sense the intolerable of Mishima's novels is quite simply the American colonization of Japan. The territorial circumstances of Mishima's characters and Travis Bickle of *Taxi Driver* are thus starkly different, one inhabiting the land of victors, the other that of the vanquished. However, in actuality there is a more or less genealogical relationship between the seers of Mishima's novels, such as the monk Mizoguchi of *The Temple of the Golden Pavilion* and the seers of post-war cinema such as Travis Bickle of *Taxi Driver*. Paul Schrader, who wrote the script to the latter, would later go on to make the biopic *Mishima*, a very poor attempt to depict the last days of the author meshed with abbreviated accounts of three of his novels. However, some time before *Mishima*, *Taxi Driver* had itself quite superbly recuperated the spirit of Mizoguchi's character on the screen: the post-war condition of a Japanese monk living in Kyoto transposed into that of an Italian-American cab driver in New York.

Both Bickle and Mizoguchi are seers depicted in their becoming conscious of the intolerability of their respective societies. These are characters that in seeing the intolerable refuse to tolerate it. From the vantage of their respective societies these are sick subjects on account of that intolerance. In this sense they both clash powerfully with the model of subjectivity on which the post-war development of both the United States and the reconstructed state of Japan depended, both grounded as they were on an ethic of tolerance. The concept of toleration derives, as we know from the works of a long line of liberal theorists of politics from Locke to Rawls, from the Latin *tolere*: to suffer, to countenance and put up with something that wrongs or harms us. Thus the liberal subject tolerates on account of its capacity to put up with and suffer that which in a more integral dimension of reality actually offends or harms it. Whether configured as it was at the end of the Religious Wars of the seventeenth century in terms of a demand to tolerate the other who worships differently to oneself, or as it became over time, a more obtuse demand to tolerate intolerable social and political practices, toleration has been conceived throughout the historical development of the liberal project as a tool for eliminating violence in the interests of political security and stability. This is a security and stability predicated on the production of a subject whose virtue rests not simply in its will to respect diverse beliefs and social practices, but in its ability to avoid countenancing that which harms it (Brown 2006). Thus his or her actions depend on an entire economy of avoiding the Bergsonian moment; of averting the gaze from the intolerable; on not seeing what lies above or below; on rendering the social world a cliché. Both Bickle and Mizoguchi testify, then, in their different ways, to the existence of another type of subjectivity, another threshold of consciousness, and another kind of perception, out of which a different type of people may emerge. Indeed one that already exists, should we care to look for it. An intolerant people of seers that desires the transformation of the conditions of its suffering.

The dumbest thing I ever heard

Modern cinema, then, irrespective of its differing territorial contexts of production, opens our eyes and sensibilities to the possibility of perceiving the intolerable, of our becoming seers. One of the primary methods by which it does this, as Deleuze argued, is by showing us seers at the expense of agents. However, there is another type of character that populates 'the soul' of post-war cinema, whom Deleuze completely ignores, and yet who is integral to the political work it performs. If we examine any of the films that we have discussed here we discover that the depiction of the seer is always achieved via his or her contextualization in a thick set of, often paranoiac or neurotic, social relations with other characters who are distinguished by their precise incapacity to see, actions of a sensori-motorized nature, a kind of generalized stupidity; cretins. What Deleuze fails to see in his focus on the seer of modern cinema is the extent to which the cretinization of sensori-motorized agency is fundamental to its political resistance.

In another recent work Ian Buchanan draws attention to Deleuze's failures to examine the 'cretinizing schlock' which in spite of what can be said of the work of great auteurs such as Hitchcock or Scorsese, undeniably makes up the bulk of contemporary cinema (Buchanan 2008: 10). Surely, Buchanan asks, if we want to understand how it is that regimes are able to mystify their publics, sustain illusionary narratives and make us tolerate the intolerable, we have to examine not so much the great works of post-war cinema but its schlock. Those films which are utterly unexceptional and which function merely to 'recycle old stories, old images, and old ideas' (ibid.: 10). This in itself is a strange failing if we consider Deleuze's broader philosophical ambitions which entailed an attempt to delineate the conditions on which peoples, individually and collectively, come to desire the conditions of their own servitude (Deleuze and Guattari 1984). Surely taking the problem of the toleration of the intolerable seriously requires that we examine the political function of cretinizing rather than just edifying cinema?

Not only is it necessary to examine cinema's cretinizing schlock, however, but also the characterization of cretineity which distinguishes the soul of post-war cinema itself. The typification of the cretin is as fundamental to the constitution of the people as is its typological seer. The typology of the seer is predicated on that which it is not: its dumb differential; its quick speaking and easy acting interlocutor. We can recognize this by returning to the three films discussed earlier. In *A Shadow of a Doubt* we encounter Uncle Charlie, a seer who in escaping from the law is forced to take refuge with his sister's family headed by a partnership of mommy-daddy cretins. Uncle Charlie's capacity to see the intolerability of the reign of Capital in 1940s America is contextualized in relation with the cretinous sister who exists oblivious to his true nature and lives out a naïve relationship with state and society, as well as with his brother-in-law who works in a bank reproducing on a daily basis the powers of capital. In *Rear Window* the seeing function of L.B. Jefferies is depicted in contrast with the cretineity of Lisa Carol Freemont, a woman who cares only for fashion and small talk. In *Taxi Driver* the depiction of the seeing function of Travis Bickle is heightened in its contrast with the cretineity of his work colleagues. In conversation with one colleague appropriately named Wizard, Travis asks for advice:

TRAVIS: I figured you've been around a lot so you could –
WIZARD: Shoot, that's why they call me the 'Wizard.'
TRAVIS: I got – It's just that I got – I got –
WIZARD: Things got you down?
TRAVIS: Yeah.
WIZARD: It happens to the best of us.
TRAVIS: Yeah, it got me real down. I just want to go out and really, really do something.
WIZARD: Taxi life, you mean?
TRAVIS: Yeah, well – No, it's – I don't know. I just wanna go out … and really – I really wanna – I got some bad ideas in my head. I just –

WIZARD: Look at it this way. A man takes a job, you know? And that job – I mean, like that – That becomes what he is. You know, like – You do a thing and that's what you are. Like I've been a cabbie for years. Ten years at night. I still don't own my own cab. You know why? Because I don't want to. That must be what I want. To be on the night shift drivin' somebody else's cab. You understand? I mean, you become – You get a job, you become the job. One guy lives in Brooklyn. One guy lives in Sutton Place. You got a lawyer. Another guy's a doctor. Another guy dies. Another guy gets well. People are born. I envy you your youth. Go on, get laid, get drunk. Do anything. You got no choice, anyway. I mean, we're all fucked. More or less, ya know.

TRAVIS: I don't know. That's about the dumbest thing I ever heard.

'The dumbest thing I ever heard.' Seers are never portrayed simply in their fugitive condition of perceiving the intolerable, but always in relation with their schmucks. Doing so allows post-war cinema to invert the master-discourse of 'the people' that distinguished classical political cinema. In *Taxi Driver* this is most overt in the scenes where Travis confronts the cretineity not just of his work colleagues but of the state apparatus more directly. This confrontation is sketched in a variety of encounters. One in his cab with the Democratic party's presidential candidate Charles Palantine (whose campaign slogan is 'We are the People'), but more poignantly with Palantine's campaign manager Betsy, who in spite of the gulf in social class separating them, he seduces. In an exchange over coffee Betsy tells Travis how he reminds her of the Kris Kristofferson lyric, 'He's a prophet and a pusher. Partly truth, partly fiction. A walking contradiction.' However, when on their first date Travis takes Betsy to a porn cinema she is horrified by the orgy of sensori-motorized actions that appear in close-up on the screen. Unable to relate to Travis's motives (for whom porn symbolizes the debasement of the sensori-motor mechanism), she rejects him. Like the arch-cretin of Thebes, Oedipus at the crossroads, the state apparatus of post-Vietnam America cannot bear the intolerable truths relayed to it by its seers. Thus did cretineity in post-war cinema become not only the site of something intolerable, but the distinguishing feature of the state apparatus itself, and consequently that which must also be destroyed.

The cretin who once was blind, now can see

Basing the foundations of the people to come on the distinction between seers and their cretins make it highly problematic to maintain, as Deleuze argued elsewhere with Felix Guattari, that this is a people which exists merely at the level of oppression, 'and in the name of the oppression it suffers' (Deleuze and Guattari 1999: 379). For in its awareness of the difference between its own capacity for sight and the relative blindness of it cretinous contemporaries, it is a people which is then led to repeat its own experience of oppression on its cretinous mass. In this sense an as instructive portrait of the process by which the people to come emerges can be found in another of Hitchcock's films, that of *Rope*. The main characters in *Rope* are two wealthy socialites, who privately decide that they belong to a minor and yet superior people capable of seeing what others cannot see, and then proceed to murder a cretinous associate on account of his inability to see what they can see. The film itself has been interpreted as a classic critique of the ideological conditions for the emergence of fascism. Indeed, if we examine many of the other seers constitutive of Deleuze's people to come, they often tend to betray deeply racist, xenophobic and misogynistic tendencies. Consider, for example, Uncle Charlie's diatribe against women in *Shadow of a Doubt*. Likewise, the depiction of Travis Bickle in *Taxi Driver* was notoriously toned down in post-production at the behest of director Martin Scorsese and scriptwriter Paul Schrader on account of their fear that his xenophobic monologues (and acts) would generate race riots when shown on American screens (Schrader 2004: 117). In which light Deleuze's representations of the constitution of the people to come may be said to have romanticized the exceptionality of the power of the seer. For in this figure do we not recognize, in fact, simply 'a mass figure, an average social character ... integrated, asocial characters ... participating in a collective, realistically attuned way of seeing things' (Sloterdijk 1987: 5)? Undoubtedly, there is much akin between Deleuze's seer and Peter Sloterdijk's cynic. The latter type, which in its ancient origins was as exceptional as Diogenes in Athens, now describes a diffuse form of subjectivity – that borderline melancholic who functions by keeping his symptoms of depression well enough under control to remain more or less able to work. Cynics, in spite of their socially diffuse positionalities, Sloterdijk is at pains to stress, 'are not dumb, and every now and then they certainly see the nothingness to which everything leads' (ibid.: 5). However, the cynic, while a seer, bearing witness to the intolerable nature of the real, also bears up to it in order to survive it. This is why Bickle, in spite of his confrontation with the intolerable nature of the power relations in which he finds himself invested, nevertheless puts up with them, accommodating himself to them, regenerating them. He is as cretinous as the colleagues he finds intolerable. It is highly instructive that the final scene of *Taxi Driver* depicts Bickle back in his cab, running the meter.

If we want to trace an account of political subjectivity within cinema on which to base a politics of resistance to the state apparatus it will be necessary, therefore, to go beyond Deleuze's own rather naïve conception of the films in which such a subject is to be found. The Danish cinematic movement known as Dogme was instigated in 1995, the year of Deleuze's death. Thomas Vinterberg's *Festen* was the first film to be certified according to its manifesto or 'Vow of Chastity' as it was called (Von Trier and Vinterberg 1995). *Festen* depicts the sixtieth birthday of the patriarch Helge for which his children Christian, Michael and Helene return to the family estate. A fourth child, Christian's twin Linda, has committed suicide. It is an exemplar of the cinema of the seer in so far as it tells the story of how Christian, the eldest son, having come to see the intolerability of Helge's authority, particularly the abuse of parental power on which it is based, then proceeds to revolt against Helge by denouncing his intolerability in front of all the guests at the birthday dinner. Similar to other seers such as Bickle in *Taxi Driver*, Christian struggles with states of paralysis and trauma, at crucial points in the film appearing overwhelmed by the task of confronting Helge's intolerability, desperately seeking the courage to act. However, *Festen* cannot be dismissed as just another example of the cinema of incapacity, as Badiou would have it, for Christian does find the courage to speak, and in speaking he does find an audience, which in turn is able to act with him. The people he addresses do ultimately heed his call, and Helge's intolerable regime of power relations and abuse is destroyed. Subsequently, however, Christian refuses the opportunity to become the new patriarch or construct another set of intolerable power relations by departing for Paris with Pia, the waitress at the dinner for whom, having freed himself from the psychic constraints of the past, he is now able to consummate a love.

At the same time it's important to register that *Festen* does not represent a return to an aesthetics of the sensori-motor mechanism in the simplistic manner that Badiou demands and identifies with political theater. This is not a heroic story of the agency of Man, because Christian is only able to overcome his paralysis through the affective alliances with, and agency of his sisters, including the dead Linda, whose own suffering is born testimony to from the grave in the form of a suicide note denouncing the oppression and abuse of Helge and the power relations around which his authority revolved. There is no escape from the fact that there is a partitioning of roles in *Festen*: Christian sees and bears witness to the intolerability of Helge, while others act in response to his testimony. However, the relation between Christian and the others is not simply that of a seer to his cretins. Christian exercises little if any sovereignty over his siblings, other guests and parties. Indeed, the process by which Helge's regime is overthrown is dependent as much on the power of those others around Christian to see and bear witness to him, to his faults and weaknesses, as much as his own integrity. One of the most crucial scenes occurs when Christian, having made the first unsuccessful attempt to speak against Helge, retreats to the kitchen to say goodbye to the chef Kim, his childhood friend, before leaving. Apparently defeated by the failure of the guests to recognize as true his denouncement of his father, Kim's words give Christian the strength to continue. 'How are you Christian?' Kim asks. 'Fine,' Christian replies. 'Fine?' responds Kim, before calling the rest of the kitchen staff together and continuing. 'Well done Christian, you've made your speech. And now you're going home. The battle's lost. Nothing has changed.' 'How long have we known each other?' Kim asks. 'Since year one,' Christian replies. 'Since year one. I've been waiting for this ever since and you just run away,' Kim observes. 'What do you want Kim?' a confused Christian asks, before the course of narrative transforms and the battle is continued to its successful conclusion.

Kim's intervention is crucial to that transformation. Christian is not only unable to act without the support of his friend and others, but he is unable to see himself without their seeing him. The seeing function is democratized as much as the figure of the cretin is rendered ambiguous in *Festen*. For Christian himself appears dumb in contrast with the clear sightedness and intelligence of Kim and the rest of the proletarian kitchen staff, whose agency is also crucial to the events as they unfold. Thus is it that *Festen* spins the relation between seeing and cretineity in an entirely different way to earlier expositions of the cinema of the seer, avoiding the taint of micro-fascism so easily identifiable in the films that Deleuze naïvely celebrated. Even the arch-cretin Michael, Christian's younger brother, who embodies all of the worst traits of Helge's regime, is demonstrated to possess the power of both agency and insight. Indeed, it is Michael's agency and willingness to turn against the father that proves crucial in the latter's downfall, with Michael eventually being the one to ask Helge to leave.

Conclusion

Deleuze's account of the modernity of cinema, including the distinctiveness of its politics, can only be understood in the context of his broader political thought and project. In the years since his death, his works have become associated with the political ideal of a stateless world, of a human-social assemblage which is utterly self-organizational, and which makes no recourse to unanimity in the advance of political struggles. Certainly Deleuze rejected the kinds of false unanimity on which the classical political ideal of 'the people' was founded. When it came, however, to confronting the political problems of his time he was insistent that a political theory and practice of the present required a new typology on which to advance its struggles. Substantial forms of political change, the vast historical cleavages and upheavals which his works were concerned with theorizing, were underwritten by collective projects. Deterritorialized multitudes are not enough (Reid 2010). The main question that motivated him, then, was that of how, in the establishment of particular regimes of power did new counter-strategic collectivities emerge? How, in turn, did such collectivities 'embark on another kind of adventure, display another kind of unity, a nomadic unity, and engage in a nomadic war-machine' (Deleuze 2002: 259)? This was not merely an historical point for Deleuze. He thought it as pertinent for the present as in the past. 'The revolutionary problem today,' he argued, 'is to find some unity in our various struggles without falling back on the despotic and bureaucratic organization of the party or State apparatus: we want a war-machine that would not recreate a State apparatus, a nomadic unity … that would not recreate a despotic internal unity' (ibid.: 260).

Deleuze's arguments as to the importance of the cinema of the seer, its new race of characters and its power to perceive the intolerable are all highly indicative in this regard. These are characters who while bereft of a political project to contribute to are nevertheless constitutive of a new kind of political imaginary. Characters in which another kind of people can be seen in its emergent properties: a people of seers. The cinema that Deleuze describes posits the existence of this people in the condition of its emergence. However, to see and extrapolate this we ourselves have to think outside of Deleuze's own treatment of this cinema, especially the taxonomic system through which he differentiates between Western and non-Western cinemas, and his conception of political versus non-political cinema. Moreover, we have to grasp this people of seers, its political practices of seeing the intolerable, and the intolerant subjectivity on which it is founded not simply in a deeply antagonistic relation with its cretinous Other. What distinguishes the political function of the cinema of the seer is its depiction of the antagonistic process by which cretins become seers, recognizing the conditions that prevent them from being able to see, as well as showing would-be seers their own cretineity. The becoming conscious not only of the intolerability of present conditions but dramaturgy of the call to destroy it through novel alliances between the full range of different subjective types is fundamental to the political function that this cinema performs.

References

Badiou, A. *Handbook of Inaesthetics* (Stanford: Stanford University Press, 2005)

Barnouw, J. *Odysseus, Hero of Practical Intelligence: Deliberation and Signs in Homer's Odyssey* (Maryland: University Press of America, 2004)

Bergson, H. *Two Sources of Morality and Religion* (Whitefish, MT: Kessinger Publishing, 2005)

——*Matter and Memory* (New York: Zone Books, 1991)

——*Creative Evolution* (London: Macmillan, 1928)

Bogue, R. *Deleuze on Cinema* (New York and London: Routledge, 2003)

Brown, W. *Regulating Aversion: Tolerance in the Age of Identity and Empire* (Princeton and Oxford: Princeton University Press, 2006)

Buchanan, I. 'Introduction', in Ian Buchanan and Patricia MacCormack (eds) *Deleuze and the Schizoanalysis of Cinema* (London and New York: Continuum, 2008)

Deleuze, G. *Cinema 1: The Movement-Image* (London and New York: Continuum, 2005)

——'Nomadic Thought', in Gilles Deleuze, *Desert Islands and Other Texts 1953–1974* (New York: Semiotext(e), 2002)

——*Bergsonism* (New York: Zone Books, 1991)

——*Cinema 2: The Time-Image* (London: Athlone Press, 1989)

Deleuze, G. and Guattari, F. *A Thousand Plateaus: Capitalism & Schizophrenia 2* (London and New York: Athlone Press, 1999)

——*What is Philosophy?* (London: Verso, 1996)

——*Anti-Oedipus: Capitalism & Schizophrenia* (London and New York: Athlone Press, 1984)

Flusser, V. *The Freedom of the Migrant: Objections to Nationalism* (Urbana and Chicago: University of Illinois Press, 2003)

Gooding, F. 'Black Light' (*Critical Quarterly* Vol.42, No.2, 2003, 4–14)

Iampolski, M. *The Memory of Tiresias: Intertextuality and Film*, trans. Harsha Ram (Berkeley and Los Angeles: University of California Press, 1998)

Martin-Jones, D. *Deleuze, Cinema and National Identity* (Edinburgh: Edinburgh University Press, 2006)

Miller, V. 'The Unmappable: Vagueness and Spatial Experience' (*Space and Culture* No.9, 2006)

Natanson, M. *Anonymity: A Study in the Philosophy of Alfred Schutz* (Bloomington: Indiana University Press, 1986)

Rancière, J. *The Flesh of Words: The Politics of Writing* (Stanford: Stanford University Press, 2004)

——*Politics of Aesthetics* (London and New York: Continuum, 2006)

Reid, J. 'Of Nomadic Unities: Gilles Deleuze on the Nature of Sovereignty' (*Journal of International Relations and Development* Vol.13, No.4, 2010)

Schrader, P. *Schrader on Schrader* (London: Faber & Faber, 2004)

Sloterdijk, P. *Critique of Cynical Reason* (London: University of Minneapolis Press, 1987)

Von Trier, L. and Vinterberg, T. *Vow of Chastity*, 1995, www.martweiss.com/film/dogma95-thevow.shtml.

6 Waltzing the limit

Erin Manning

The scene returns three times. In hues of amber and grey-black, three ani-mated[1] figures emerge from the sea. We see the first figure from behind, a standing naked male body holding a gun, walking out of the water toward an amber-grey shelled-out cityscape. Two more figures lie on their backs in the water. Then the face, a face that will haunt us with its detached familiarity, fills the screen, looking off slightly to the right.

A body framed by water, rippling black-amber, rises, shells brightening the amber-hued night sky. The image pulls back, the cityscape now framed by two feet peaking out of the water. Then we are close once more, facing the rising bodies, accompanying them as they walk out of the sea toward the city.

Two bodies, and finally a third, have now made their way out of the water. Bombs fall on the scene of destruction but we don't hear them, the audio-scape carried by the music that will haunt this scene, and with it, the film, from beginning to end. In amber light we watch the bodies dress. Then, the tone shifting from amber to grey, we accompany their climb into the city, where, still fastening their clothing, they weave into the streets, streets with posters of Bashir's face, streets full of mute, anguished women, women whose voices we won't hear until the very last scene. Then, as the camera turns, turning its back on the women, we are faced, again and once more, with the face, a full-screen close-up of the soldier's impassive face.[2]

Twice more we will see the stark amber sky and the soldiers dressing, but never again will we see this scene from beginning to end. Yet as we watch it, we will feel as though it repeats itself frame for frame: every time we will once more have the experience of following the soldiers walking up the stairs into the city, under the posters of Bashir, into the crowds of mourning women, a repetition framed, always, by the face.

The repeated scene of the bodies rising out of the water begins as a promise: it looks like a flashback. As with all flashbacks, we are lulled into the feeling that there will be a *dénouement*, that the scene will grow into its content, rather than withdraw again and again into the expressionless face. Coming as it does soon after the first scene – the dreamscape of amber-grey-black dogs barking, of violence on the cusp of playing itself out, the city caught in a web of fear – we assume that this scene of bodies emerging from water will hold the key to the missing facts that memory holds at bay. We are almost certain the scene will provide the clues to the Sabra and Shatila massacre, that the rising bodies moving into the amber-grey night of war will let us know how the repressed returns.[3]

However, the repressed does not return.[4] We are witnesses not to the victims of truths now uncovered, but to sheets of experience exposing at once the singular horror of the Sabra and Shatila massacre and the impossibility of containing it within an explanatory narrative. What returns is not the past but the future, the ineffable more-than. Toward this future is the figure of the face, the face we can never fall into, the face that resists affective recognition, the face that leads us incessantly across, onto the surface of an imagescape that folds, twists, undoes and recreates itself at the complex intersection where life-living comes to expression.

Despite how haunted we are by the face and its reappearance – especially when we realize that it is the face of Ari Folman, the soldier/filmmaker/ memory-driver of the film – the face never sticks. The face does not produce the interiority for the film, does not become the centre as the affective image around which the narration turns. It appears and disappears, remaining flat, an impersonal surface that marks the passage from now to now, from singularity to singularity, in a deferred rhythm without pre-conceived connection, without attachment to time-as-such, without territorializing on a 'personal' body. The face resists catharsis.[5]

Yet at first we cannot know this, and so we are almost certain the scene of the rising bodies will provide the clues to the Sabra and Shatila massacre, that the face staring into the amber-grey night of war will let us know how the repressed returns. What we find instead is that we are witnesses to what Deleuze calls 'the power of the false,' that which 'replaces and supersedes the form of the true, because it poses the simultaneity of incompossible presents,

Figure 6.1

or the coexistence of not-necessarily true pasts' (Deleuze 1989: 131). The many-ness of expressibility in all of its entangled unfoldings is what is at stake here. This is why, despite appearances to the contrary, it is soon revealed that this is not a film 'about' the Sabra and Shatila massacre, not a film that attempts to 'return' to the past to resolve the massacre's fascistic unfolding. It is a film, rather, that surfaces the complexity of time to make felt what cannot be straight-forwardly resolved, a film that asks experience in the making to encounter its own uneasiness, its own ineffability in the face of the incompossibility of truth.

Waltz with Bashir (Ari Folman, 2008) is an animated film about living memory, about life's opening onto memory as forgetting, about the impossi-bility of memory's causal narration, about the ineffability of violence's con-tainment within the frame. It is a drama of amber and grey-black that leaks onto all memory-surfaces, until it ends, finally, on the blues and grays of archival documentation with one startling image of orange, a dead girl's body on the sandy road of the Sabra and Shatila refugee camp. *Waltz with Bashir* is a film replete with singularities that do not add up, that cross over into sheets of experience that cannot ever manage to tell the whole story, once and for all, the story of how memory and war coincide.

The face

Waltz with Bashir is about how the virtual plane – what Deleuze calls the metaphysical surface[6] – of the film brings life back not as a human face, not as a past converted into a present, but as a movement across. By presenting the face in its withdrawing from the imagescape, *Waltz with Bashir* creates a tight circuit between what presents itself and what remains virtual, returning us to the image's own movement, to the affective tonality of the imagescape's haunting amber-black-grey, thus creating an opening for what Deleuze calls *a life*, the barely active stirrings of life at the limit. To bring *a life* to the fore, the human face must remain deterritorialized, collective: when territorialized on a 'personal' body of the individual, the face too strongly proposes a terri-tory, an interiority. In *Waltz with Bashir*, the face that returns, the impassive face of the soldier/filmmaker, is felt as the surface of its own collectively tran-sient becoming. It does not overcome. It is *a life*, affective resonance in the intensive passage between surfaces of experience. *A life*, Deleuze reminds us, happens not through transcendence, but on the transcendental field itself. 'Whenever immanence is attributed *to* subject and object, which themselves fall outside the plane [of immanence], the subject being taken as universal, and the object as any object whatsoever, we witness a denaturing of the transcen-dental ... And we witness a distortion of immanence, which is now contained in the transcendent' (Deleuze 2007: 389). *A life* is immanence felt in the stirrings of actualization. Force of potential, force of life.

The characters in *Waltz with Bashir* are faces, but faces as flat surfaces, as markers for the force of fabulation, a telling poised at the limit of articulation, a telling, as one character explains, of a past 'not in my system.' Fabulation is about the event, the event of time: fabulation is not the telling of a narrative in the form of the 'what was' (the transcendent) but the expression of 'the *act* of legending.' This act creates not a truth but an opening onto the aberrant movement of time where the surface of the film itself begins to 'fiction,' to 'legend' or fabulate, where the character (the surface) begins to 'fabulate without ever being fictional' and where the filmmaker cannot but '"intercede himself"' from the real characters who wholly replace his own fiction through their own fabulations' (Deleuze 1991: 150, translation modified). What emerges via the face in *Waltz with Bashir* are stories fabulating themselves, creating themselves in the merging of events that do not constitute a clear continuity, events replete with fantasy and dream, reconstruction and confusion.[7] 'Do you recognize this picture,' the filmmaker asks, 'no' the impassive face responds; 'was I always there?' he asks another, 'yes.' The impassivity of the faces of the characters as they relay their selective memories tinged with forgetting invites a moving-across into the texture of memory itself. The telling does not sink into the myth of an attainable past. It moves through events in the making, creating a collective surface for the telling. In the fabulation that ensues, the face resists empathy at any personal, individual level. For the face here is not the locus of human expression, but the metaphysical surface through which events pass; the movement of the events of the film bubble at its impassive surface inviting us to move across into the collective event that is the imagescape itself. We cannot get inside the faces, so we move across their surfaces into the texture of the becoming-image, the becoming-image of a forgetting that is all but a past uncovered. Shards of meaning coincide, but no ultimate meaning is revealed. *Waltz with Bashir* is a web of futures in the making more than a depth of remembrance, once and for all. What we see is not the past bubbling to the surface, but life itself active in the immanence of the future-arising, *a life* on the verge of appearance at the very intersection where immanence transcends itself and merges with the actuality of the ineffable.

A life is how the drama of the political expresses itself in *Waltz with Bashir*. It is Nietzsche's 'was that life? Well then once more'[8] and Massumi's *bare activity*.[9] It is the force of agitation that pushes the virtual to the limit, the dark precursor that propels the doubling of transcendence and immanence into the pure experience[10] of the now. It is the activity of the metaphysical surface and, as such, it is the force of expression of the transcendental field.

The concept of the transcendental field radically challenges standard notions of transcendence. Where transcendence relies on the already-existent platform of spacetimes of experience in order to overcome them, the transcendental field is a pre-individual topological surface that spurs aberrant movements out of which spacetimes are created anew, aberrant because there can never be a pre-imposed path for how life can and will emerge.[11]

A transcendental field can never be known as such; however, it can be felt through the singular series – the lives – that bring it momentarily into appearance: 'Singularities are the real transcendent events, and Ferlinghetti calls them "the fourth person singular" … Only when the world, teaming with anonymous and nomadic, impersonal and pre-individual singularities, opens up, do we tread at last on the field of the transcendental' (Deleuze 1990: 103).

Waltz with Bashir's relentless imagescape of amber-grey-black steers us into an uneasy realm. It does not give us anything to hold onto and yet it pushes us across. It forces us to think, as Deleuze would say, pushing thought to the beyond where it is no longer about content, but about the creation of movements of thought. Thought in its bare activity, thought at the cusp where it merges with feeling.

Forcing thought to its limit where the thinking and the feeling are one, *Waltz with Bashir* activates a protopolitics that merges, uncertainly, with the politics the film can never get beyond, pushing the political to its limit, a limit from which it returns – if it returns – as the dramatic image of its own bare activity, broken into shards of light, amber-grey. There is no face to latch onto, no expression with which to empathize and so we keep moving. *Waltz with Bashir* proposes more than it provides, offering affective tonality before content, providing color and force-form before it gives us a figure, a body as such. *Waltz with Bashir* thus propels us across the infrahuman topological surface of the image, forcing us to think not simply *what* but *how* – what surfaces is also how it surfaces.

What – as allied to *Being* – is the question of transcendence, the question of interiority and depth, while *how* – as allied to process, or *becoming* – is the question of the transcendental field. There are no questions that cannot be dangerous in their own right, that are protected from returning to habits of thought, but there are few starting points as lethal as the totalitarianism of Being: 'I' is a habit, and where it leads is toward the supremacy of the human.[12] Being and the human cannot be disengaged, and with the human at the center, the frame is already in place for the eclipsing of the complexity of other ecologies, of other surfaces of experience. Foregrounding instead the metaphysical surface as the *how* of experience in the making opens the way for a different proposition. For *how* does not delimit a field according to pre-existing parameters: it opens it to its outside, to the outside as it curves back in on the topological surface that never quite contains it. *How* brings us back to the protopolitical and the dark precursor which is its movement of thought, to politics at the very cusp of its appearance, at the bare edge of its agitation. *How* does not guarantee against the return of fascism or the microfascist tendencies the political can and does call forth. However, it at least offers an opening onto the potential of a forking, onto *a life* welling at the winding surface that is the singular limit between now and now.[13]

The ineffable

To the physics of surfaces a metaphysical surface necessarily corresponds. Metaphysical surface (*transcendental field*) is the name that will be given to the frontier established, on the one hand, between bodies taken together as a whole and inside the limits which envelop them, and on the other, propositions in general. This frontier implies, as we shall see, certain properties of sound in relation to the surface, making possible thereby a distinct distribution of language and bodies, or of the corporeal depth and the sonorous *continuum*. In all these respects, the surface is the transcendental field itself, and the locus of sense and expression (Deleuze 1990: 125).

The transcendental field filters into experience as the virtual agitation of life welling. It is not yet delineated into subject or object: it moves intensively across, preindividually, aberrantly creating remarkable points that emerge, eventually, as the subjects and objects of the next now. It resonates with these singular events of becoming, propelling series into actualities that carry with them the germ of its intensive surface.

The transcendental field in *Waltz with Bashir* expresses itself as the emergent surface that is the repeated and varied contrast of amber-grey-black. This contrast is felt as a field of resonance where color becomes sonorous continuum – its surface the rhythm for the seeing-hearing of *a life* coursing through. While the amber-grey-black returns, always, in moments of recollection, it is not the content of the scenes that feeds forward from the transcendental field but the quality, the rhythm, the resonance, of the imagescape itself. The imagescape pulses through, pushing forward and across, moving us with it, resonating with the unseen, the ineffable. For the image resonates with the forgetting at the heart of memory, the forgetting at whose limit life begins to bubble to the surface.

Never conscious of itself, the transcendental field is the qualitative duration of the without-me of relation, of life-living. Radically empirical, it emerges, barely, at the interval of feeling and felt. When we feel it, what we feel is the cut of the interval, the between of its singular appearance here and now. In *Waltz with Bashir* we feel this quality of the active interstice in the intensive surfacing of amber-grey-black, we feel it in the resonant field created by the contrast of the bright and the dull, we feel it as the intersection where the impossibility of strategically coupling then and now expresses itself. Throughout *Waltz with Bashir*, we are never really out of this interval for we never rest in the amber-grey-black. Its stark contrast moves us each time anew, reminding us that the past cannot be doubled onto the present, that what emerges appears in the multiple now of life in the making, of life fabulating.

Sheets of the present move at various rhythms, creating different sonorous continuums and affective tonalities, and with them come different resonant fields. Take the scene between the filmmaker[14] and Ori, the friend-therapist. In stark departure from the grey-amber-black tones of the earlier scenes of the film, this scene, in which Ori describes a memory experiment, is in greens and pinks. The experiment is as follows: people are shown pictures from their childhood. They figure as children in these pictures and the events are real – they actually happened. Then, the experimenters give them a false image. This image still has them as the protagonist but the environment is invented. They were never really there. As Ori relates the experiment to the filmmaker, the scene shifts to a child in an amusement park, the child like a cut-out in a field of clowns and Ferris wheels, all this in bright candy colors. This is one such 'not really real' image: the amusement park is not one the child ever actually visited. Eighty percent of the people who take this experiment, Ori explains, claim really to have been there when they see themselves in the picture. The remaining twenty percent – those who are unsure of whether they were really there – are invited to go home and think about it. When they return, and upon seeing the picture of 'themselves' in the amusement park once again, they 'remember' the amusement park. As Ori says, 'memory is dynamic, it's alive.'

This scene briefly takes us 'out' of the story of war. An aside on memory, it feels like a film within the film. We relax in the assumption that we are pausing outside the atrocities of war while we are being taught a lesson about the slippery quality of memory so that when we return to the 'real' film, we will expect less from the 'truth' of recollection. However, just when we are certain that this is simply an academic exercise into the inevitability of memory's failures, and that this scene is cast apart from the real events of the film, the scene itself begins to fabulate: a washed-out version of the amusement park scene briefly becomes the backdrop to Ori and the filmmaker's conversation, the Ferris wheel and the clown appearing out the window behind the filmmaker's back. The amusement park has made its way onto the surface of the now, into the story of how war and memory can never strictly coincide. Memory has already begun working its sly tricks. The force of fabulation has once more infiltrated the transcendental field of the film.

This short, washed-out amusement park scene haunts the film. We see it, but they don't – the filmmaker and Ori continue to speak about memory as though nothing had happened, as though their discussion hadn't already changed the imagescape's course. The appearance of the amusement park behind the filmmaker's shoulder cuts into the past/future circuit he is working so desperately to unravel, bringing a new surface to a complex topological field of recollections

Figure 6.2

of the forgotten past and dreams of the unimagined future. Then, a few seconds later, the semblance of the amusement park gives way once more to the dreary backdrop of an outside garden, things back 'as they should be.' Yet this instance of memory's intrusion into the future-present will continue to resonate at the edges of the film's metaphysical surface. Like the dogs of the first amber-grey-black scene, it never returns as such. Never again do we even see its colors – the bright pinks and greens of the clowns and the balloons. Nonetheless, this scene has altered the field, multiplying time's supposed linearity. '[T]here is no other crime than time itself,' writes Deleuze (1989: 37). The amusement park image marks time/memory as aberrant movement. 'What aberrant movement reveals is time as everything, as 'infinite opening,' as anteriority over all normal movement … ' (Deleuze 1989: 37).

The transcendental field does not transcend time. It fields time's creation in the event. To transcend time would be to posit linear time in order to redraw time's passage as an inside and outside of experience that moves seamlessly from past to present to future. This would assume an omnipresent (human) body, documenting, remembering, orchestrating, witnessing. This is transcendence, operative always on the molar stratum of experience where life appears as pre-defined. The metaphysical surface, on the other hand, has no preconstituted spacetime. It has virtual circuits, impossible flows, ineffable becomings, wash-outs, active always on the molecular stratum where life is still in the making. Events as they come to expression merge with this metaphysical surface in infinitely dynamic ways. Dynamic events are full of holes, or better, of folds. They propel subjects and objects into the world, but they are not presupposed by them. Actively emergent from the transcendental field of experience, events do not create form once and for all, they create openings for the force of a taking-form. This is memory: the dynamic force of life-living in the uneasy forming.

Transcendence builds memory from without, feeding the past 'fully-formed' into the container of the present. To transcend spacetime is to move outside spacetime to force a mode of life on living. Transcendence cleaves morally, separating fields of experience into representations of good and evil. It is a back-gridding procedure that creates a totality, a totalitarian, tautological experience.[15] The transcendental field, by contrast, has no direction except toward the event, and no form in itself – it folds into the event forming.

Desiring surfaces

Let's return to the first scene of the film. The only dream in the film, this first scene is strangely disconnected from every other event, and yet its surface quality imbues all future imagescapes. This scene creates the mood of the film, its contrast, color and affective tone. For two minutes we move to the threatening rhythm of twenty-six dogs, their growls and panting in tandem with the synthesized sound of drums mixed with aggressive barking, the image finally centering on an amber sky, a grey building, a lone, distant face at a window looking out onto the street.[16] Moving alongside the dogs, our gait is one of horizontality, a threatening movement across, relentless, from now to now to now.[17] Never is there a clear sense of the status of this now. The now is always moving. The movement is before, behind and across and we move with it, horizontalizing the topological surface of pure experience. The dogs surround us on this horizontalizing plane even as we move with them, following them in their fight to the death. In this terrifying moving surround, we see amber eyes as placeholders of certain versions of events; we experience the mobilization of discrete singularities, and yet nothing stays still as we at once participate in and fear the mobile surface, the abstract surface of the amber-grey-black that continuously moves across.[18]

As the opening scene gives way to future amber-grey-black scenes of memory and forgetting, we become somewhat distanced from the horror of the dogs, but the dogs have set the tone and we cannot but feel that, in the end, there is no distance, no break in the movement across, only the semblance of a strange, detached calm.[19]

This uneasy movement between surfacings, topological and horizontal, between affective tonalities, lull and anguish, between calm and agitation, terror and beauty, is active, always, in the contrast, amber-grey-black. The amber-grey-black is a backdrop that is never strictly a background, forcing the viewer into a continued seeing-feeling across strata: we are drawn into a backgrounding-foregrounding resonance, we are lulled by the warmth of the amber, but cannot tear ourselves away from the nightmare of the inky black, the threatening night sky, the destroyed world of grey asphalt. So with each return of the amber-grey-black, a version of the dogs return, their eyes amber, their fur grey, the sky amber, the streets grey, their sound amber-grey-black, the sonorous continuum resonant on the mobile surface of the imagescape.

The amber-grey-black is the fourth person singular, as Ferlinghetti calls it. It is the desiring machine that moves us across the surface of the image, not so much feeding the narrative as fuelling the intensive absence of a linear reminiscence. It promises no mimicry of itself, no representation, no absolute

Figure 6.3

recognition, no ultimate tying of loose ends. It keeps us poised at the limit, that edge where terror haunts the image. This edge is never transcended. It remains the affective tonality of what cannot be expressed: the transcendental field of a micropolitics in the making.

The fourth person singular is not I. It is a desiring machine that cuts across: 'desire, by its very nature, always has the tendency to "leave the subject" and to drift' (Guattari 1977: 49, my translation). A desiring machine is a machine in the sense that it cuts, assembles, produces. It creates desire, and more desire, pushing the surface to the limits of its desiring potential. In *Waltz with Bashir* the desiring machine of the film creates an opening for transversal linkages without giving the fabulation moral standing, for desiring machines are 'machinic montage[s] that bring into conjunctions semiotic chains and an inter-crossing of material and social fluxes,' never situating them strictly on the side of good or evil (ibid.: 54, my translation). Desiring machines only propel: they promise nothing. They creates openings, intervals, fluxes of potential relation. They propose; they risk; and they move.

The fourth person singular is the protagonist of *Waltz with Bashir*, a protagonist that flirts with microfascisms of pure reminiscence as much as with the impossibility of activating the past in the present, a protagonist that cannot be resolved or recognized as such. Like all topological surfaces, the fourth person singular does not promise resolution. It desires folds. It assembles singularities. It is nomadic. 'What is neither individual nor personal are, on the contrary, emissions of singularities insofar as they occur on an unconscious surface and possess a mobile, immanent principle of auto-unification through *nomadic distribution*, radically distinct from fixed and sedentary distributions as conditions of the syntheses of consciousness' (Deleuze 1990: 102).

The dogs are an example of a desiring machine. They are a multiplicity that moves across experience in the making. They drive the film: they are relentless impetus, movement across at the topological surface of memory and dreams. As such, they are markers, remarkable points not for the transcendence of the past – the unraveling of memory, the locating of its source – but for the future anterior, the becoming of the 'it was' of the 'not yet.' They are desiring machines for a potential to come. We never know what they can do.

Waltz with Bashir thus begins off-kilter, the amber-grey of the dogs moving into the ineffable event of memory's desire. Memory crashes along the surface. It gallops, its claws scratching into the dark grey parchment to reveal not the surface's depth but its present scarring. Yet memory can create new forms. The metastable quality of its movement across is replete with its urge for transcendence. Desire can go both ways. This is the danger: that memory will fight to the death for recognition of itself as pure past, that it will create its own vortex of transcendence, that it will seek the hole of putrid history, creating new microfascisms in the making with the frenzy of vicious dogs out for revenge. This is totalitarianism at work. It stops thought.[20]

Anything that flirts with transcendence risks totalitarianism, and while fascism and totalitarianism do not strictly collude, fascism is seduced by the aura of transcendent truth that is situated in the myth of a past, fully formed. Fascism produces singularities that retell stories of belonging, that create regressive attachments. It tells dark stories as though they happened in the light of day and repeats these stories, creating doctrines from them. Fascism predicts the ending and moves toward it, suicidally. The quest is regressively circular. The search for the past that never was cannot but create the self-destruction of presents in the making. *Waltz with Bashir* flirts with each of these tendencies but in the end I think it resists them. Uneasily, out of joint, it proposes something quite different from the microfascisms that lure it: an uncertain field, a memory that leads nowhere but to its dynamic futurity.[21]

At the limit: folding surfaces

'The living lives at the limit of itself, on its limit' (Simondon 1964: 260–64, quoted in Deleuze 1990: 104). The impassive face that culminates the scene of the men rising out of the water marks a limit. This limit is not a boundary. It is a cleavage, an interval that opens back onto the surface of the film's ima-gescape. The face that creates no interiority haunts this surface. Because we cannot hold onto this surface, because its affect does not easily translate to emotion, into a circumscribed entity, enveloping recognition into itself, because we cannot sink into it, we instead feel with its resonant contrast, its back-grounding-foregrounding, its movement with the limit of memory expressing itself not as content, but as tonality. We feel not for the life of this human body, but for the force that cuts across it, for *a life*, the burgeoning of activity across surfaces of life-living. We don't feel empathy.[22] For the impassive face calls forth a protopolitics not of personal identification, but of co-constitution where what is staged is less a face-to-face encounter than an encounter with the beyond of the face, a beyond that calls everything into question including the place of the human in experience.

   A life is not strictly of the human. *A life* is not interiority. It is pure surface. It cannot be lived as such. It moves across, its volumetric surface folding. It is pure experience, pure opening onto potential. It promises nothing.

   A life is felt in *Waltz with Bashir* as the activity of memory's deformation in the event's coming to itself. It is wholly impersonal, yet singular. The dogs move through it but never come to rest in it. 'It's a haecceity, that is no longer indivi-duation, but singularization: life of pure immanence, neutral, beyond good and evil, since only the subject that was incarnated in its midst made it good or bad' (Deleuze 1990: 361). Absolute movement. Aberrant movement. 'The entire mass of living matter contained in the internal space is actively present to the external world at the limit of the living ... to belong to interiority does not mean only to "be inside" but to be on the "in-side" of the limit ... At the level of the polarized membrane, internal past and external future face one another' (Simondon 1964: 260–64, quoted in Deleuze 1990: 104).

   Aberrant because it does not evolve in any linear sense. It changes. The surface senses not the past but its presenting, its making future of the interior/

exterior fold, the expression of its limit as singularity. 'Singularities are distributed in a properly problematic field as topological events to which no direction is attached' (Deleuze 1990: 104). How singularities resolve into the present-passing has to do with the interval between memory and forgetting, 'the *memorandum* which is at the same time afflicted with an essential forgetting, in accordance with that law of transcendental exercise which insists that what can only be recalled should also be empirically impossible to recall' (Deleuze 1994: 140). The problem: 'solutions are engendered at precisely the same time that the problem determines *itself*' (Deleuze 1990: 121). *Waltz with Bashir* takes us far away from empirical memory. It creates memories out of lived relations, in the relation itself. Radically empirical, memory in *Waltz with Bashir* moves with the forgetting that is essential for the creation of a problem worth having, a problem that forces thought to the surface, across the surface.

Between the scenes

Between the scenes, in the stark contrast of nows, *Waltz with Bashir* introduces a serial interlude: a music video. In each case, music overlays the scene, a scene imbued with paradoxes of and in time. The first of these 'music videos' takes place on the 'love boat': 'Then the war started and they put us on that damned "love-boat",' Carmi recalls. OMD play and we are transported into the 1980s with the reminiscent tune of 'Enola Gay.'[23] We watch as men dance on the boat, drinking. The scene happens in a beyond of description, images unfolding without explanation for forty-five seconds. Forty-five seconds to pan in from a remote distance to a close-up of the partying on the boat. Forty-five seconds until the love boat explodes and the water turns from black to red. Forty-five seconds until Carmi speaks again: 'I saw my best friends go up in flames before my eyes.' However, even as we hear the voice and we see the red water, even as we attempt to situate ourselves in the between of the living room in Holland where the discussion takes place and the capsizing boat, what we actually feel is not the explosion. We feel a strange sonorous blue quiet: we watch Carmi being taken away from the scene onto the body of an immense blue water-woman, we watch as they drift together away from the love boat, their coupled bodies as blue as the blue water, the blue sky, the blue boat. It is from this vantage point, from Carmi's perspective, lying on the woman's larger-than-life swimming body, that we see the exploding boat at last, that we see war planes drop the bombs, as though for the second time. It is through his eyes (his head turned away from us) that we watch what at first we only heard: the scene turning blood-orange, bodies, boat, ocean colored by the event. With the world once more turned amber, we watch with him, his face resting on her stomach in the ocean, looking into the distance, impassive.

The music videos that appear sporadically in *Waltz with Bashir* are a mode of accessing the strange interval between remembering and forgetting. We feel this interval sonorously, in a strange betweenness of color and sound, in the discordant rhythm of the feeling-telling. These music videos create an eerie fissure in time, transporting us through sonorous events into the tight circuit of the virtually actual, leading us, as music can, into the affect of a recollection that is also of our own making. Until the voice-over returns – and it always does – we waver in the between that music can call forth, a between that places us fully in the feeling of the past, in the present. In the music video scenes, this sonorous continuum overlays the film's surface, multiplying the strata. The music videos play with audio-vision at the limit where the pure experience of the time-circuit vibrates, inviting us to feel the forgetting as it happens: 'Transcendental memory ... grasps that which from the outset can only be recalled, even the first time: not a contingent past, but the being of the past as such and the past of every time. In this manner, the *forgotten* thing *appears* in person to the memory which essentially apprehends it. It does not address memory without addressing the forgetting within memory' (Deleuze 1994: 140).

Forgetting is memory's sonorous continuum, a sonorous continuum created through sheets of repetition – the music video, the amber-grey-black, the bodies rising out of the water – each of which is imbued with a persistent refrain. These are differential refrains that play on repetition with a difference: the Bach Piano Concerto #5 repeats three times, the Schubert sonata is replayed in different versions throughout the film, the amber-grey-black returns again and again, yet each is interpolated with the surfacing imagescapes such that they are never exactly the same twice. The sonorous continuum resonates in the circuit of time folding in on itself.

Memory as forgetting poses a problem that cannot be worked out in a linear fashion, a problem that is not so much its content than its persistent refrain, its persistent difference. The problem of memory is its affect, the way affect resides both here and there, in the play of sensation of time's shifting surface. To remember we have to forget the *what* of memory and shift to the how of its strange vibrating surface. To remember, as Nietzsche reminds us, we must forget. Otherwise, we fall into the clutches of the transcendent traps of nostalgia, guilt and resentment that is memory's 'what,' memory's tight grasp on the containment of a unique capsule that promises to move through time unchanged. This is not how *Waltz with Bashir* plays with memory. Through the music video, *Waltz with Bashir* brings memory to life in the resonance of the sonorous now of forgetting. It tells a story in sheets of affect, a story that never quite fits together, where events are more like hyperlinks than continuities in linear time. In *Waltz with Bashir*, to remember is to activate an interval for forgetting that folds across the metaphysical surface at the limit where the future-passing unravels. Memory thus tunes toward actuality, making felt forgetting's sonorous continuum, 'the locus of sense and expression,' sonorous in the sense that it is a direct experience of time as rhythm, a pure rhythmic image of sensation (Deleuze 1990: 125). This limit where forgetting meets the event is where sense 'doubles up,' creating 'the production of surfaces, their multiplication and their consolidation' (ibid.: 125).

If memory is trapped in an air-tight cell of linear narrative, its consolidation will create black holes, traps of depth where resentment colludes with the

nostalgia and guilt of the 'if only.' In *Waltz with Bashir*, the music video inter-
rupts this tendency, pushing us into forgetting's divergent strata, distracting us
as the amusement park did, feeding the imagescape forward toward more,
more-than.

Deleuze calls forgetting the 'nth power of memory' (Deleuze 1994: 140). Forgetting is how memory expresses itself in the event of the now. Without the
nth power, without forgetting as the dark precursor of memory in the making,
memory risks falling into transcendence, into the infinitely regressive search
for meaning. This brings with it a nihilist will to power that holds to pre-imposed
associations and recognitions, making superficial links between a pre-constructed
then and now, bridging regression into a linear flow. Such nihilism holds onto
the past as though it could be transported fully formed into the present, as though
it could be known as such, and recreates the present in its image. Then, it
polices this image, holding it to its unchanging self. *The Being of the what*. The
music video in *Waltz with Bashir* subverts this tendency. The love boat fades
into the impossibility of remembering, drifting into the amber-grey foreground
of the ineffable as it moves across the shifting surface of the future-passing.

The second music video begins with a man walking onto the beach holding
a gun. Looking straight at the camera, the sun rising, the soldier takes his gun
and uses it to play air-guitar to the tune of Cake's 'Beirut,'[24] the words altered
from its original 'I bombed Korea.' This scene as it unfolds is a provocative
re-play of the beginning of *Apocalypse Now*.[25] In this, the most obvious of the
music video series, the no-time of military down-time is foregrounded, making
the crystal of time felt, riffing as it does on the unassignable limit where the
virtual and the actual coincide, 'each playing the role of the other' (Deleuze
2007b: 149, translation modified). We are thirty-six minutes into the film and
have just taken part in the telling of an event replete with the terror of war
and watched as a lone soldier swims to safety under the threat of air raids.
'I didn't do enough,' he says. 'I wasn't the hero type who carries weapons
and saves everyone's life.' After that, music, and the image of planes crashing,
boys surfing. No obvious connection to the previous dark black-amber scene
of the soldier's almost-drowning, of the broken soldier who will never have
done enough. Instead, blue-green water, grey-yellow sky and sand, plans being
made for the massacre of Sabra and Shatila by commanders eating breakfast
while talking on the phone, games of beach badminton being played in the
distance. 'I bombed Sidon today,' the music croons as bombs fall like stars
from the sky and a soldier makes sunny-side-up eggs on a hot metal remnant
of a bombed-out car. Half-naked men surf. 'I almost went home in a coffin,'
the music continues, the soldiers' arms raised up in a dance of victory or renun-
ciation as they run into the star-studded sky. Then, as quickly as it emerged,
the music video fades back into the piecing together of forgetting, back to the
voice-over and the impassive face. The surface moves again.

The next music video is of a completely different order. It is subtle and
graceful, with Bach's concerto #5 overlaying a surreal scene of soldiers walking in slow-motion through a forest, their fatigues melding into the dappled

green of the leaves, their faces impassive in a tense atmosphere of fear. Juxta-posed to the previous music video of macho images of men surfing and killing to rock music, this music video plays on the uneasy silence where beauty and terror coincide. For one minute, we watch as soldiers move very slowly, their guns poised, their bodies tense, while in the background, juxtaposed to the slowness of the soldiers' movement, we catch a quick glimpse of two children crouching under trees, running from one hide-out to another, looking for the perfect aim. Then, still in slow-motion, one of the children launches a missile and we watch as it moves slowly, slowly, through the two straight lines of sol-diers walking toward us, targeting the tank behind them. The missile inches in flight between them, Bach's concerto playing uninterrupted, the missile's sudden hit causing the soldiers to fall forward in a collective choreography of bodies lowering, their faces still impassive. Then, in unison, the soldiers raise their faces and continue to move forward, crouching along the ground, crawling off into the distance.[26]

This music video is yet another fissure in the surface of the film, the trans-cendental field now imbued with a new sense of danger – the danger of the unthinkable limit between silence, beauty and death as it moves not in the soldiers' individual bodies but across the shifting surfaces of their collective becoming-body. Despite appearances, this is not an aestheticization of death, not a micro-fascist tendency to 'let art flourish – and the world pass away' (Benjamin 2002 [1936]: 122).[27] For such an aestheticization would privilege the individual, the One. Death is everywhere here, but in the more-than: it is felt in the tense attention of the killing field, in the shadows of the forest becoming cemetery, in the collective becoming-body of the biogrammatic sur-face of the transcendental field where memory and forgetting, movement and rest, beauty and terror coincide. The music video is not an aestheticization of death but the calling forth of the uncanny between out of which the then-now of experience emerges. It is active in the relation, in the movement of sound and color, its bodying choreographed as collective, its protopolitics felt as the very edge where the terror of war is most ineffable and the memory of its violence most ungraspable. It is in this relation, in the collective movement of the transcendental surface, that the welling of the political at its bare-active limit emerges and persists.

Becoming-body

Intensity of feeling in *Waltz with Bashir* emerges on the volumetric surface of the becoming-body, the sensing body in movement, of the film itself. This becoming-body resists the quintessential sensitive surface by refusing to terri-torialize on the human face, except, perhaps, at the last scene, where the ani-mation gives way to documentary footage. In this amodal field of experience, the becoming-body as surface is its own intensive multiple movement across. It resists moving into *a* body, a personalized human body. It remains instead a biogram on the transcendental field's topological surface.

That the film moves between bodies in becoming, shaping the emergence of *a life* not as body but as biogram,[28] does not suggest that it disregards the body. Quite the contrary. The biogram of the film makes *Waltz with Bashir* all about the body, all about the intensity of life welling. What *Waltz with Bashir* resists is the subjectification of *this* body, the stultification of *this* personal experience as mapped through the recognition of the face as the quintessential affective image. At the limit of the now of events diverging where sense and memory coincide in an active forgetting, the becoming-body is an attractor for the creation of nodes of resonance, of sonorous continuums where *a* face has not yet congealed. This is why the face in *Waltz with Bashir* eludes us. It is not yet fully formed. Until the last scene.

The biogram of *Waltz with Bashir* is a moving of preindividual life across the folds of the surface of experience in the making. The becoming-body as biogram plays at the interstice of individuation and singularity, trembling on the resonant circuit of the virtual/actual now of pure experience, appearing as a tonal difference that pushes the narrative along: the body not as content but as crystal of potential. The biogram constitutes not a unique body, but a body-emergent across series, the force of life that can never return to the body as One. Force of life: where life is not yet individual or person but collective individuation. Here, where the actual and the virtual coincide in a tight circuit, there is no morality, there is only life-living, *a life*. Morality belongs to the discourse of individualized politics where perpetrators and victims are identified not as bodies in the making, but as fully formed nodes of a politics already constituted, a politics that transcends the now of experience.

Bare activity is the term Brian Massumi gives to the politics-in-germ of the becoming-body. Politics-in-germ bubbles on the pre-individual level as the singularly felt edging into life-living of the body-becoming. Bare activity is not biopower. It is the biogrammatic tendency of an edging into bodyness, of the surface welling into a singularity across series. 'Biopower's "field of application" according to Foucault is a territory, grasped from the angle of its actually providing liveable conditions for an existing biological being. [Bare activity] operates on a proto-territory tensed with a compelling excess of potential which renders it strictly *unliveable*.'[29] On the edge of the livable: *a life*.

A life percolates. Unlike some of *Waltz with Bashir*'s critics, we must not mistake '*a life*' with the life of the filmmaker, overlaying it with Ari Folman or with a generalized version of the Israeli or the Palestinian body. This is not what churns at the edges of the film. *A life* is the bare activity of the surface folding, of the background foregrounding. *A life* pushes through the plane of immanence, always on the verge of appearing, making itself felt, but never 'as such.' Beyond good and evil. Protopolitical, preindividual, *a life* shapes the sensing surface. We are caught by it, but only peripherally, for it has always already moved beyond in a welling of a new proto-territory. It is activation on the edge 'at [the] intensive limit of life' (Massumi 2009). It is the waltz in *Waltzing with Bashir*.

The waltz: two men crouched on the edge of a road in a grey, shelled cityscape fight over a gun in the midst of heavy artillery. Imminent danger all around:

soldiers shoot wildly, their anguish palpable. The sky is amber against the grey of the buildings and the dusty asphalt. We see fire in the distance. The soldier rises, the gun he has now managed to get a hold of at his side. We watch, tense, as the soldier moves into the suicidal path of bombs and bullets. The sound of a Chopin waltz playing in the background intensifies. The soldier begins to cross the street to the rhythm of the music in a three-step, all the while firing the gun into the air. Five seconds, ten seconds, the image focused on his feet, one-two-three, one-two-three, the bullet casings falling around him as he continues to shoot into the sky. We hear a gunshot whizzing by but the soldier's seemingly invincible body is the only one the image cares about, the ima-gescape dancing with him amidst the gun-flame amber in the grey-light sur-round. As the waltz gains in speed, the casings continue to pollute the earth around him and the image turns and turns, waltzing with the soldier as the sky darkens, its amber shadows intensifying in step with the image's focus in on the soldier's tight circle, one-two-three, one-two-three. Twenty seconds.

Then the voice-over returns to address what is happening, but similarly to the earlier music videos, this scene cannot be explained, cannot be comprehended. So our attention remains focused on the soldier's movement, his becoming-body dancing, *a life* quivering to the surface.

As the soldier's dance comes to an end, the image is taken over by the larger-than-life poster of Bashir's face, gazing off-screen, pock-marked with bullet holes. We sense a shift: from the micropolitics of the waltz to the macropolitics of everything Bashir represents as the recently elected president, as the mur-dered Phalangist leader, as the dark precursor to a war already in the making. Bashir's face, larger than life, takes over the screen until we are looking straight at him, another face that eludes us, that will not look at us, but this is less an impassive face than a face uninterested in us: Bashir's gaze is turned away, turned to the prelude, perhaps, of the Sabra and Shatila massacre, a massacre we will neither fully see, nor directly connect to, nor ever fully comprehend. Sixteen seconds with Bashir's face looking away, a non-merging with its exten-sive surface, the macropolitical surface of the Lebanon war.

What is the status of Bashir's face, filling the screen? How does this face that refuses to face us coincide with the incessant return of the impassive face that looks straight at us? What kind of circuit does Bashir's face superimposed on the anguished waltz of the mad soldier create?

Bashir's face is not unexpressive, but nor is it engaged. It looks off into a distance that cannot be fathomed – we cannot see what he sees. Here is a proposition: Bashir's face creates the initial delimitation of a territory.[30] This territory is where the massacre will take place: it is a specific place with a date and a history and an aftermath. Bashir gazes toward the macropolitical, his gaze directed toward the transcendent unity which is the state, the unity from which he derives the power to make decisions such as who is included and excluded from the realm of the political. Yet his face is not there – it is here, here in the dance, here in the vertigo where the macro and the micro coincide, where the affective tonality of *a life* coursing through this life makes itself felt.

Bashir's face marks the passage from the abstract plane of experience where memory and war collide without coinciding (the soldier's face) to the plane of organization where war proliferates as the actual violence of destruction. The soldier and Bashir's face: an uneasy pairing of bare activity and representation dancing at the limits where the micro and the macro coincide, at the dangerous limit where the micropolitical potentially territorializes into fascisms in the making.[31] For '[f]ascism is inseparable from a proliferation of molecular forces in interaction, which skip from point to point ... There is fascism when a war machine is installed in each hole, in every niche' (Deleuze and Guattari 1987: 214).[32]

Waltz with Bashir gives life to the bare activity of the political bubbling to the surface of the transcendental field at the same time that it warns that surfaces are not purveyors of moral truths. In the immensity of Bashir's face filling the screen and dwarfing the soldier, we sense that protopolitics are always potentially fascist politics, and yet we also feel the uncanny surplus of the waltz's movement undermining the straightforward narrative of political predetermination. From the waltz to Bashir, from the soldier's face lost in the reverie of his mad movement to the calm certainty of Bashir's distant gaze, a political drama is set forth that creates a tight circuit of molecular potentials and micropolitical captures.

As Ari Folman was creating *Waltz with Bashir*, microfascisms were playing themselves out in different ways across political constituencies, as they have a tendency to wherever there is a transcendent capture, be it liberal or neoliberal, conservative or neo-conservative. At the liberal edge of the spectrum 'we' insist on a politics of recognition based on a benevolent responsibility *for* the other that builds on dichotomies of inclusion/exclusion, perpetrator/victim, and reifies the human in the name of race, identity, gender. Not necessarily fascism, but certainly a tending toward fascism in the name of a universal figure of the human. As Guattari underscores, the universal as a tendency activates forms of microfascism in the name of desire to have the final word on the moral and the immoral, right and wrong, and this tending toward universalizing is with us, always. 'Fascism happened and it never ceases happening. It travels through the finest weaves; it is in constant evolution. It seems to come from the outside, but it finds its energy in the heart of each of our desires' (Guattari 1977: 62, my translation). Fascisms are war machines that fill the holes and gaps of potential, sedimenting the open topological surface of the transcendental field. Fascisms are a strange interplay of rigidity and suppleness – rigid disciplinings that reek of totalitarianism, supple choreographies of surface cells in the making. *Waltz with Bashir* does not protect us from the microfascist edges of politics. Indeed, it takes us again and again to their limit. What *Waltz with Bashir* does is refuse to know in advance how the consequences of the undeniable horror of the massacre play out, and where the ongoing fascisms of politics in the making are located. In so doing, it makes felt how fascisms never reign simply on the macropolitical surface of experience – they crawl between, across strata of experience, resurging in forms and forces less obvious than those in the macropolitical realm but no less insidious.

This is what *Waltz with Bashir* does: it complexifies the stakes by resisting the settling of fascism within one or another of the camps; it resists personalizing the political. Go back to the waltz scene, the scene of bullets flying and a soldier dancing, and see once more how the impassive face of Bashir is superimposed onto the agitations of *a life*. Note how, by superimposing Bashir's face, enormous and compelling, onto the backdrop of a mad dance of a soldier's undoing, *Waltz with Bashir* activates and makes felt the originary difference at the heart of all dephasings. How it makes felt that there is much more at stake than simply one surface of experience. How it makes felt that what surfaces is also how it surfaces.

The drama of the political

For eighty-eight of *Waltz with Bashir*'s ninety minutes, the face remains impassive, resists empathy, undoes recognition. Or it looks away. This is the brilliance of *Waltz with Bashir*, that it waits, creating sheet upon sheet of experience, surface upon surface of feeling, contrast after contrast, dephasing after dephasing, amber-grey-black upon amber-grey-black, pushing us across the limits of the sonorous continuum, *before* it brings us face to face with the documentary footage of the last two of the ninety minutes. It is this, the intensive passage between abstraction and recognition merging in the recognizable face of horror, that makes the final scene of the film with the flesh-and-blood face of the wailing Palestinian woman so powerful, so terrible.

The final scene leading up to the documentary footage of the Sabra and Shatila massacre takes thirty minutes to unfold, beginning with the long, slow close-up of Bashir's bullet hole-infested face framing the dancing soldier's incessant one-two-three. For thirty minutes a back and forth in time from a lawn in Holland to a couch in Israel. Then, finally, we arrive at the scene of the Sabra and Shatila massacre.

When we arrive, the scene is set: fascism beckons. 'You know that picture from the Warsaw ghetto? The one with the kid holding his hands in the air? That's just like the long line of women, old people and children looked.'

The victims are walking toward us, their bodies black against the amber night sky. We are looking straight toward the child's face – the child who reminds us of the child from the Warsaw ghetto – his hands up in the air. The child walks slowly toward us, one, two, three, four, five, six, seven, eight, nine, ten seconds, but though we recognize his gesture, his slow walk reaching toward a memory in the making, we cannot quite see him, we cannot quite make him come to life, to our life. For his face remains shadowed by the amber-black. Colour-light before face, surface before content. Yet we know the content and it haunts us: we are there, back at the camps, in the fascisms of our memories.

We enter the camp, this camp, its surfaces almost completely amber, the air like an amber gauze of sand and light, and we walk behind the women, the women we've seen three times before in the scene of the bodies rising from the

Figure 6.4

water, but this time the women are walking away from us, screaming, wailing, clutching their bodies, holding their heads. We cannot see their faces.

Moving through them, we find ourselves beside their anguish, our pace now a little in advance of their movements. We dread what we are about to see. For in the distance we see *him*, facing them, the soldier-filmmaker, his face filling the screen, his previously impassive face slowly falling apart. As we approach, as the face beckons larger and larger, we see that the face is no longer pure surface: it is leaking, breathing, chest heaving up and down, mouth slightly open, eyes roving. We feel the face's breakdown, the loss of its contours, and through this intensive folding we feel the whole metaphysical surface of the film folding into expression. However, it is not expression of content: we do not see what he sees, our backs still to the women. What he sees: the ineffable, the ungraspable, the horror.

Then we do see. We see with our own eyes. We see the wailing Palestinian women through the documentary footage taken in 1982. One Palestinian woman's face fills the screen, growing larger than life, larger even than the space of the frame. Then the face moves away from us, into the devastation of the massacre. Now another face looks straight at us, screaming, wailing into the eye of the camera in a language so many will never fully comprehend. In a rush we feel everything, we feel the amplitude of the transcendental surface now active on the surface of life, this life: we feel the terror, the empathy, the guilt, the shame, the horror. Yet we feel it not solely in their name, but in the fullness of our taking part; we feel it as our own movement across the surface of the ineffability of experience. This shift from animation to documentary footage shakes our relation to the image. We feel-see the horror.

In two minutes, the metaphysical surface of the film has completely shifted. Everything has come undone, but this is not the film's first undoing. The series

Figure 6.5

of undoings that occur throughout the film keep the circuit tight between affect and emotion, holding us to the now of experience in the making. These undoings are what keep us from taking the stance of the dispassionate observer, that keep us from falling into our *selves*. We watch-with, we feel-with the terror of a life fleeting, consumed, subsumed by the horrors of war. So we become responsible *before* the event, in the face of it, in its incessant coming-to-act, as Deleuze would say. For what *Waltz with Bashir* has instantiated with its roving imagescape and its relentless sonorous continuum is emphatically not a responsibility *for* the event, as though the event could be captured and circumscribed.[33] This is not to say that the coupling with fascisms in the making is not always there, at the ready, as are the risks of becoming responsible *for*, of taking a universalizing stance from beyond the event of *a life*'s unfolding. The specter of the boy with his hands raised, the recall of Warsaw, looms large. A rigid segmentarity. However, still the film resists, I believe, and it is this resistance that is most haunting.

The documentary footage barely lasts one minute, its blues and grays pausing in the end on an image of orange, a dead girl's body, before we are taken back to black screen of the animated film, back to amber credits, back to the Schubert that has returned more than once, differently each time, activating the sonorous continuum of our experience in the watching. Before the credits, though, the screen remains black, a blackness that lasts an eternity of twelve seconds. We do not know where we stand.[34] The ground trembles with the responsibility before life. We cannot comprehend the imagescape. It washes over us, black, a surface alive with the haunting sonorous continuum of a horror uncharted, a surfacing that now gives time for the re-creation of a circuiting back to each and every amber-grey-black image of the film. We are back, rising out of the water, walking into a city at dawn, terrified and deadened by the difference of repetition. We are back, rising out of the water, dressing on the edge of the sea, holding our hands up in the nightmare of Warsaw, lost in an image that refuses to situate us. So *Waltz with Bashir* resists the resolve of a dogmatic political stance, leaving us instead at the very heart of the drama of the political barely active.

'Everything changes when the dynamisms are posited no longer as schemata of concepts but as dramas of ideas' (Deleuze 1994: 218). *How?* is the dramatic question. In its departure from the transcendental *what?*, the differential *how?* is with what *Waltz with Bashir* is concerned. How: how to conceive of relations of force over and above a power structure that puts the individual at the center?

Relations of force are relations in their incipiency. They are tendencies in the making. Their will to power is a fight to the death between the metaphysical surface and transcendence. Transcendence often wins, because in the end it is easier to give up on the amber-grey of the face-as-surface, to turn away from the ineffable, to make the individual the starting and the end point, to background the uncertainty of relations still in-forming, to place blame, to live in resentment, to be a victim, to be guilty, to be innocent.[35] Yet to make the personal political – to opt for transcendence – is radically to underestimate the power of fascism and its unique ability to morph into folds of experience as yet unthought.

There is no question: responsibility must be taken, consequences must be faced. The macropolitical cannot be ignored. However, the edge, the differential, where the molar and the molecular meet is equally vital. For it is here, where the bare-active forces of the political agitate beyond the realm of the personal or the individual, that difference is felt at its most acute.

Waltz with Bashir is a political drama the strength of which is that it plays itself out at the uneasy intersection of *a life* effervescing and politics' potential reterritorialization on the face of fascism.[36] *Waltz with Bashir* refutes an easy solution. There is no promise here, nor even the certainty that it isn't fascism that rears its ugly head as the film comes to a close. Yet it is also here, it seems to me, in the uncertainty, that the potential looms for something yet to come that has not yet found its name, its face: a politics in the making.

In providing us with the opportunity to think about the *how* of protopolitics, *Waltz with Bashir* calls forth the future, but not a ready-made one; an uncertain one. In doing so, it resists territory's refrain, creating the opportunity for an ongoing conversation across surfaces of war and violence, an ongoing conversation not only about past wars or ongoing massacres, not only about the ineffability of the Israeli–Palestinian conflict and its micro- and macrofascist tendencies, but also about the danger of 'new forms of microfascisms: the simmering of familialism, at school, in racism, in ghettos of all kinds' (Guattari 1977: 62, my translation).

Waltz with Bashir does this by taking a protopolitical stance: we must be wary of identifying too strongly with the face, for the face is a dangerous proposition – either we recognize it as our own, or we turn away from it in horror.[37] The face must remain a topological surface equal to all other surfacings:

it must not territorialize too quickly onto an identity, onto an individual, onto the Jew or the Palestinian. Because if it does, we will have positioned ourselves in advance, and we will already have succumbed to the most potentially racist of subject-object positions.

Beyond the face is where the politics of the more-than can begin, but we must walk the tightrope carefully, remembering all the while, as Deleuze and Guattari remind us, that there are no micropolitical experiments impervious to capture by macropolitical tendencies and vice versa: 'everything is political, but every politics is simultaneously a macropolitics and a micropolitics' (Deleuze and Guattari 1987: 213).

Beyond the human

On the dangers of macropolitical capture, we can learn, perhaps, from the troubling about-turn of Emmanuel Levinas, whose ethical philosophy is constructed on the ineffability of the face, but for whom, as a Zionist Jew, the face of the Palestinian was, in the end, too much to face.

Levinas's ethical philosophy is constructed around the concept of the face-to-face encounter where 'the face is present in its refusal to be contained' (Levinas 1961: 194). His ethics underscore the idea that the face cannot be comprehended or encompassed and he is clear that the face must not be thought as 'content' – that it ultimately cannot be grasped or touched as such. The face is always the face of the Other, it is that which underscores 'the incomprehensible nature of the presence of the Other' as the first revelation of the absolute difference of the other, a relation that is 'maintained without violence, in peace with this absolute alterity' (Levinas 1961: 195, 197).

So far, the face as Levinas conceptualizes it is very reminiscent of the face in *Waltz with Bashir*. It refuses to be contained and operates as the topological surface of difference. Where *Waltz with Bashir* significantly diverges from Levinas is in its emphasis on the infrahuman and on the question of the response/ responsibility. In Levinas, the absolute alterity of the face, that 'puts me in a relation with being,' calls forth a need for a response, and there is no question that this is a response directed at another human (Levinas 1961: 212). Relations abound and encounters multiply in *Waltz with Bashir*, but these encounters are between abstract surfaces – face color, face sound, face dance, each of them operational in the tight circuit where the virtual and the actual coincide and differential relations play themselves out. Were *Waltz with Bashir* to demand 'a response,' a human-to-human encounter before all else, it would risk falling right back into the transcendence of political pre-positionings. In order to create an opening onto the drama of the political where relations of force are what is at stake, and not individual power, *Waltz with Bashir* must do everything to *avoid* making the pre-composed, pre-narrated body of the human the center of life-living.

This is the topic of the conversation that takes place between Levinas, Alain Finkielkraut and Shlomo Malka in the aftermath of the Sabra and Shatila massacre. The discussion begins with the question of response and responsibility, underscoring, as far as I am concerned, the dangers of an ethical philosophy that humanizes experience and seeks to comprehend it in a gesture of recognition of its humanity.

Shlomo Malka begins the conversation by quoting a talk of Alain Finkielkraut's where Finkielkraut says, 'We are all split between a feeling of innocence and a feeling of responsibility, both of which are anchored in our traditions and our ordeals. I do not yet know which of the two, innocence or responsibility, we will choose as Jews. But I believe that our decision will determine the meaning that we give to the ordeal of genocide' (Malka 1989: 290).

Taking this quote as a starting point, Malka asks: 'Levinas, you are the philosopher of the "other." Isn't history, isn't politics the very site of the encounter with the "other," and for the Israeli, isn't the "other" above all the Palestinian?' Levinas responds: 'Prior to any act, I am concerned with the Other, and I can never be absolved from this responsibility' (Malka 1989: 290). Continuing on the subject of responsibility toward 'those "who have done nothing",' and focusing on the concept of an 'original responsibility of man for the other person,' Levinas underscores the fact that 'my *self* ... is never absolved from responsibility toward the Other' (ibid.: 290–91).

This statement of Levinas turns the stakes of the discussion toward the specific question of the Jew and the Palestinian and the responsibility of Zionism in the face of the Sabra and Shatila massacre. Is it a responsibility *for* or a responsibility *before*? Can there be any question of innocence? Levinas responds: 'in alterity we can find an enemy, or at least then we are faced with the problem of knowing who is right and who is wrong, who is just and who is unjust. There are people who are wrong' (Malka 1989: 294). From the thinker for whom responsibility is always the question of the response elicited by the face of the other yet who claimed that the face must always remain without content, do we not experience here the stark reterritorialization on the face against which Deleuze and Guattari warn in their work on faciality?[38] Isn't the question of responsibility once again a question of whose face? Is it not the face of the other that we now see as wrong?

This is precisely what *Waltz with Bashir* resists: nowhere in the film is there a reterritorialization on the face of the other. By the time the Palestinian women's faces appear, it can no longer be a question of territory, the surfaces far too intermeshed. *Waltz with Bashir* thus resists the two tendencies at play here in the bringing together of ethics and politics: the staging of the politico-ethical solely in the body of the human and its responsibility *for* the other it faces. Responsibility *for* reeks of benevolence, a dangerous kind of liberal humanist 'generosity' that maintains the other as either victim or perpetrator, keeping the strata rigid. Being responsible *before* is a different proposition. To be responsible *before* is to engage at the non-human limit of the barely active where *a life* is restlessly agitating. On the cusp where the surfaces of life-living resonate, on the sonorous continuum of the ineffable, responsibility *before* means that we cannot already have positioned ourselves, that we are indeed, as Deleuze suggests, sorcerers creating life, and more life.[39]

To create more life is to produce difference. It is to resituate memory in the act of the telling that opens life-living to the pure experience of the welling *now*. 'Recollection introduces difference into the present in the sense that recollection constitutes, each subsequent moment, something new' (Deleuze 2004: 45, translation modified). The drama of politics at the heart of *Waltz with Bashir* is the recursive *now*, the terrible now of the tense, war-infested street where the soldier erupts from his war-self into a dance, the eerie now of the love-boat's dance exploding into blood-red ocean, the strangely quiescent now of Bach dancing in the forest. This drama of time, in time, is not theatrical. *Waltz with Bashir* does not *represent* war, or memory, or suffering. It does not express it on a stage that is separate from its happening. It lives it, on the very edge of life where life takes on the resonant political drama of *a life*.

Notes

1 *Waltz with Bashir* was made first as a non-animated video based on a 90-page script and then transformed into animation (with 2,300 illustrations drawn by art director David Polonsky and his three assistants). The animation format is a combination of Flash animation, classic animation and 3D. In an interview with Erica Abeel from indieWIRE, Ari Folman discusses his use of animation for this film (with the exception of the last scene of the film, which is documentary archival footage of the Sabra and Shatila massacre). He says: 'I had the basic idea for the film for several years, but I was not happy to do it in real life video. How would that have looked like? ... If it could be done in animation with fantastic drawings, it would capture the surreal aspect of war. If you look at all the elements in the film – memory, lost memory, dreams, the subconscious, hallucinations, drugs, youth, lost youth – the only way to combine all those things in one storyline was drawings and animation. You know, the question most frequently asked since Cannes is "why animation?" And it's a question that's absurd to me. I mean, how else could it have been done? ... [With animation] you can go from one dimension to another ... I think you get enormous freedom with animation and illustrations. It's a really great language for me, the best. You can imagine everything.' www.indiewire.com/article/oscar_09_waltz_with_bashir_director_ari_folman/.

2 In fact, this scene is almost identical to the final scene of the film, except that in the last scene, the camera will not turn its back on the women, and the face will open itself to the unthinkable suffering of the massacre.

3 Deleuze speaks of the necessity for 'the actual image [to] enter into relation with its *own* virtual image as such; from the outset pure description must divide in two, "repeat itself, take itself up again, fork, contradict itself". An image which is double-sided, mutual, both actual and virtual, must be constituted ... We are in a situation of an actual image *and* its own virtual image, to the extent that there is no longer any linkage of the real with the fictional, but *indiscernibility of the two*, a perpetual exchange ... And just as the real and the fictional become indiscernible in certain very specific conditions of the image, the true and the false now become undecidable or inextricable: the impossible proceeds from the possible, and the past is not necessarily true' (Deleuze 1991: 274–75, translation modified).

4 This is not a film about personal redemption. In response to a question about the 'therapeutic' aspects of making this film about 'his' experience as a soldier in the Lebanon war, Ari Folman says: 'I'd say the filmmaking part was good, but the therapy aspect sucked.' www.indiewire.com/article/oscar_09_waltz_with_bashir_director_ari_folman/ Elsewhere, underscoring the dynamic aspect of experience, he says: 'My

belief is that any kind of filmmaking is therapy; but, it's dynamic. You're actually *doing* something.' theeveningclass.blogspot.com/2009/01/waltz-with-bashir-evening-class.html.

5 In his excellent work on anime, Thomas Lamarre works with the concept of the 'superflat,' suggesting that it is the very flatness of the animated image that creates the potential for a certain kind of metamorphosis and timing. He writes: 'This is because, if one thinks about flatness in terms of two-dimensional surfaces, then the logical question becomes: how does anything happen in this surface world? How does anything come forth or vanish? And how is such change expressed. Clearly, events and change can be expressed only in terms of an interaction of surfaces, as a movement of surfaces on surfaces, as shift from surface to surface. I should like to stretch Murakami's superflat, and think of a superflat that entails flat interactions or flat articulations. That is, the superflat becomes a quality of movement, change or transformation. In effect, the supposedly flat and depthless characters and figures in *anime* are superflat. In their very flatness, they are traversed by a potential for interaction, motion and transformation. They move on a specific field of forces' (see 'From Animation to Anime,' *Japan Forum* 14(2) 2002: 329–67, 338). While *Waltz with Bashir* does not fit into the category of anime, the use I am making of the idea of surface resonates with Lamarre's analysis, and is informed by it. See also his important book *The Anime Machine – A Media Theory of Animation* (Minneapolis: Minnesota University Press, 2009). Here, Lamarre develops much more thoroughly than I do here the concept of animation and its potential as a visual and cultural practice.

6 See Gilles Deleuze, *Logic of Sense*, trans. Mark Lester and Charles Stivale (New York: Columbia University Press, 1990).

7 In the English translation of Deleuze's cinema books, fabulation is translated as story-telling, which in its common definition departs from the way Deleuze is using the term. Fabulation, or the 'function of fabulation' is a concept Deleuze takes from Bergson that departs from the idea of narrative to touch on the question of what Deleuze calls 'the power of the false.' It is also implicitly aligned to the notion of intercessor, which Deleuze defines as the conduit for expression. Deleuze writes: 'Whether they're real or fictional, animate or inanimate, we must create our intercessors. It's a series. If we do not form a series, even completely imaginary, we are lost. I need my intercessors to express myself, and they could never express themselves without me: when we work we are always many, even when it is not obvious' (Deleuze 1995: 125, translation modified). Fabulation follows directly from this notion of a manyness of expression. In Deleuze's text on intercessors, it is through Pierre Perrault's work that Deleuze activates the concept of fabulation. He writes: 'The fabrication of intercessors in a community stands out in the work of the Canadian cinematographer Pierre Perrault: I gave myself intercessors, and this is how I can say what I have to say. Perrault thinks that, if he speaks alone, even if he invents fictions, he's bound to come out with an intellectual discourse, he won't be able to get away from a 'master's or colonist discourse,' an established discourse. What is needed: to catch someone else 'legending,' 'caught in the act of legending.' Then a minority discourse, between two or several, begins to form. We here come upon what Bergson calls 'fabulation ... To catch people in the act of legending is to catch the movement of the constitution of a people. Peoples do not preexist' (Deleuze 1995: 126, translation modified). This ties in with what Deleuze writes in *Cinema 2*: 'When Perrault is addressing his real characters of Quebec, it is not simply to eliminate fiction but to free it from the model of truth which penetrates it, and on the contrary to rediscover the pure and simple *function of fabulation* which is opposed to this model. What is opposed to fiction is not the real; it is not the truth which is always that of the masters or colonizers; it is the fabulatory function of the poor, insofar as it gives the false the power that makes it into a memory, a legend, a monster' (Deleuze 1991: 150, translation modified).

8 Friedrich Nietzsche, *Thus Spoke Zarathustra: A Book for None and All*, trans. Walter Kaufmann (New York: Penguin Books, 1967), 157.

9 On his concept of bare activity, see, amongst others, Brian Massumi, *Semblance and Event: Activist Philosophy and the Occurent Arts* (MIT Press, 2011).

10 'Pure experience' is the term William James gives to the virtual-actual nexus of experience in the making. He writes: 'The instant field of the present is at all times what I call the "pure" experience. It is only virtually or potentially either subject or object as yet. For the time being, it is plain, unqualified actuality, or existence, a simple *that*' (James 1996: 23).

11 Ari Folman also speaks of the movements of the film as being aberrant, referring especially to the strange gait of the animated characters. He says: 'Look at the motion. People don't walk in reality like they walk in this film. It's a different kind of walk we developed, slow and awkward. We had problems in animation creating this slow movement. It's much easier to make action scenes.' www.indiewire.com/article/oscar_09_waltz_with_bashir_director_ari_folman/.

12 In the preface to the forthcoming Chinese translation of *A Thousand Plateaus*, Brian Massumi writes: 'What is at issue philosophically is never the empirical question of "what" something is (the question of being). It is the pragmatic question of "how" things go (the question of becoming-oriented). What is always at issue philosophically is this pragmatic question, taken to the limit of thought' (Massumi 2010: 12).

13 In *Cinema 2*, Deleuze connects a cinema that creates time (creating thought) to one that departs from a certain fascism of the cinematographic. Citing Artaud, he writes: 'the image must produce a shock, a nerve-wave which gives rise to thought' (Deleuze 1991: 165). Microfascisms are challenged by the 'as yet unthought' allowing us to 'discover the identity of thought and life' where 'the whole is the outside' and 'what counts is the interstice between images,' 'a spacing which means that each image is plucked from the void and falls back into it' (ibid.: 179).

14 While it is clear that the film-maker 'represents' Ari Folman, we never actually get to know the character. We know only that he was a soldier and now makes films and that this is a film he is moved to make. 'I'm just a filmmaker!' he says when Boaz seeks his help about the dog-nightmare. 'Can't films be therapeutic?' Boaz asks? The filmmaker does not answer directly, except to say that he has not had any flashbacks: 'The truth is, that's not stored in my system,' he says, referring to the Sabra and Shatila massacre. 'You never think about it?' Boaz insists. 'No, no ... no,' the filmmaker responds, his face impassive. They hug and go their separate ways. 'I'll think of something,' the filmmaker says. *Waltz with Bashir* is the force of thought this thinking propels.

15 For more on back-gridding and experience, see Brian Massumi, 'Concrete is as Concrete Doesn't,' in *Parables for the Virtual: Affect, Movement, Sensation* (Duke University Press, 2002).

16 The 'techno' sound for this scene was made from ninety-eight tracks reduced to five, Ari Folman explains in an interview. www.indiewire.com/article/oscar_09_waltz_with_bashir_director_ari_folman/.

17 The graphic novel *Waltz with Bashir* is completely different from the film, despite the fact that the images are original animated drawings and the text is the same. Without the movement across of the cinematic imagescape, the affective tonality of the surface as *a life* does not come through. In the graphic novel, the text takes over and the images become aids or representations to the story. As a result, the characters take on a more standard 'personality' and the story thus becomes more traditional in its telling. This is not to suggest that only cinematic images have movement. For stills that are immanent with absolute movement, see any of Leni Riefenstahl's photographs from *Olympia* (this question of the still-in-movement is further developed in Erin Manning, *Relationscapes: Movement, Art, Philosophy* (MIT Press, 2009)).

18 On the topic of movement and anime, Thomas Lamarre writes: 'Animation then becomes something other than a process of animating figures, of drawing all the stages to produce seamless movement. It is a process of inventing machines of movement – machines of walking, of talking, of running, leaping, flying, and so forth – that take up all manner of objects.' See 'From Animation to Anime,' *Japan Forum* 14(2) (2002), 329–67, 339.

19 For more on semblance and event, see Brian Massumi, *Semblance and Event: Arts of Experience, Politics of Expression* (MIT Press, 2011).

20 Deleuze and Guattari write: 'The plane of immanence is not a concept that is or can be thought but rather the image of thought, the image thought gives itself of what it means to think, to make use of thought, to find one's bearings in thought … Thought demands "only" movement that can be carried on to infinity. What thought claims by right, what it selects, is infinite movement or the movement of the infinite. It is this that constitutes the image of thought' (Deleuze and Guattari 1994: 37).

21 I say this being fully aware of the many conflicting responses to the film and the disavowal of the film from many left-wing groups in Israel, Palestine and abroad. That *Waltz with Bashir* is a film that awakens paradoxical responses is its strength, I believe, and its politics. Critiques follow two major lines: a lack of political commitment (see Todd Brown below), and the absence of Palestinians in the role of writing history (resulting in its incapacity to do justice to the horror and its lack of responsibility) (see Naira Antoun). The second critique is the more interesting one, and the one to keep in mind here. My reading of the film does not seek to disqualify such a critique, but to reproblematize the question of memory, experience and the political via the affective surface created by the film. Whether or not the film ultimately does justice to the horror of the massacre cannot be the question, it seems to me, as *nothing* could do the massacre justice. How movements of thought are generated by art, how surfacings are complicated through the qualitative expressions of the transcendental field art can activate is what I hope to address here. The key question, it seems to me, is one that concerns attending to the differential of molar/macro questions and molecular/micro questions. I agree with Antoun that the issue of taking responsibility is always at stake. This is an example of a macro question that must be addressed. The problem is that when only this stratum is addressed, we quickly fall into the personalization of politics, a personalization that appeals to the transcendent plane of the state. See below how Antoun herself falls into this trap, suggestion that the face in *Waltz with Bashir* is a personal face, and building her argument on exclusion based on this notion of the refacialization of politics.

Todd Brown writes: 'In many ways, this is the hardest review I've ever sat down and committed myself to writing. I regret watching Ari Folman's Waltz with Bashir. No, it's not because it was a waste of time. It wasn't because it was bad filmmaking. On the contrary, it is filmmaking at its finest. Waltz with Bashir is, at the very least, an astounding animated documentary with incredible originality and breathtaking impact, a film that must be watched by anyone with even a passing interest in world affairs or Middle Eastern History … While Waltz with Bashir occupies the upper end of the scale in terms of quality filmmaking, it incredibly dominates the lower end of the political propaganda spectrum with its insidiousness … While I applaud Folman for attempting to face up to the guilt of the Sabra and Shatilla Massacre, this film falls utterly short of making any commitment on the issue, instead choosing to weasel out of the grasp of responsibility which even Israel's own Kahan Commission had assigned to the IDF' (twitchfilm.com/reviews/2009/10/waltz-with-bashir-reviewwal.php).

Naira Antoun writes: 'To say that Palestinians are absent in *Waltz with Bashir*, to say that it is a film that deals not with Palestinians but with Israelis who served in Lebanon, only barely begins to describe the violence that this film commits against Palestinians. There is nothing interesting or new in the depiction of Palestinians –

they have no names, they don't speak, they are anonymous. But they are not simply faceless victims. Instead, the victims in the story that *Waltz with Bashir* tells are Israeli soldiers. Their anguish, their questioning, their confusion, their pain – it is this that is intended to pull us. The rotoscope animation is beautifully done, the facial expressions so engaging, subtle and torn, we find ourselves grimacing and gasping at the trials and tribulations of the young Israeli soldiers and their older agonizing selves. We don't see Palestinian facial expressions; only a lingering on dead, anonymous faces. So while Palestinians are never fully human, Israelis are, and indeed are humanized through the course of the film ... In the final analysis, this is what *Waltz with Bashir* is about: the evasion of responsibility. It is not that the self-reflection offered by the film is only partial, and that we would simply be nay-sayers to be dissatisfied with it. Because there is no sense of what the Israeli role in Lebanon was, because it is about ethically and morally redeeming the film-maker and his contemporaries – and by extension the Israeli self, military and nation, the Israeli collective in other words – because of all this, the film is an act not of limited self-reflection but self-justification. It is a striving towards working through qualms to restabilize the self as it is currently constituted; it does not ask challenging questions that would destabilize that self' (electronicint ifada.net/v2/article10322.shtml).

22 Empathy is not affective. It is an emotion that operates within the register of the first person singular, where 'I' see 'you,' where subject and object are predefined. As I will outline at the end of the chapter, is 'responsibility for' the other and not 'before' the other, an ethics of recognition rather than a desiring machine for collective individuation. Being responsible 'before' the other involves the embrace not of an other qua human other, but of a tendency toward becoming. We are responsible before in a collective individuation that resonates on the cusp of the actual and the virtual where experience begins to take form.

23 Enola Gay is the name given to the B-29 superfortress bomber that dropped the first atomic bomb on Hiroshima.

24 'I Bombed Korea' is reworked into 'Beirut' by Zeve Tene.

25 *Apocalypse Now*, directed by Francis Ford Coppola, 1979.

26 This scene is strangely reminiscent of the dappled forest scenes and classical music of Terrence Malick's *Thin Red Line* (1999).

27 '"Fiat ars – pereat mundus" says fascism, expecting from war, as Marinetti admits, the artistic gratification of sense perception altered by technology. This is evidently the consummation of *l'art pour l'art*. Humankind, which once, in Homer, was an object of contemplation for the Olympian gods, has now become one for itself. Its self-alienation has reached the point where it can experience its own alienation as a supreme aesthetic pleasure. Such is the aestheticizing of politics, as practiced by fascism Communism replies by politicizing art' (Benjamin 2002 [1936]: 122).

28 Deleuze's concept of the diagram (particularly as he develops it in relation to Francis Bacon's work in *Logic of Sensation*), is closely allied to my use of the bio-gram. See also Brian Massumi, 'Strange Horizon,' in *Parables for the Virtual: Movement, Affect, Sensation* (Durham: Duke University Press, 2002).

29 See Brian Massumi, 'National Enterprise Emergency: Steps Toward and Ecology of Power,' *Theatre, Culture and Society*, special issue on Foucault (2009).

30 'The territory is the surface form extruded by the life-priming of bare activity. It is the effective form of expression of what Deleuze and Guattari would call a cutting edge of deterritorialization, understood as the processual suspension of prior gridd-ings remitted to the formative commotion from which they emerged.' See Brian Massumi, 'Perception Attack: The Force to Own Time,' in *Ontopower: Potential Politics and the Primacy of Preemption* (Duke University Press, forthcoming).

31 For more on the relationship between the political and politics, see Jacques Rancière, *Disagreement*, trans. Julie Rose (Minneapolis: Minnesota University Press, 1999).

32 See also Foucault's introduction to Deleuze and Guattari's *Anti-Oedipus*, which he calls a 'handbook for anti-fascist living.' He writes: 'how does one keep from being fascist, even (especially) when one believes oneself to be a revolutionary militant? how do we rid our speech and our acts, our hearts and our pleasures, of fascism? how do we ferret out the fascism that is ingrained in our behavior?' (Deleuze and Guattari 1983: xiii).

33 'Writers are sorcerers because they experience the animal as the only population before which they are responsible in principle. The German preromantic Karl Philipp Moritz feels responsible not *for* the calves that die but *before* the calves that die and give him the incredible feeling of an unknown *Nature-affect*. For the affect is not a personal feeling, nor is it a characteristic; it is the effectuation of a power of the pack that throws the self into upheaval and makes it reel. Who has not known the violence of these animal sequences, which uproot one from humanity, if only for an instant, making one scrape at one's bread like a rodent or giving one the yellow eyes of a feline? A fearsome involution calling us toward unheard-of becomings. These are not regressions, although fragments of regression, sequences of regression may enter in' (Deleuze and Guattari 1987: 240, my emphasis).

34 Comprehension suggests a holding-together of 'facts' with a sense of 'objectivity.' On the subject of objectivity and its relation to filmmaking, Ari Folman says: 'I don't believe in objectivity. There is no objectivity in filmmaking. Logically, it cannot exist. The basic fact that you go into an editing room with 200 hours of footage and by the end of the editing process come out with a film that is 50 minutes or an hour negates objectivity.' theeveningclass.blogspot.com/2009/01/waltz-with-bashir-evening-class.html.

35 On the topic of blame, in answer to Erica Abeel's question, 'Why didn't you hold the leadership more to account? Sharon was complicit, after all, he allowed the massacre to happen,' Ari Folman responds: 'I didn't want to make any statement about the leadership. I wanted to recreate the world of the ordinary soldier. There was a commission that found Sharon guilty, he was banned from office for life, then he came back as Prime Minister, came back as a hero, think of it. Those things happen in Israel … Bottom line, for me it was not a revenge film against Ariel Sharon. As for why he didn't stop the massacre, he's asleep now, so we can't ask him. The whole plan for Lebanon was so sick, to my mind. What the master plan was nobody really knows.' www.indiewire.com/article/oscar_09_waltz_with_bashir_director_ari_folman/. I quote this to emphasize the push and pull between the molar and molecular as it plays out both in *Waltz with Bashir* and in my reading of it.

36 For a thought-provoking article on *Waltz with Bashir*, see Gary Kamiya, 'What Waltz with Bashir Can Teach Us About Gaza,' www.salon.com/opinion/kamiya/2009/01/13/waltz_with_bashir/index1.html.

37 For a more sustained exploration of the horror of the face with respect to Levinas's and Deleuze and Guattari's theories of faciality, see Erin Manning, 'Face to Face with the Incommensurable: Srinivas Krishna's Lulu,' in *Ephemeral Territories: Representing Nation, Home and Identity in Canada* (Minnesota University Press, 2003).

38 See Deleuze and Guattari's chapter on faciality, 'Year 0: Faciality,' in *A Thousand Plateaus*, trans. Brian Massumi (Minneapolis: Minnesota University Press, 1987).

39 Deleuze and Guattari write: 'Memories of a Sorcerer, I. A becoming-animal always involves a pack, a band, a population, a peopling, in short, a multiplicity. We sorcerers have always known that,' in *A Thousand Plateaus*, trans. Brian Massumi (Minnesota University Press, 1987).

7 Politics on the line

Leonie Ansems de Vries

Introduction

Fascism, Deleuze and Guattari suggest, implies a molecular regime distinct from molar segments: not the rigidity of state molarity but both the suppleness and the dangers of the line of flight. In their conceptualisation of social and political relations as a play of lines in dynamic interaction, lines crisscross and clash as well as mix and merge; lines create and connect, abort and destroy; lines function to capture, demarcate, defend and uphold a territorial domain of limits and bounds, order and organisation; and lines challenge, undermine, perturb and destroy domains or order(ing)s of organisation and organisations of order(ing). If power and resistance, creation and destruction, operate on the same line(s), then the problem is not so much that forms of resistance come to resemble the regimes of power they seek to counter, but rather that the gravest dangers lie in the capacity of a single line to turn any direction. The same line(s) constitute the milieux of strategies of both power and resistance hence neither their course nor their outcome can be predicted in advance. Besides, the movement that holds out the greatest promise of creative becoming – of modes of movement and relationality affirmative of life – also poses the gravest danger of ending in death and destruction. The political *problematique* that emerges with Deleuze and Guattari's conceptualisation of lines is accordingly this: if what holds the most promising creative potential also carries the most serious danger of destruction, and if the course of movement can be neither controlled nor predicted, then how to produce a politics of affirmative becoming without either getting bogged down in a regime of molar fascism or falling foul to a fascistic logic of destruction?

In his Preface to Deleuze and Guattari's *Anti-Oedipus*, Michel Foucault describes this text as a book of ethics that responds to the major enemy of fascism. Being 'anti-oedipal', Foucault writes, 'has become a life style, a way of thinking and living' to rid our speech, acts, hearts and pleasures of fascism. '*Anti-Oedipus* is an *Introduction to the Non-Fascist Life*' (Foucault 2004). It could be said that Deleuze and Guattari continue this project in the second volume of *Capitalism and Schizophrenia*, *A Thousand Plateaus*, in which they take up, pursue and perturb a Spinozan ethics to create a style of politics/life free from fascism. Yet this work also indicates that the danger of fascism looms incessantly and its force destroys irrevocably. Everything happens on the same lines: the line of 'destruction pure and simple' at once is/becomes a line of transversal connection creative of affirmative difference.

Deleuze in turn finds an articulation of the problem of fascism in Foucault's writings. In *Foucault*, he writes that the question of resistance to power is (for Foucault) that of how to 'cross the line': how to create transversal lines of resistance rather than integral lines of power? What troubled Foucault is that transversal relations of resistance continue to become restratified and encounter or even *construct* knots of power. If we must attain a life that is the power of the outside, what tells us that this outside is not a terrifying void and that this life, which seems to put up a resistance, is not just the simple distribution within the void of 'slow, partial and progressive' deaths? (Deleuze 2006).

Put differently, the question is how to avoid warding off one form of fascism (macro-fascism) by getting bogged down in another form of fascism (micro-fascism) or, as Deleuze and Guattari put it, '[w]hy does desire desire its own repression, how can it desire its own repression?' (Deleuze and Guattari 2004: 236–37). Only micro-fascism, they reply in *A Thousand Plateaus*, provides an answer to this global question: it is because everything happens on lines inextricably entangled and crossing over into one another:

> It is not that these lines are pre-existent; they are traced out, they are formed, immanent to each other, mixed up in each other, at the same time as the assemblage of desire is formed, with its machines tangled up and its planes intersecting. We don't know in advance which one will function as a line of gradient, or in what form it will be barred.
>
> (Deleuze and Parnet 2006: 100)

Expressed in terms of a play of lines constitutive/disruptive of the social and political field, fascism emerges as a problem more complex, mobile, immanent and relational than a conflict between fascistic and anti-fascistic forces, or a (dualist) opposition or interaction between micro- and macro-fascisms. Moreover, connecting lines to the notion of the milieu(x) reveals the significance of the temporal dimension of this fundamentally political *problematique*. Whilst the effort to ward off both macro- and micro-fascistic tendencies – and hence the conversion of one into the other – consists in rendering visible and knowable their possible future courses, the problem is that this cannot be predicted in advance, at least not without recourse to fascism. Put differently, whilst the effort consists in laying out in advance how the line will pass, the problem is that the line cannot come to pass when everything is laid out in advance: the play is foreclosed when the line of flight – both the most vital force against fascisms and its most dangerous producer in its capacity to push it to a state of total destruction – is immobilised. Because lines entangled in a complex play of movements and relations can turn anywhere, one must establish and predict where or how the line will pass; however, this cannot be done without producing the forces from which one seeks to escape. Hence arises the political paradox, in which the line of flight constitutes both the greatest promise and the most perilous danger. As Deleuze and Parnet put it, '[e]verything is played in uncertain games' (Deleuze and Parnet 2006: 100).

In order to draw out the stakes of this play – its fascistic dangers as well as its political promise – this chapter seeks to engage, create and perturb the complexity, mobility and relationality of Deleuze and Guattari's politics of lines by connecting it, first, to their biophilosophy revolving around the notion of the milieu and, second, to the Spinozan ethics of bodies they produce. An introduction to the politics of lines in the second section will serve to explicate the political *problematique*. It also raises the question of the historical specificity of regimes of lines. The third section connects the play of lines to the notion of the milieu in order to expose the complex mobile relationality of the forces at play, and to explore how practices of biopolitical governance securitise the becoming of forces this entails. Connecting the milieu, on the one hand, to Foucault's conceptualisation of the *dispositif* of security and, on the other, to Dillon and Reid's notion of the 'emergency of emergence' will explicate how the contemporary acknowledgement of the primacy of the line of flight provokes the hyperbolisation of liberal fascisms. The final section probes a response to this seemingly inescapable problem of fascism through Deleuze's Spinoza. Does an ethico-politics of bodies understood in terms of relations of movement/rest and powers to affect/to be affected hold the promise of a life beyond fascism? Through lines, milieux and movements, it will emerge that one can only *become* yet never *be* free from fascism, which leaves us on uncertain lines.

A politics of lines

> Whether we are individuals or groups, we are made up of lines and these lines are very varied in nature.
>
> (Deleuze and Parnet 2006: 93)

The ninth plateau of *A Thousand Plateaus*, '1933: Micropolitics and Segmentarity' articulates a politics of lines in which the line of flight plays a crucial role as both vital force and movement of destruction, promise and danger. Both this plateau and the chapter 'Many Politics' in *Dialogues*, a co-authored text by Deleuze and Claire Parnet, conceptualise the social and political field as a set or multiplicity of lines which are irreducible to one another (Deleuze and Parnet 2006: vi). A third exploration of the politics of lines can be found in the tenth plateau of *A Thousand Plateaus*, entitled '1730: Becoming-Intense, Becoming-Animal, Becoming-Imperceptible … ', in which Deleuze and Guattari contrast the line to the point. Here the focus will be on the field of lines.

'We are segmented from all around and in every direction', Deleuze and Guattari (2004: 230) write in the ninth plateau. We are segmented in a binary fashion (e.g. social classes, man/woman, adult/child, etc.), a circular fashion (in ever wider circles: neighbourhood, city, country, world), and in a linear fashion, on the basis of straight lines,

> of which each segment represents an episode or 'proceeding': as soon as we finish one proceeding we begin another, forever proceduring or pro-cedured, in the family, in school, in the army, on the job. School tells us, 'You are not at home anymore'; the army tells us, 'You are not in school anymore'.
>
> (Deleuze and Guattari (2004: 230)

These three modes of segmentarity are interrelated, bound up with and crossing over into one another, and change according to one's perspective. The distinction to be drawn politically is, however, not between these types of segmentarity. Nor, Deleuze and Guattari explain, on the basis of the differ-ence between segmentation and centralisation for the modern political system is a regime of both centralisation and segmentation. All segmentary lines are modes of order(ing) related to a plane of organisation. A more productive distinction is that between rigid and supple, or molar and molecular, seg-mentarities – segmentarities which are at once opposed and entangled: they overlap, coexist and cross over into one another. For instance, aggregates of perception or feeling involve a molar organisation and rigid segmentary, yet there is simultaneously 'an entire world of unconscious micropercepts, uncon-scious affects, fine segmentations that grasp or experience different things, are distributed and operate differently' (Deleuze and Guattari 2004: 235).

It is in this context that Deleuze and Guattari claim that 'everything is poli-tical, but every politics is simultaneously a *macropolitics* and a *micropolitics*.' It is of importance to note that the distinction between macro and micro, or the molar and the molecular, is to be understood in terms of organisation and movement rather than size or scale. Macro-politics or molar organisation relates to the capture of spatio-temporal and relational order(ing) in seg-mented, binary and homogenised categories, and the centralisation of interior space; molecularity can be understood as the (dis)order(ing) force that both underlies and uproots this order(ing). Micropolitics constitutes a third move-ment that is in addition to the two lines described above; there is a line of flight – or a movement in-between – which is primary. Three different types of lines thus traverse, mark out and disrupt the social and political field descri-bed by Deleuze and Guattari: lines of molar segmentarity, lines of molecular segmentarity, and lines of flight. The first are binary machines – social classes, sexes, ages, etc. – which cut across and collide against each other, bringing about a dualist organisation of segments. The status of molecular lines 'seems to be completely different', Deleuze and Parnet write. For instance, their seg-ments are 'proceeding by thresholds, constituting becomings, blocs of becom-ing, marking continuums of intensity, combinations of fluxes' (Deleuze and Parnet 2006: 98). Lines of molecular or supple segmentarity thus make fluxes of deterritorialisation shoot between the binary segments. These lines do not synthesize the binary segments but constitute a third which comes from else-where and disrupts binarism. Hence the molecular line does not arise through adding segments to molar organisation. Rather it is a matter of tracing another line that is in the middle.

Thus within a (Cold War) conception of world order segmented between East and West, molecular destabilisation occurs on a north–south line. No great ruptures, but the little crack coming from the South: '[a] Corsican here, else-where a Palestinian, a plane hijacker, a tribal upsurge, a feminist movement, a Green ecologist, a Russian dissident' (Deleuze 1995: 98). Put differently, lines of molar segmentarity effect movements of territorialisation, whereas mole-cular segmentarity relates to relative deterritorialisation. Territorialisation refers to the organisation, ordering and capture of space, time and relations; to impose upon the forces of life an order of categorisations and limits. This operation of delimitation, which establishes a frame and demarcates an inside and an outside, renders chaos the opposite of order; and the order of organi-sation the opposite of disruptive forces endangering the organisation of order and life. Movements of territorialisation are deeply entangled with processes of deterritorialisation, which uproot and challenge the binary order of natur-alised identities and categorisations and, Deleuze and Guattari contend, are prior rather than derivative (Deleuze and Guattari 2004: 10–11).

Finally, lines of flight are abstract molecular lines with an incessant ten-dency to escape; mutant flows that flee the interiority of order(ing). Whereas fluxes of deterritorialisation emitted through supple segmentarity are rela-tive – i.e. simultaneously compensated by reterritorialisations, returning them into a molar equilibrium – lines of flight emit absolute movements of deter-ritorialisation and decoding. These lines are without beginning or end and do not pass from one point to another; they pass between points, continuously moving in-between (*au milieu*) (Deleuze and Parnet 2006: 98ff). It is this creative line of disorder(ing) which, according to Deleuze and Guattari, defines the social field.

What constitutes a molar regime of governance, organisation of order or a state is not some consensual agreement of parties or men – i.e. molar segments; what underlies and renders possible so-called political order is a rupture, a movement of disorder(ing), the force of which is captured and striated into a molar line reproductive of order(ing). In other words, the creative force of disorder(ing), the line of flight, is made to work productively for the reproduc-tion of a particular regime of order such as the state. Deleuze and Guattari accordingly emphasise that the line of flight is primary in society; lines of flight do not flee from but constitute the social field. 'It is always on a line of flight that we create' (Deleuze and Parnet 2006: 102). It can be said that the line of flight comes first, whilst the other types of lines are derivative; however, its primacy is not chronological for reterritorialisations occur simultaneously.

Deleuze and Guattari thus highlight the primacy of movements and relations over constituted forms and organisation/organisms. What comes first are the movements of flight, which constitute the social field by tracing out its boundaries and gradations (Deleuze and Parnet 2006: 101). '[W]hat is primary is an absolute deterritorialization, an absolute line of flight, however complex or multiple ... ' (Deleuze and Guattari 2004: 63). Hence the disordering force of absolute movement is explained not by the failure of the molar line, but rather the absolute speed of the line of flight constitutes the prior, intrinsic force of (dis)order(ing) that both disrupts and constitutes the potential of the ordering of life politically. Beneath the segmentation and binarity of macropolitics one finds micropolitical flows; there is always something that flees or escapes. From a micropolitical perspective, society is defined not so much by its contradictions as by its lines of flight: it flees all over the place.

Yet, it is only in relation to the stabilising function of reterritorialisation – a return to molar organisation – that the line of flight gains its creative productivity; without reterritorialisation the line of flight may turn destructive – abolitionary or suicidal (Deleuze and Guattari 2004: 239, 253). The play of lines comprises a continuous, complex play of mobile and relational forces. Despite prioritising the line of flight, Deleuze and Guattari stress that the three lines coexist and continually transform into one another, and that all happens at once. 'It is in terms not of independence but of coexistence and competition *in a perpetual field of interaction*, that we must conceive of exteriority and interiority ... ' (Deleuze and Guattari 2004: 398). The three types of lines are entangled, caught up and immanent to one another; engaged in a complex play of movements and relations productive/disruptive of political (dis)order(ing). The complexity, immanence, mobility and relationality of this play furthermore entail a rejection of dualism in favour of 'a multiplicity of dimensions, lines and directions in the heart of the assemblage' (Deleuze and Parnet 2006: 100). Politically, what counts is not the difference between individual and collective, nor between natural and artificial, nor between organisation and spontaneity; the differences that count pass between the lines. That is to say that attention must turn towards the play of movements/relations of, on and between the lines rather than to the dualistic oppositions that occur in molar segments.

To summarise, the three types of lines that constitute/disrupt the political field, which also explains, according to Deleuze and Parnet,

> why we sometimes say that there are at least three different lines, sometimes only two, sometimes only one which is very muddled. Sometimes three because the line of flight or rupture combines all the movements of deterritorialization, precipitates their quanta, tears from them the accelerated particles which come into contact with one another, carries them onto a plane of consistence or a mutating machine; and then a second, molecular line where the deterritorializations are merely relative, always compensated by reterritorializations which impose on them so many loops, detours, of equilibrium and stabilization; finally the molar line with clearly determined segments, where the reterritorializations accumulate to form a plane of organization and pass into an overcoding machine.
>
> (Deleuze and Parnet 2006: 102)

It has become apparent that the line of flight, whilst simple and abstract, at once constitutes the most complex and tortuous – and accordingly most dangerous – line (Deleuze and Parnet 2006: 94). Moreover, '[i]n a multilinear system, everything happens at once' – in one move, the line breaks free of points, coordinates and localisable connections (Deleuze and Guattari 2004: 328, 322) – with the implication that '[n]o one can say where the line of flight will pass' (Deleuze and Parnet 2006: 276). Does it remain consistent; does it get bogged down or arrested into another line; does it turn abolitionary? One cannot predict in advance what may happen on the line. Each type of line has modes of movement and organisation – of order(ing) and disorder(ing) – specific to it, which can nevertheless be evaluated only in relation and in play with the other lines. Each type of line accordingly carries its own dangers.

Resort to the seeming predictability of segmentised categories on the molar line ('a rigidity which reassures us') will not suffice to avoid the dangers and insecurities intrinsic to the tortuosity of the line of flight. The rigidity of segmentised categorisations such as the reduction of life's vital and creative complexity to dualistic choices, and the (fascistic) politics to which this may lead, is specific to the macro-fascism that occurs on the line of molar segmentarity. It turns us into 'creatures which are most fearful, but also most pitiless and bitter'. These excesses give impetus to and render of great pertinence resistance against molar regimes of power. At the same time, however, it will not suffice simply to blow up the molar line in a movement of deterritorialisation or flight. 'Even if we had the power to blow it up,' Deleuze and Parnet ask, 'could we succeed in doing so without destroying ourselves, since it is so much part of the conditions of life, including our organism and our very reason?' Resisting macro-fascisms must be an effort of long labour and immense prudence – an effort not simply to explode, but to manipulate, soften, divert and undermine the molar line – directed at prevailing forms of order(ing) and organisation both in the form of the state or order of governance and in the form of the organisms that we are ourselves.

The line of supple segmentarity not only carries the dangers of the molar line in miniaturised form but also holds its own. Referred to by Deleuze and Guattari as the 'black hole phenomenon', this form of micro-fascism sees one passing thresholds of deterritorialisation too quickly, without taking sufficient precautions; one constructs a black hole, 'with a self-assurance about his own case, his role and his mission … : the Stalins of little groups, local law-givers, micro-fascisms of gangs' (Deleuze and Parnet 2006: 104). Finally, lines of flight, in addition to the macro-fascistic dangers of the first line and the micro-fascisms of the second, also have the most dangerous potential of turning into lines of abolition – of destruction of oneself and of others. The examples cited by Deleuze and Guattari/Parnet suggest that lines of flight are more prone to end in suicidal destruction than to produce life-affirmative movements of becoming. To the question why their examples are all of lines of flight turning out badly, Deleuze and Guattari/Parnet reply that it is precisely because they are real and not imaginary – i.e. not due to the intervention of other lines but on their own account;

on account of the abolitionary force intrinsic and specific to them: 'Kleist and his suicide pact, Hölderin and his madness, Fitzgerald and his destruction, Virginia Woolf and her disappearance' (Deleuze and Parnet 2006: 105).

The three types of lines, albeit distinct in their modes of movement and organisation – and hence in the dangers intrinsic to each – are entangled in a complex play of movements/relations, in which lines clash and merge, fracture and mix, produce and destroy and turn into one another. According to Deleuze and Guattari/Parnet, it is this complexity, relationality and mobility that explains why resistance against the stifling power of macro-fascistic forces is often productive of yet more and different fascisms (in molecular form). It is as a function of the deep entanglement of lines in play – and hence of modes of being and becoming – that desire desires its own repression. The problem of fascism accordingly becomes a complex play ungraspable and irresolvable through dualistic oppositions such as fascism versus non-fascism or macro-fascism versus micro-fascism.

An answer to the question why desire desires its own repression is therefore to be found in the entanglement of lines or of modes of being and becoming: because everything happens on the same lines, which are inextricably caught up in one another *and* continuously clashing *and* turning into one another. Due to the complexity, relationality and mobility of this play, one cannot predict in advance what will happen on the line(s). One cannot know beforehand where or how a line(-play) will run, turn, mix, clash, abort, create, destroy, become, etc. Here arises the political paradox. How to construct a politics when the greatest promise at once constitutes the most perilous danger, and when one cannot know in advance how things will (continue to) turn?

The introduction of the concept of the milieu will serve to shed more light on this political *problematique* of lines in play. Albeit not articulated in those terms by Deleuze and Guattari /Parnet, the play can be described usefully in terms of milieux. Put succinctly, the molar line of rigid segmentarity establishes a territorial order (the milieu as territorial *environment*), whilst the line of supple segmentarity (the milieu as a *medium* of action) swings between this order and the line of flight (the milieu as *movement in-between* (*au milieu*)). Articulated thus, the play of lines expresses the political paradox *qua* fascism: the line of flight is both most creative and most dangerous, and hence not salvatory in itself, whereas molar segmentarity constitutes both a requirement and the impossibility of the becoming of the line of flight. This problem equally confronts regimes of governance and forces of resistance. How to govern or resist if lines continue to cross over into one another, and if the outcome cannot be predicted in advance? How to govern or resist if the chances are rife that one may end up in a black hole or on a line of destruction?

If everything happens on the same line(s), the distinction to be drawn is not between lines of governance as opposed to lines of resistance. Rather, attention must be paid to the movements and forces at play in particular milieux. For example, how do lines and milieux produce, create, delineate and adjudicate in the different orders of governance identified by Foucault – sovereignty, discipline and security? Deleuzean onto-political productions of lines and milieux run the risk of disregarding the evolution of forms of (liberal) rule and the specificity of the ways in which the lines play out in different regimes of power. Foucault's *dispositif de sécurité* serves to ground and contextualise the plays of lines. It also raises the question of what marks out the contemporary order, specifically in relation to the entry of complexity in the domains of life and politics: how to govern if life is emergent, continuously becoming beyond the bounds of its own being?

Is this the end (of the line)?

> It is an abstract line, a pure movement which is difficult to discover, he never begins, he takes things by the middle [*par le milieu*], he is always in the middle [*au milieu*] – in the middle of [*au milieu des*] two other lines? Only movements concern me.
>
> (Deleuze and Parnet 2006: 95–96)

Carrying such profound and unavoidable dangers, do lines of flight necessarily end in destruction? Deleuze and Parnet indeed suggest that 'all creation comes to an end in its abolition, which was fashioning it from the start' (Deleuze and Parnet 2006: 105). Is this the end? Does destruction lie at the end of the line? The notion of the void as well as the examples of suicidal lines of flight Deleuze and Guattari/Parnet cite (Kleist, Fitzgerald, Woolf, etc.), indeed appear to mark a definite end. Starting from the idea of a play of lines produces a different thought. If lines are produced and entangled in play, continuously encountering, creating, destroying and crossing over into one another, and if (re)territorialisation is always already *en route* a deterritorialisation, then is there not something beyond the line of flight? If the line of flight is a line without beginning or end (always in the middle [*au milieu*]), then how can it be that the turning destructive of the line of flight appears to present the ultimate end: death, destruction pure and simple?

The complexities and paradoxical nature – the promise and the dangers – of the line of flight emerge with more clarity in terms of milieux. Like the play of lines, the Deleuzean notion of the milieu serves to express the simultaneity, relationality and immanence of productive and destructive forces; of creativity, becoming, foreclosure, striation and abolition; of macro- and micro-fascistic tendencies and non-fascistic movements. Although Deleuze and Guattari do not develop a comprehensive theory or conceptualisation of the milieu, their reference to the concept in relation to, for example, organic strata and becoming in *A Thousand Plateaus* nevertheless provides the tools to create a politics of milieux.

In the 'Notes on the Translation and Acknowledgements' of *A Thousand Plateaus*, Brian Massumi draws attention to the difference between the French and the English terms 'milieu', of which one must be aware when engaging Deleuze and Guattari's writing on the milieu. Whereas in English the term refers to 'environment', in French, the milieu continues to reflect its various historical meanings, namely 'surroundings' (or 'environment'), 'medium' and 'middle'. Deleuze and Guattari's use of the term combines all three conceptions (Massumi 2004: xvii). As an environment the milieu refers to all that surrounds an organism or body and to all in which it is immersed. Whilst often considered solely in spatial terms and in relation to, yet distinct from, the organism, the milieu-as-environment constitutes a complexity of spatio-temporal and relational (or affective) dimensions. Second, the milieu-as-medium refers either to an instrumental medium of action, or to a relational force in-between (*au milieu*). The critical distinction between these conceptions lies in this: the milieu understood as instrumental means in pursuit of a specified end is laid out between points (e.g. beginning-destination), which defines its utility – that is to say its function lies in specifying, in rendering predictable and knowable, the direction and destination of movement; the movement in-between constitutes a relational force without beginning or destination. Finally, the milieu-as-middle has a double connotation, too; it refers either to the movement in-between of the milieu-as-medium introduced above, or to a static centre. Although Deleuze and Guattari's conceptualisation of the milieu combines these various aspects, emphasis is placed on its mobile and relational qualities. The milieu, they write, consists of qualities, substances, powers and events; intensities and affects (Deleuze 1998: 61).

Foucault's genealogical tracing of the concept and the practice of the milieu in the lecture series *Security, Territory, Population* provides a different account of the movements at play. For Foucault, the milieu exemplifies a particular configuration of power, a *dispositif* of security. This apparatus functions on the basis of the fostering and management of circulations: 'it was a matter of organizing circulation, eliminating its dangerous elements, making a division between good and bad circulation, and maximizing the good circulation by diminishing the bad' (Foucault 2007: 18). As such, the milieu *qua dispositif* does not encompass the full complexity of the forces at play; it heeds the strategies or deliberate interventions of governance only.

Foucault's conceptualisation of the milieu focuses on its manifestations as a space of circulation (environment) and medium of action. *Security, Territory, Population* sketches the development of a distinctly liberal governmentality. By tracing the genealogical shift from a problematisation of power centred on the exercise of sovereignty over a territory to one concerned with the regulation of populations via the notion of the milieu, Foucault places the historical emergence of the concept and practice of the milieu in the context of a number of interrelated developments, or problems, in the eighteenth century, which he describes as problems of circulation and action at a distance. In mechanics, for example, Newton is occupied with the question of how one body sets another into motion without direct physical contact, which he seeks to resolve via the idea of an ether that permeates all matter and space. At around the same time, the economic and commercial rise of the town prompts its opening up to various forms of movement and the need to intervene only from a distance. In the economic realm of the market, the biological domain of health/disease and the political field of governance, too, notions of circulation and action at a distance arise in the context of what Foucault terms the problem of security (Foucault 2007).

Roughly speaking these movements can be divided into a threefold development. First, the problems related to the rise of the town give rise to new practices of security or mechanisms for the regulation of circulation based on the notion of *laissez-faire* – i.e. by planning a milieu. In mechanics the conceptual notion of the milieu arises with the questions of the medium of action and action at a distance. Third, this mechanical notion is subsequently adopted in and adapted to biology, as a result of which it is transformed into an absolute concept and becomes intrinsically related to man/the species: man and his environment or milieu. Rather than a strictly chronological occurrence or a uni-linear causal sequence, these movements emerge via a complex conjunction of conceptual and practical factors, circumstances and developments (Foucault 2007: 21).

Foucault summarises the appearance of a *dispositif* of security both as the problem of the town and in the context of the emergence of, first, a different economy of power and, second, a different political personage, which is the population. Of relevance in the context of this chapter is the function of the milieu as a medium of action that facilitates the governance of the population on the basis of its understood natural capacities and requirements. Governance operates on the basis of a 'freedom of circulations' – a *laissez-faire*. Fostering and managing circulations must operate from a distance because a series of natural and artificial givens must be taken into account. As that within which circulation is carried the milieu expresses the relation between man and environment as a conjuncture of geographic, climatic and physical elements and the human species insofar as it has a body and a soul (Foucault 2007: 21, 23). If he wants to change the human species rather than the individual physical body, Foucault explains, the sovereign must act on the milieu; he must intervene at the intersection between 'nature' (as physical elements) and the 'nature' of the human species – i.e. at the point where the milieu becomes the determining factor of nature.

The milieu as conceptualised by Foucault thus risks becoming synonymous with the *dispositif* of security. As a response to urgency, a *dispositif* has a strategic function, that is to say it operates as a manipulation of relations of forces, an 'intervention in the relations of forces, either so as to develop them in a particular direction, or to block them, to stabilize them, and to utilize them' (Foucault 1980: 195–96). Foucault's concept of the milieu precisely refers to the manipulation of forces through their regulation on the basis of their understood nature, which is manifested in the fostering and management of circulations.

The milieu of security is the space in which a series of uncertain elements unfold (Foucault 2007: 20). It refers both to a multivalent and transformable framework that requires regulation and to the regulation of (a series of) events within this multivalent framework. That is to say that the milieu concerns both time and space since the temporal problem of uncertainty explains the necessity to plan a milieu of security:

> The specific space of security refers then to a series of possible events; it refers to the temporal and the uncertain, which have to be inserted within a given space. The space in which a series of uncertain elements unfold is, I think, roughly what one can call the milieu.
>
> (Foucault 2007: 20)

The problem of security in the eighteenth century is, both spatially and temporally, a problem of action at a distance. According to Foucault, governance can be understood as the continuous effort to order a field of force relations: 'to govern ... is to structure the possible field of action of others' (Foucault 2002: 341). If the problem of governance is the indeterminacy of life and the unpredictability of future events, then the effort of governance is to render knowable and predictable the temporal uncertainty of the future; and in order to regulate a future series of events they must be inscribed into a space (Deuber-Mankowsky 2008: 139). In order to make predicable events temporally distant the present must be connected to the future through a straight line, which is drawn out spatially. Time is introduced as a chief operative factor; however, its becoming nature – its unpredictability – must be regulated through conversion into a space of circulation.

Understood as a medium of action and the element in which it circulates, the milieu of security on the basis of free circulations constitutes an attempt to capture temporal insecurity within a given space. The freedom of movement on the basis of which governance governs thus remains subjugated to a principle of order and ordering within a specific spatio-temporal domain that is laid out in advance. Here we touch upon a principle distinction between two different understandings of the milieu as a medium, as well as the distinction between Deleuze and Guattari's and Foucault's conceptions of the milieu. The milieu as medium can function, on the one hand, as a means-end strategy in which the end is specified *a priori* and, on the other, as the movement in-between, without beginning or destination. The former refers to the *dispositif* of security. Despite the attempt to let things take their natural course, governance must specify in advance which nature it seeks to foster and manage, and within which bounds it may circulate. The milieu constitutes a medium of action instrumentally linking means to end. In distinction, the milieu prioritised by Deleuze and Guattari, the milieu understood as force in-between, has beginning or end. This is the line of flight, which continuously becomes, and becomes beyond its own bounds: its movement cannot be captured and remains elusive *qua* movement.

Foucault's conceptualisation of the practices of governance in terms of a *dispositif* of security serves to contextualise Deleuze and Guattari's onto-political creation of lines. Nevertheless, the identification of the milieu with the *dispositif* suffers from the reduction of the milieu to strategies of power, leaving little space for attention to the creative forces of becoming which, according to

Deleuze and Guattari, constitute the very movement of milieux. In the Foucaldian milieu, there is little space for resistance beyond the strategic integration of forces into modes of ordering. Moreover, as discussed below, practices of liberal governance have themselves transformed in response to evolving conceptualisations of life, now prioritising complexity, relationality and emergence. Whilst the productivity of Foucault's *dispositif* lies in the possibility to differentiate between historical manifestations of governance and the specificity of liberal practices of security, it fails to encompass the complexity of the forces at play. Michael Dillon and Julian Reid's (2009) examination of contemporary manifestations of liberal rule and war demonstrates the importance of paying attention to the disruptive force of complexity – the movement in-between – as an operative principle of liberal governance.

Before turning to their analysis, the temporal dimension of the difference between manifestations of the milieu as instrumental medium of action and force of movement in-between must be further explored. The distinction is astutely articulated by Henri Bergson, who distinguishes between the way in which our intellect seeks to capture movement and our lived duration. Contrary to our motionless and fragmentary view of it – taken from a position outside of time – life, Bergson explains, 'progresses and *endures* in time' (Bergson 2005: 58). Moreover, '[t]he more we study the nature of time, the more we shall comprehend that duration means invention, the creation of forms, the continual elaboration of the absolutely new' (Bergson 2005: 13). Despite the continuous becoming of life – what Bergson calls 'creative evolution' – concerned primarily with practical action, the human intellect focuses only on moments, positions, states in order to establish where movement is going and to determine its end. That is to say we are interested in the 'unmovable plan of movement rather than the movement itself' (Bergson 2005: 329). Because 'our interest is directed, before all, to its actual or future positions, and not to the *progress* by which it passes from one position to another, progress which is the movement itself', we take 'snapshots' of what is continuously passing, in perpetual becoming (Bergson 2005: 170).

By taking instantaneous views at intervals, the intellect, starting from immobile states, seeks to reconstruct movement by putting together 'immobilities'. Here lies the problem for, Bergson contends, it is an illusion to think that one can construct 'the unstable by means of the stable, the moving by means of the immobile' (Bergson 2005: 171, 297).[1] This illusion, which is essentially an effort to lay out in space succession in time – to capture the future by representing its duration as already rolled up in the past – Bergson describes as a natural mechanism of the intellect (Bergson 2005: 370, 371). This mechanism furthermore informs scientific method, ancient as well as modern. What Bergson terms the 'cinematographical method' refers to a conception of movement that isolates moments (e.g. the positions T1, T2, etc. on a line), and has no concern for what happens in the intervals. Science accordingly misses the movement insofar as movement is becoming: 'real time … as the very mobility of being, escapes the hold of scientific knowledge' (Bergson 2005: 358).

Both the natural mechanism of the human intellect and the mechanistic Scientific Method involve an effort to render movement visible and knowable through its capture in positions and states – i.e. in immobilities – and, by determining its direction and end, attempt to reconstruct movement from immobile states. This implies an *a priori* construction of the Whole that is it lays down the end in advance (Bergson 2005: 172–73). Movement, which is mobile *qua* durational force, thus gains a spatial determination and is accordingly immobilised. As Deleuze writes in his book on Bergson, 'one misses the movement because one constructs a Whole, one assumes that "all is given", whilst movement only occurs if the whole is neither given nor giveable' (Deleuze 1986: 7).

It is this endeavour to capture movement in immobile states through the insertion of durational forces into a spatial framework that Foucault identifies as characteristic of the *dispositif* of security. By seeking to render visible and predicable the uncertain force of movement in the interest of practical action (i.e. the governance of order) movement is immobilised. It is an attempt to contain and order the tortuous unpredictability of the line of flight through its capture in a segmentary order. However, spatialised within a domain of circulations, time cannot come to pass; it cannot become. In Bergson's words, '[t]ime is invention or it is nothing at all' (Bergson 2005: 371). The production of a milieu of security through inserting into space the temporal uncertainty and undecidability implies an attempt to determine in advance the course and bounds of movement.

From a Bergsonian and Deleuzean perspective, the attempt to render movement visible is precisely what immobilises it. *A priori* determined, movement becomes static and reproductive rather than creative, and the becoming of life is foreclosed. Becoming – and according to Deleuze and Guattari life is a matter of becoming – involves continuous transformative processes, which challenge and break the ordering of order through connections, mixtures, ruptures, cracks, etc., which involve heterogeneous elements and forces. Hence the course, potentialities and limits of order(ing) and the whole of which it forms part can neither be predicted in advance nor definitively established: they continuously change, adapt and transform in ways unexpected and changing. It is the nature of movement that it is always already different. This is what Deleuze and Guattari refer to when they speak of becoming, the line of flight or the movement in-between (*au milieu*).

> A line of becoming is not defined by points that it connects, or by points that compose it; on the contrary, it passes between points, it comes up through the middle ... a line of becoming has neither beginning nor end, departure nor arrival, origin nor destination ... A line of becoming has only a middle [*un milieu*] ... A becoming is always in the middle; one can only get it by the middle. A becoming is neither one nor two, nor the relation of the two; it is the in-between ... [Becoming] constitutes a zone of proximity and indiscernibility, a no-man's-land, a nonlocalizable relation sweeping up the two distant or contiguous points, carrying one into the

> proximity of the other – and the border-proximity is indifferent to both contiguity and to distance.
>
> (Deleuze and Guattari 2004: 323–24)

Without point of origin or (predetermined) destination this line is the absolute speed of movement (Deleuze and Guattari 2004: 290, 323). Rather than a centre (*milieu*) (which can be pointed out) or a connective line to be localised between points, i.e. a medium (*milieu*), the milieu-as-middle moves as an indiscernible, non-localisable passage. The point Deleuze and Guattari wish to make is, precisely, that movement itself, *qua* movement, is by nature imperceptible, below or above the threshold of perception: 'movement itself continues to occur elsewhere' (Deleuze and Guattari 2004: 309–10). One arrives too early or too late. Movement becomes visible only afterwards, when it is stratified or territorialised into an order of organisation such as an organism, subject or space of security. That is the *effects* of movement are perceptible, nevertheless, movement itself – the force of the line in-between – is by definition unlocalisable.

This is precisely the problem, for how to organise an order, how to foster and secure life, when its becoming is elusive, uncertain and unpredictable? Liberal governance responds to this problem by means of the endeavour to make knowable and predictable the uncertainty of future events through planning a milieu of security. In other words, the problem of governance is the problem of the passing of time and the becoming of life that is passage of time, or duration. Governance must work with and on the basis of, yet keep within bounds and circulations, life's tendency to pass, i.e. to move, relate, connect, transform and become beyond boundaries and across limits. This conversion of the force of becoming into an instrumental medium of action establishes an order of segmentary lines; it is the conversion of the risk of micro-fascistic destruction into the certainty of macro-fascistic segmentation.

Deleuze and Guattari prioritise movements and relations, arguing that forms of organisation and governance are derivative. In their conception of life as becoming they gain inspiration from the complexity sciences. Complexity theory, a critique of the dominant 'Newtonian' model of scientific thought, starts out from the notion of the primacy of radical relationality and the impossibility of complete understanding due to the self-organising and emergent properties of complex systems such as the living being (Dillon and Reid 2009: 72; Marks 2006: 10–11). Deleuze and Guattari's prioritisation of movements and relations over constituted forms thus provides a critique of the macro-fascism of modes of (liberal) governance. However, the question of how to govern life given its emergent, self-organising and radically relational character has become central to contemporary liberal thought and rule, too.

Dillon and Reid's *The Liberal Way of War* details how the liberal ways of rule and war are intimately connected and co-constitutive, as well as how the contemporary liberal way of rule/war is deeply influenced by developments in the complexity sciences. The integration into liberal analyses of governance of notions such as complexity and emergence suggests a move away from its characteristic anthropocentrism towards an account of mobile and relational forces. Dillon and Reid's work offers an ingenious account both of the emergence of complex emergence in the information and life sciences, which transforms the way in which life is understood, and of how this new conceptualisation of life comes to inform the liberal way of rule and war. If life is complex, emergent and radically contingent – i.e. if life continuously becomes, and becomes beyond its own limits – then liberal rule, which governs on the basis of life's understood capacities and requirements, must accordingly adapt. Yet – and this is the paradox of liberal rule/war Dillon and Reid wish to lay bare – preoccupied with the fostering and regulation of life based on a particular yet naturalised notion of what life is, that is to say concerned with securing and determining the uncertainty that constitutes life's temporal nature, life's becoming is readily understood as a becoming dangerous to itself (Dillon and Reid 2009: 146).

Dillon and Reid invent the notion of the 'emergency of emergence' to explicate the problematic nature of this paradox. Acknowledging the emergent – and hence indeterminable and unpredictable – nature of life, its fostering and management on the basis of security/freedom becomes a constant effort at 'emergency governance' (Dillon and Reid 2009: 86–88).[2] The problematic nature of the paradox of liberal emergence, which arises when the order of life becomes understood in terms of circulation, complexity and connectivity, is adeptly articulated also by Dillon and Lobo-Guerrero. Biopolitical governance operates on the basis of circulations: more circulation means greater connectivity; increased connectivity in turn begets an increase in complexity; and finally, the more things interconnect, circulate and complexly adapt, the more contingent they become (Dillon and Lobo-Guerrero 2009: 10–15). Hence, Dillon and Lobo-Guerrero explain, contingency is now conceived *the* property of species life as well as a mode of governance that takes life as its referent object, for politics must govern on this basis. Liberal governance, as an effort to make knowable and predictable, has evolved into governance through emergency because its referent object is complex, emergent and contingent. In Dillon and Lobo-Guerrero's words, 'the complex adaptive emergence of the contemporary understanding of what it is to be a living thing is the emergency of its continuous emergence' (Dillon and Lobo-Guerrero 2009: 10).

Here emerges the crux of the problem for the effort to make live entails the lethal business of waging war on life. The task of liberal rule, Dillon and Reid write, is:

> not only to adjudicate membership of the species. It decides, implicitly or explicitly, whom to correct and whom to punish, as well as who shall live and who shall die; what life-forms will be promoted and which will be terminated; and all so that life can be made to live the emergency of its emergence.
>
> (Dillon and Reid 2009: 87)

In other words, 'good emergence has to be distinguished from bad, desired emergence from unwanted emergence' (Dillon and Reid 2009: 109), and to recall Foucault's observation, the good must be maximised; the bad diminished, or indeed eliminated. Hence the paradox emergent with liberal emergence is that to foster life also means to wage war on it. That this paradox lies at the heart of political modernity was of course already conceptualised by Foucault. Taking cue from Foucault's work, Dillon and Reid demonstrate the hyperbolisation of this paradox in the contemporary liberal way of rule and war. Their analysis reveals, in addition, that both the fostering of and the war waged on life become ever more excessive and lethal as the capacities to understand and manipulate life advance. Thus, rather than assuaging the problem of fascism, as Deleuze and Guattari's prioritisation of movements and relations might suggest, the liberal complexity turn has triggered the hyperbolisation of liberal fascism.

Rather than embracing and exploring the political potentials of the becoming of life, liberal governance remains premised on the centrality of a particular order(ing) and the imperative to secure, reproduce, naturalise and universalise it. Due to the continued understanding of politics and life in terms of its capacities and requirements for (self-)governance and (self-)organisation, life's contingent, complex and emergent nature is conceived an emergency, and governance crisis management. Moreover, as emergency becomes the *modus operandi* of politics and life and hence the operative principle of governance, it must be sustained in order for governance to operate:

> It is neither possible, nor in fact desirable, to bring an end to the emergency or, in effect, to diminish its rage. For the emergency is now definitive of the condition of the every day life of species life. Life, here, is the emergency; and emergency does not so much present an object to be governed as set the very operant conditions of governability as such.
>
> (Dillon and Reid 2009: 89)

The primacy, irreducibility and unpredictability of movement qua movement throws up a political paradox for both Deleuze and Guattari and liberal governance: how to organise a politics when its movement, *qua* becoming, is imperceptible and fleeting; an unlocalisable passage that can be captured, ordered or organised only after the event, and only by immobilising it? We find (and create) ourselves on uncertain grounds, in a continuous, intangible play between macro-fascisms of molar rigidity in which the course and limits of movement are laid out in advance and life is produced and inhibited thus; and the prospect of micro-fascisms of the void, in which the flight of the moving line ends in (suicidal) destruction. How to forge a politics, create a style of life, that avoids falling foul to either fascistic movement?

Deleuze and Guattari's approach is one of experimentation and caution. The question is, however, whether it offers a movement beyond the destructive effects of liberal fascism *qua* emergency governance? Do they seek to overcome the impasse at all; do they wish to specify what may lie beyond, or how to move beyond fascism given their belief that one cannot predict in advance how the line will pass? If the line of flight has no beginning or end, then the void is *au milieu de*, in the midst of things, which would suggest that it is fruitless to ask whether all creation ends in destruction, and whether that is 'the end'.

> Even if all creation comes to an end in its abolition, which was fashioning it from the start, even if all music is the pursuit of silence, they cannot be judged according to their end or their supposed aim, for they exceed them in all dimensions. When they end up in death, this is a function of the danger proper to them, and not of their destination.
>
> (Deleuze and Parnet 2006: 105)

Going through the middle

How do Deleuze and Guattari propose to resolve the paradox of life's tendency to create, order and destroy on the same line(s)? Can their prioritisation of the line of flight answer the current fascism of emergency governance, which is equally informed by the prioritisation of radical relationality? Deleuze and Guattari's starting premise is that life is always already in the middle; wherever we are, we are always already in a middle – in a milieu and *au milieu*. If '[t]hings do not begin to live except in the middle' (Deleuze and Parnet 2006: 41), then one cannot start at the beginning and follow through to the end. Rather than laying down (founding) terms or principles from whence relations and politics arise, Deleuze and Guattari propose to study movements and relations in terms of their speeds, affects, intensities and (re)productive and (dis)ordering effects.

The aim or destination of movement is not the point and not the danger either. In order to assess the productivity/destructivity of a line one must study the line itself; its speeds and slownesses, its intensities, its effects. Put in Deleuze's Spinozan terms, lines are to be studied in terms of their relations of movements and rest and their powers to affect and to be affected. Deleuze and Guattari thus turn towards the question of the body, which they oppose to the organism. Whilst the organism constitutes a stifling molar regime, the body is made up of movements and relations. Dismantling the organism, they write, is a matter of 'opening the body to connections that presuppose an entire assemblage, circuits, conjunctions, levels and thresholds, passages and distributions of intensity, and territories and deterritorialisations' (Deleuze and Guattari 2004: 177). Via Spinoza, Deleuze defines a body in terms of its latitude and longitude – that is to say, according to the kinetic and the dynamic principle. The first proposition:

> tells us that a body is defined by relations of motion and rest, of slowness and speed between particles. That is, it is not defined by a form or by

functions. Global form, specific form, and organic functions depend on relations of speed and slowness. Even the development of a form, the course of development of a form, depends on these relations, and not the reverse. The important thing is to understand life, each living individuality, not as a form, or a development of form, but as a complex relation of differential velocities, between deceleration and acceleration of particles. A composition of speeds and slownesses on a plane of immanence … It is … a matter of … how to live: it is by speed and slowness that one slips in among things, that one connects with something else. One never commences; one never has a tabula rasa; one slips in, enters in the middle [*au milieu*] …

(Deleuze 1988: 123)

The dynamic proposition, too, stresses that '[y]ou will not define a body (or a mind) by its form, nor by its organs or functions, and neither will you define it as a substance or a subject'. Rather than subjects, bodies are capacities for affecting and being affected (Deleuze 1988: 123–24). The question, accordingly, is 'of what is a body capable?' The problem is that one cannot know this in advance because life is becoming.

Understood through Deleuze's Spinoza a body never stands on its own; it is not an entity with certain properties, an internal organisation and external boundaries that distinguish it from other entities and the environment. Rather a body is defined by its modes of relationality; by the kinds of connections that are established and the modes of engagement of which these movements are productive. It is a question of what a body can do – of its relations of movement and rest as well as its powers to affect and be affected, which is to say that what a body can do is not fixed or determined but a matter of becoming(s).[3]

Of relevance in conceptualising bodies are therefore not organs, functions, species or genus. In a lecture on Spinoza Deleuze asserts that:

[i]f you consider beasts, Spinoza will be firm in telling us what counts among animals is not at all the genera or species; genera and species are absolutely confused notions, abstract ideas. What counts is the question, of what is a body capable? And thereby he sets out one of the most fundamental questions in his whole philosophy … by saying that we don't even know what a body is capable of … a body must be defined by the ensemble of relations which compose it.[4]

Significant for Deleuze is the question of the powers of the body that pertain to it. Most important is to know which encounters agree with one's body; and most beautiful 'is to live on the edges', at the (joyful) limit of one's powers to be affected. Because this limit differs for each body – 'What counts is what your power is for you' – no formula can be specified that is good for each and every body. Moreover, a body being defined in terms of relations of movement and rest and powers to affect and be affected, degrees and limits of power continuously change. Deleuze thus accords to Spinoza an ethics of becoming.

Spinoza becomes the thinker who poses the question of what a body can do in terms of movement/rest and powers to affect/be affected. Hence, what a body can do is a matter of its relationality. Defining the body thus, the political *problematique* re-emerges:

> We know nothing about a body until we know what it can do, in other words, what its affects are, how they can or cannot enter into composition with other affects, with the affects of another body.
>
> (Deleuze and Guattari 2004: 284)

This ethological question of a body's mobile and relational capacities is an ethical one because one cannot know in advance of what a body is capable. Not knowing in advance how a body may move and relate, an approach *au milieu* presents at once the most creative and the most dangerous approach. Whilst experiment is their adage, Deleuze and Guattari also warn that one must remain cautious. For example, processes of stratification that produce organisms are both beneficial and unfortunate: strata limit, capture and foreclose, yet strata simultaneously produce a platform for creative becomings. 'Is it not necessary,' Deleuze and Guattari (2004: 289) ask, 'to retain a minimum of strata, a minimum of forms and functions, a minimal subject from which to extract materials, affects and assemblages?' Without strata there are no forms, substances or organisations: we are 'disarticulated', 'chaos pure and simple'. Hence Deleuze and Guattari stress that every effort at destratification such as 'going beyond the organism, plunging into a becoming', must be undertaken with extreme caution for 'a too sudden destratification may be suicidal or turn cancerous' (Deleuze and Guattari 2004: 54).

Deleuze and Guattari do not simply advocate the creativity of bodies or milieux of becoming over the rigidity and stasis of organism of centralisation and molarity. The stratification of movement into orders of organisation is both beneficial and unfortunate, as the example of contemporary liberal rule and war demonstrates. The stratification of life's becoming may invoke war on life, yet by providing a stabilising order, processes of organisation simultaneously prevent forces of becoming from turning destructive and enable further deterritorialising movements, different becomings. Rather than a diametric opposition, what emerges here is a play of milieux, a play of lines which clash, merge, mix, become, destroy, produce, fracture, etc.

The force of becoming, the movement in-between is not salvatory in itself: one must remain aware, in each instance, of the movements, intensities and effects produced – i.e. of the kind of milieux in which one finds oneself, or in which one may lose oneself. It is not enough merely to set off on a line of flight, to gain absolute speed, to attack the organism, state or order of governance as a suffocating form of organisation. In such acts of resistance it is, moreover, not enough merely to remain cautious not to replicate or reproduce the very modes of movement and forms of order and organisation that one resists and thereby produce a rigidification of extant order(ing) – i.e. to ward off macro-fascistic forces. Movements of resistance of the genre of the line of flight must, most crucially, also be effected ethically in the sense of a careful assessment of their effects in order to avoid a micro-fascistic suicidal turn.

Where does this leave us? How to draw the line? What is Deleuze and Guattari's guidance for the creation of a non-fascistic life? How to respond to the destructive effects of liberal fascism *qua* emergency governance, which exemplifies the lethal effects of attempts to turn the line of flight into a regime of governance precisely in order to counter its destructive potential? Deleuze and Guattari do not provide an answer or propose a solution to this political *problematique* of life's entanglement in and on lines simultaneously productive, destructive, stratifying, creative, stifling, becoming and suicidal. Their creation of lines and milieux suggests that one can only become yet never be free from fascism: the non-fascistic life exists only in becoming. One cannot arrive at a life beyond fascism, one can only create it, and its creation remains a continuous and continuously uncertain effort. Given its open and uncertain character, the question remains whether this style or ethics of experimentation can offer a response to the destructive effects of a liberal fascism that operates on the same lines. One can draw the line anywhere (Deleuze and Parnet 2006: 103).

Notes

1 Bergson makes a similar argument in *Matter and Memory*. See: Henri Bergson, *Matter and Memory* (New York: Zone Books, 1991), 191. See also: Suzanne Guerlac, *Thinking in Time. An Introduction to Henri Bergson* (London: Cornell University Press, 2006), 159ff.
2 See also: M. Dillon and L. Lobo-Guerrero, 'The Biopolitical Imaginary of Species-being' (*Theory, Culture & Society*, Vol. 26, No. 1: 2009), 10ff.
3 See also: K. Ansell Pearson, *Germinal Life. The Difference and Repetition of Deleuze* (Oxford: Routledge, 1999), 12.
4 Gilles Deleuze, 'Spinoza, 24/01/1978', *Les Cours de Gilles Deleuze*, www.webdeleuze.com (accessed 10 June 2010).

References

Ansell Pearson, K. *Germinal Life. The Difference and Repetition of Deleuze* (Oxford and New York: Routledge, 1999)
Bergson, H. *Creative Evolution* (New York: Cosimo, 2005)
——*Matter and Memory* (New York: Zone Books, 1991)
Deleuze, G. 'What Children Say', in *Essays Critical and Clinical*, trans. Daniel W. Smith and Michael A. Greco (London and New York: Verso, 1998)
——'Spinoza, 24/01/1978', *Les Cours the Gilles Deleuze*, www.webdeleuze.com (accessed 10 June 2010).
——*Bergsonism* (New York: Zone Books, 1991)
——*Cinema I, The Movement-Image* (London: The Athlone Press, 1986)
——*Foucault* (London and New York: Continuum, 2006)
——*Negotiations: 1972–1990* (New York: Columbia University Press, 1995)
——*Spinoza: Practical Philosophy* (San Francisco: City Lights Books, 1988)

Deleuze, G. and Guattari, F. *A Thousand Plateaus. Capitalism and Schizophrenia* (London and New York: Continuum, 2004)

Deleuze, G. and Parnet, C. *Dialogues II* (London and New York: Continuum, 2006)

Deuber-Mankowsky, A. 'Nothing is Political, Everything Can Be Politicized: On the Concept of the Political in Michel Foucault and Carl Schmitt' (*Telos* No.142, Spring 2008, 135–61)

Dillon, M. and Lobo-Guerrero, L. 'The Biopolitical Imaginary of Species-being' (*Theory, Culture & Society* Vol.26, No.1, 2009)

Dillon, M. and Reid, J. *The Liberal Way of War. Killing to Make Life Live* (London and New York: Routledge, 2009)

Foucault, M. *Power/Knowledge. Selected Interviews and Other Writings, 1972–77* (New York: Pantheon, 1980)

——'The Subject and Power', in James D. Faubion (ed.) *Power, The Essential Works of Michel Foucault 1954–1984, Volume 3* (London: Penguin, 2002)

——'Preface', in Gilles Deleuze and Félix Guattari, *Anti-Oedipus. Capitalism and Schizophrenia* (London and New York: Continuum, 2004)

——*Security, Territory, Population, Lectures at the Collège de France, 1977–78* (Basingstoke: Palgrave Macmillan, 2007)

Grosz, Elizabeth A. *The Nick of Time: Politics, Evolution and the Untimely* (London and Durham: Duke University Press, 2004)

Guerlac, S. *Thinking in Time. An Introduction to Henri Bergson* (Ithaca and London: Cornell University Press, 2006)

Marks, J. 'Introduction', in *Deleuze and Science*, special issue (*Paragraph, A Journal of Modern Critical Theory*, Vol.29, No.2, 2006)

Massumi, B. 'Notes on the Translation and Acknowledgements', in Gilles Deleuze and Felix Guattari, *A Thousand Plateaus. Capitalism and Schizophrenia* (London and New York: Continuum, 2004)

8 Fascist lines of the tokkōtai

Nicholas Michelsen

Introduction

In fascism the State is far less totalitarian than it is suicidal.

(Deleuze and Guattari 2004b: 254)

Gilles Deleuze and Felix Guattari, confirming a claim by Paul Virilio (1998), argue that fascist states are definitively suicidal. This argument appears in a cartographic analysis of National Socialism as the assemblage of three desiring-political 'lines'. In *A Thousand Plateaus*, Nazism is interpreted as conjugating a *molar* line (which defined Hitler's state as totalitarian), a *molecular* line (which identified the Nazi movement as characteristically 'microfascist'), and a *line of flight*. The Nazi line of flight is understood as an intrinsically catastrophic trajectory, which set the state on a suicidal path, concluding with Hitler's telegram 71 declaiming 'If the war is lost, may the nation perish' (Deleuze and Guattari 2004b: 255; Virilio 1998: 41). Deleuze and Guattari argue that recognising the presence of this suicidal trajectory does not simply hone our horror of the Nazi event; rather, they suggest that state fascism is always suicidal inasmuch as it conjugates the three lines.

The claim that state fascism is always suicidal has been challenged as unsustainably deriving a universal theory from peculiarities of the Nazi event (Holland 2008). The historical singularity of Nazi suicidalism certainly seems to limit the utility of their schema for identifying or charting the emergence of fascisms elsewhere. As a consequence, Eugene Holland (2008: 94) suggests that we may discard the third line, and its attendant concept of fascist suicidalism, whilst retaining the rest of Deleuze and Guattari's theoretical edifice to chart the 'resurgence of something like old-fashioned fascism' today.

In response to this and other critiques of the third or suicidal fascist line, this chapter seeks to clarify the cartographical nature of Deleuze and Guattari's approach. It will argue that Deleuze and Guattari's concept of state-fascism, as distinct from state-totalitarianism, is crucially an assemblage of all three lines. For Deleuze and Guattari (2004b) *all* political assemblages are built on three lines, each of which carries an integral danger (see also Deleuze 2002). Suicide is the danger that lurks on *any* line of deterritorialisation, alongside microfascism as the danger of molecular striation, and totalitarianism the danger of molar striation. Fascism is defined as the realisation of the dangers on all the lines of the political simultaneously. The chapter argues, therefore, that suicidalism (the danger on the third line) is integral to the Deleuzoguattarian theory of fascism, and this is essential if we hope to mobilise them to think about fascisms today.

Responding to Holland's critique, the chapter will demonstrate that the Deleuzoguattarian schema is an effective conceptual toolbox for mapping the dynamics of fascist events other than Nazism. The Meiji regime that took Japan into the Second World War was certainly defined by unique cultural, historical and institutional dynamics. Yet, like Nazi Germany, Meiji may be lucidly mapped in Deleuzoguattarian terms as a machinic assemblage of the three lines to build a 'suicidal-state'. Meiji Japan certainly set out on 'a road that finally brought the country to self-destruction on a colossal scale in World War II' (Ohnuki-Tierney 2002: 61). Its *tokkōtai*, or special-attack corps, more commonly known as the *Kamikaze* (divine wind), seem iconically to embody Meiji's eventual flight towards self-abolition.

Charting the dynamics of Meiji fascism clarifies the status of Deleuze and Guattari's claim that fascism carries an integral politics of suicide. To mistake the suicidal line of flight for no more than an historical contingency of Nazism is to neglect a crucial dimension of their account of fascism *per se*. This is critical if we wish to pursue, with Holland (2008), a Deleuzoguattarian programme for the analysis of fascisms today. Deleuze and Guattari imply that fascist lines are to be found not simply in state-totalitarian assemblages which make the molar and molecular resonate together, but in *global* innovations on the third line that transform such territorial formations into the machine-parts of a suicidal 'peace machine' (see also Virilio and Lotringer 1997; Virilio 1998).

The first and second fascist lines

> Fascism implies a molecular regime that is distinct both from molar segments and their centralisation.
>
> (Deleuze and Guattari 2004b: 236)

In *Anti-Oedipus*, the first volume of Deleuze and Guattari's magnum opus *Capitalism and Schizophrenia*, fascism is articulated as lying at one pole of the fundamental political dichotomy between paranoia and schizophrenia that structures the work. As John Protevi puts it, 'fascism is largely addressed architectonically, as a pole of desires ... fascism is on the side of paranoia and reterritorialisation, the counter-pole to schizophrenia and deterritorialisation' (Protevi 2000: 168). In this sense fascism may be understood as the fundamental adversary engaged by the text (Deleuze and Guattari 2004a: xv).

In *Anti-Oedipus*, fascism is that which finds manifestation in the repressive or paranoiac functions of any social, political, economic and psychological assemblage (Land 1993: 66). Fascism names the myriad seductions of para-noiac sensibility – from the reactionary lure of political identity, to the over-codings affected by the family unit on the individual psyche. Fascism is the general tendency of desire towards paranoiac enclosure, stability and terri-toriality. As Michel Foucault puts it, *Anti-Oedipus* is the account and critique of 'the fascism in us all, in our heads and in our everyday behaviour, the fas-cism that causes us to love power, to desire the very thing that dominates and exploits us' (Foucault in Deleuze and Guattari 2004a: xv).

We are enjoined to cultivate our escape from fascism through a programme of desiring political schizophrenisation, to challenge fascistic enclosures with intellectual, artistic, organisational, familial, collective and individual deterri-torialisations, so as to release the *molecular complexities* obscured by the para-noiac tendency of desire. Not even the *molar* unity of our egos can be assumed as unproblematic; that unity is constructed only through the over-coding of a crowd of *molecular* sub-selves. The ego is built only on the effacement of prior self-difference, on the obscuration of the dynamic multiplicity of pro-ductive desiring-machines which are the condition for the possibility of being/becoming-human.

In *A Thousand Plateaus*, the second volume of *Capitalism and Schizophrenia*, this account of fascism is given greater specificity. Nick Land argues that 'a massive shift takes place in the diagnosis of National Socialism, which is dislodged from the general category of fascism, and subjected to a more specific analysis' (Land 1993: 73). Actual 'historical fascism' is, as both Protevi (2000), and Foucault remark, almost entirely absent from the earlier text. In *A Thousand Plateaus*, however, Nazism is articulated as its paradigmatic enun-ciation (Protevi 2000: 167). Fascism is no longer a virtual, catch-all concept, but apparently one which must be reassessed according to its precise historical parameters.

A Thousand Plateaus explicitly distinguishes fascism from 'molar' totalitar-ianism. After all 'there are totalitarian states, of the Stalinist, or military dicta-torship type, that are not fascist' (Deleuze and Guattari 2004b: 236). Deleuze and Guattari argue that the 'concept of the totalitarian state' is macro-political; it concerns 'rigid segmentarity and a particular mode of totalization and centralization' (Deleuze and Guattari 2004b: 236). Totalitarianism is built when the 'localised assemblage' of the state is subjected entirely to an 'abstract machine of over-coding', causing all social flows to come under a unified, centralised, vertical and hierarchical bureaucratic structure (Deleuze and Guattari 2004b: 254). The dangers implicit to such a formation is clear; an absolute rigidity in sociality, a truth defined from above; collectivised 'values, morals, fatherlands, religions'; the paranoid certainty of purified selfhood as against difference; a politics characterised by 'fear' (Deleuze and Guattari 2004b: 250).

For Deleuze and Guattari, the National Socialist state was obviously tota-litarian. Nazism built a *molar line* which segmented society under a rigid bureau-cratic and identitarian uniformity. Nazism involved more than this molar totalitarian segment, however. Under Nazism the molar line was conjugated with a molecular segmentarity. This second, 'molecular line' of fascism was central to the rise of Nazism and to its eventual trajectory or machinic dynamics.

The second or molecular fascist line addresses the fact that Nazism *began* as a 'mass-movement: a cancerous body rather than a totalitarian organism' (Deleuze and Guattari 2004b: 236). Historical 'fascism is inseparable from a proliferation of molecular forces in interaction, which skip from point to point, *before* beginning to resonate together in the national socialist state'. This marks the socially dispersed historical flows that allowed the emergence of National Socialism at that particular moment in time, and identifies why the masses 'desired it'. To understand the rise of Nazism, Deleuze and Guattari argue, we must move *below* the concept of top-down state authoritarianism to the emergence of the social movement that built its popular appeal upon a narrative of national rebirth; we must explain, in other words, the failure of Weimar democracy as a desiring machine.

Deleuze and Guattari argue that the National Socialist movement began as a cloud of tiny 'microfascist' formations, wherein flows of signification were segmented into 'micro-black holes' of paranoiac enclosure. Such molecular paranoia was dispersed in the narcissism of social sub-groups, ex-soldiers, cities, rural networks, schools, families and beer halls, building the powerful mass-mobilisation machine, under Hitler's charismatic leadership, that took power, overthrowing Weimar, to establish the totalitarian regime of the Third Reich.

At this point, the microfascist movement was conjugated with a molar line under a 'central black hole' that defined Nazi fascism as a macro or state process. The microfascist social machine continued, however, to 'resonate' within German society. In this way the molecular line enabled the Nazi regime's characteristic reach into the micro-capillaries of social life. By containing a supple resonance machine within the 'closed vessel' of the totalitarian state the regime incorporates a 'fluidity' which contrasts fundamentally with the 'classical centralisation' of Stalinist totalitarianism (Deleuze and Guattari 2004b: 236, 246).

The Nazi totalitarian state acts as 'resonance chamber' within which the tangle of microfascisms that established it were put to work (Deleuze and Guattari 2004b: 247). As such, the regime plugged the social-movement into its state function, attempting to over-code and order its microfascist dynamics (which entail variously disordered quanta). In doing so, the Nazi regime maintained a resonating molecular machine within society on which it would draw to enact its genocidal project. Without these resonating 'microfascisms' at his disposal, Hitler's regime would have been unable to achieve its '*unequalled* ability to act upon the masses' (Deleuze and Guattari 2004b: 236, my emphasis).

For Deleuze and Guattari, fascism is a political assemblage of desire and not simply a category of state organisation. They argue that 'It's too easy to be antifascist on the molar level, and not even see the fascist inside you, the fascist you yourself sustain and nourish and cherish with molecules both personal and collective' (Deleuze and Guattari 2004b: 237). There is a fascism of the in-group, which haunts all social movements, and leads to a micro-authoritarianism masquerading as its opposite, even, or especially, in those which pretend to a revolutionary avant-gardism (Thoburn 2008: 99). However, there is also fascism at work in the very dynamics of being. We are constantly prone to allowing our constitutive flows of desire to circulate exclusively around particular objects; individuals; ideas; self-images; aesthetic experiences, like heavy weights on a rubber sheet, sucking desire into gravitic black holes from which it cannot escape. Such a cancerous paranoid molecularity is deemed to be latent to our present societies:

> Reproducing in miniature the affections, the affectations, of the rigid ... supple segmentarity brings dangers of its own that do not merely reproduce in small scale the dangers of molar segmentarity ... A multitude of black holes may very well not become centralised, and acts instead as viruses adapting to the most varied situations, sinking voids in molecular perceptions and semiotics. Interactions without resonance. Instead of the great paranoid fear, we are trapped in a thousand little monomanias, self evident truths, and clarities that gush from every black hole and no longer form a system, but are only the rumble and buzz, blinding lights giving any and everybody a mission of self-appointed judge, dispenser of justice, policeman, neighbourhood SS man.
>
> (Deleuze and Guattari 2004b: 251–52)

Whilst such a diffused micro-paranoia is dangerous of itself, the radical danger revealed in Nazism is that 'microfascisms have a specificity of their own that can crystallise into a macrofascism' (Deleuze and Guattari 2004b). The Nazi party rose to power precisely by such a microfascist social movement rising up from below and establishing a totalitarian apparatus. That microfascist social movement then took on the characteristics of an enormous resonance machine within the German state. Nazism achieved its characteristic power over social minutiae by nurturing its molecular resonance machine within the void of the totalitarian state (Deleuze and Guattari 2004b: 246). The microfascisms already extant within democratic societies allow us to assemble into desiring machines for our own repression given the correct historical and institutional circumstances.

It is crucial to note that the difference between Nazism and other totalitarianisms is in this regard, for Deleuze and Guattari, largely a matter of degree. *All* totalitarian states set up a paranoid 'resonance' between the 'centralised' and the 'segmentary' (Deleuze and Guattari 2004b: 247). There is always a 'molar side and a molecular side' in totalitarianism (Deleuze and Guattari 2004b: 248). Nazism certainly *radicalised* the simultaneity of the two lines for Deleuze and Guattari, inasmuch as its molecular segmentarity (microfascist social movement) originally set up its resonant molar totalitarianism (as opposed, for example, to it finding its genesis in a military coup), and that molecularity was placed at the centre of Nazism's socially penetrative mechanisms of rule. Nonetheless, they state explicitly that *all* totalitarianisms seek to set up a resonant molecularity that does not simply 'seal, plug or block' subversive tendencies but channels popular flows into the service of paranoiac state function. Indeed, 'the stronger the molar organization is, the more it induces a molecularization of its own elements' (Deleuze and Guattari 2004b: 237).

Both fascist states and totalitarian states make the molar and the molecular resonate together. This suggests that a category fascism, if it is to be clearly distinguishable from totalitarianism (rather than being its extreme limit), must involve more than molar-molecular resonance. For Deleuze and Guattari it is important to recognise that the interaction between the molar and molecular is neither intrinsically totalitarian nor fascistic. *All* political forms have molar and molecular (paranoiac) dimensions: as a political party, for example, will comprise a general identity coextensive with multiple internal distinctions, factions, cliques, think-tanks, differential priorities, and thus potential policy directions. Totalitarianism and fascism maximise the rigidity of molar identity and set all the molecular distinctions to resonate within its bounds; this is the paranoiac danger which haunts all political forms, which assemble molar and molecular lines.

Up to this point it seems that *A Thousand Plateaus* can be read as a straight-forward reaffirmation of *Anti-Oedipus*, adding greater clarity and distinction to the concept of fascism as paranoiac. The politics of paranoia builds itself on two lines (state totalitarianism and microfascism), which can occur independently but are conjugated together with unprecedented radicality in fascism-proper, when a state-totalitarianism builds a microfascist resonance machine, or 'even worse' when a microfascist social movement sets up a totalitarian state apparatus (Deleuze and Guattari 2004b: 253). In this regard, Nazism might be understood as a particularly *radical* and socially entrenched form of totalitarianism, in which the dangers inherent to both molar (state despotism) and molecular (a socially diffuse microfascism) politics are conjugated together.

Eugene Holland takes up Deleuze and Guattari's account at this point to argue that, for the identification of *contemporary* fascisms, what is crucial is the 'transmission from movement to regime which occurred when the molar and molecular lines conjugate' to give birth to Nazism as a particularly radical form of totalitarian politics (Holland 2008: 78). Certainly 'fascism require[d] popular mobilisation', but it also requires concretisation in a state-totalitarian body to form a macrofascism. A directly comparable assemblage of molar and molecular fascist lines in the G.W. Bush administration suggested to Holland that we witnessed the 'advent of 21st century fascism in the United States' (Holland 2008: 74).

Holland bases this argument on an identification of the 'born-again Christian social movement', of which he views G.W. Bush as the representative, as paradigmatically microfascistic. There is a 'striking' correspondence, he argues, between the psychodynamics of that born-again Christian movement and the German Friekorps. The Freikorps, as Theweleit (1987) outlined, were characterised by a process of 'splitting' negative internal signifiers onto external objects within a palingenic narrative. This focus on 'palingenesis' and a functionally derived rejection (scapegoating) of a determined other (the Jew) may therefore be understood as suggestive of the structure of microfascism (Holland 2008). Holland points out that the born-again Christian movement in the United States also entailed a palingenic narrative of religious conversion/ redemption, 'weak ego-synthetic abilities; they tend to see everything in stark, absolute terms of black and white, good versus evil', and an 'extreme tension between superego demands for absolute and unwavering adherence to a simplistic homogenising moral code, and multifarious drives and desires arising from the complexities and ambiguities of heterogeneous human existence in a mass mediated global consumer society on the other', with 'the homosexual' replacing 'the Jew' as determined other. We see, in other words, the very microfascist complexes that were definitive of the psychodynamics of the Nazi regime at work in the psychodynamics of the born-again Christian social-movement in the United States. These microfascisms were set to resonance with the molar state apparatus by the Bush administration.

Positing such psychodynamic correspondence with Nazi microfascism is not, Holland accepts, sufficient reason 'to declare the fundamentalist Christian Bush regime "fascist"' in the Deleuzoguattarian sense (Holland 2008: 89). Rather, departing from Deleuze and Guattari's account, Holland finds further significant parallels with Nazism's genesis out of an emotive sense of defeat (Versailles), and (totalitarian) behaviour in power, which confirms the validity of the fascist referent for describing the Bush administration. The born-again Christian social movement emerged from a series of highly emotional defeats, beginning with the 'Scopes trial', but continuing with 'Roe vs. Wade' and the failure in Vietnam. These defeats established a religious-conservative 'resonance machine', with a powerful media wing, which set out to 'take back America'. Actually taking power under Bush, that desiring machine sought to consolidate its rule in a characteristically paranoid and, in tendency, totalitarian manner. The Bush administration developed a politics rooted in fear; using security, after 9/11, as a tool for 'strengthening the state repressive apparatus' at home and abroad, and as a justification for the widespread suspension of rights. This conjugation of a molecular microfascist segmentarity with a molar totalitarian tendency, identifies, according to Holland (2008), the Bush administration as a macrofascist (i.e. extremely totalitarian) assemblage in the Deleuzoguattarian sense. That resonance between the molecular and the molar suggested, to Holland, the reappearance of 'something like old-fashioned fascism' in America (Holland 2008: 94).

Whilst Deleuze and Guattari certainly identified the horrific excesses of Nazism with its resonating molar-molecular machine, Holland neglects the central reason they thought that its assemblage of the molar and molecular was quite *so* dangerous in the Nazi case. Holland is correct to note the paranoiac and indeed fascistic potential of a state that sets itself up in resonance with a socially dispersed religious fundamentalism. Indeed, *any* radical conjugation of the molar-totalitarian and molecular microfascist will produce a uniquely paranoiac assemblage. Significantly for this paper, however, to construct the Bush administration as fascistic, Holland *excises* the third constitutive line of Deleuze and Guattari's schema which marks Nazism's character beyond the conjugation of totalitarianism with microfascism. This occludes the fact that, for Deleuze and Guattari, the politics of fascism are never exhausted by the paranoiac function (i.e. making molar and molecular lines resonate within the closed vessel of totalitarianism). Nazism entailed a third line, a suicidal line of flight, which brings into play a completely different 'abstract machine'.

The third line

There are not just two kinds of line but three.

(Deleuze and Guattari 2004b: 244)

The third line of fascism (its 'suicidal line of flight') completes the schema developed in *A Thousand Plateaus*. Deleuze and Guattari argue that in relation to the third fascist line 'the dangers of all the other lines pale by comparison'. Furthermore, they are clear that whilst the third line *emerges from* the supple yet nonetheless territorial (i.e. paranoiac) segmentations of microfascist molecularity, its dynamics are *deterritorialising* or *schizophrenic*. For Deleuze and Guattari, the Nazi fascist event entailed a suicidally schizophrenic 'war-machine taking over the state' (Deleuze and Guattari 2004b: 254).

Deleuze and Guattari explicitly bind this element of their account into the hypothetical framework developed in the *Treatise on Nomadology*, in which paranoiac 'state apparatus' is distinguished from essentially schizophrenic 'war-machines' (Deleuze and Guattari 2004b: 253). In the *Nomadology*, a state apparatus is identified as determined by an 'abstract machine of overcoding'. State orders, they argue, are fundamentally based on a regime of interiorisation, hinging on the two-headed disciplinarity of policing and taxation that allows a territory to be organised and dominated. States striate space, so as to code and over-code desiring flows to serve a despotic function. The state is an abstract machine for molar and molecular striation.

War-machines, on the other hand, are determined by an 'abstract machine of mutation'. This abstract machine is qualitatively and 'quantifiably' different in function to the machine of paranoiac overcoding, deterritorialising desiring flows rather than reterritorialising them (Deleuze and Guattari 2004b: 564). 'The war-machine' is the diagram of any and every function which actualises an abstract machine of mutation. Any assemblage which emits lines of flight, 'quanta of deterritorialisation' or 'mutant flows', whether social, cultural, aesthetic, political or/and economic, is understood by Deleuze and Guattari as having built a war-machine to do so (Deleuze and Guattari 2004b: 253).

War machines, as they define them, set up a 'smooth space' within which (social, economic, sexual, artistic) flows can circulate and spring up at any point. This is why they are intrinsically linked to creativity or productivity for Deleuze and Guattari (always a function of deterritorialisation). The fundamental function of the war-machine is to construct and occupy smooth space for unconstrained flux. Deleuze and Guattari ascribe the 'invention' of the war-machine to nomadic, pre- or non-territorial social systems. This must not be taken to imply that war-machines are solely built by pre-modern nomadic societies. When any practice is productive of new flows it has necessarily built a smooth space, and thus employs a war-machine; there are purely aesthetic war-machines such as writing and music. War machines maximise fluxion by allowing a form to occupy geography (whether physical, intellectual, artistic, or social) without building an interiorised (striated molar-molecular) territory upon it.

Actual war, as an exercise of force, appears in this hypothetical discussion as the means by which nomadic orders build and defend smooth spaces against territorial state apparatus. War is what war-machines engage in when faced by the interiorising (reterritorialising) praxis of a state apparatus. War, as such, is originally an *anti-state function*. By extension, war is understood as only the 'supplement' of the war-machine, rather than its originary purpose or fundamental essence. War is directed at the paranoiac barriers to nomadic fluxion, and originally serves no other purpose than to allow a war-machine to build and occupy smooth space.

War machines are only given war as their exclusive object *by* states. State apparatus seeks to harness the capacity to wage war to aid in the construction of territoriality. Consequentially they seek to capture, under their system of interiorisation, the war-machine. In doing so, they over-code that war-machine with its supplemental destructive function (as in Clausewitz's dictum, making war serve as a means to state ends). When a state apparatus co-opts a war-machine it short-circuits it, 'divest[ing] the war-machine of its power of metamorphosis', and 'substitute[ing] destruction for mutation' (Deleuze and Guattari 2004b: 253).

Once affected, this capture *of* a war-machine *by* the state apparatus is instantly vulnerable to a counter-coup due to a 'catastrophic charge' released (Deleuze and Guattari 2004b: 253). Once a war-machine is given war as its sole objective it can all too easily, Deleuze and Guattari argue, set off on a line that is so absolute in its focus that the state in question is no longer able to determine and code its directionality. Harnessing war 'as a means to a state end' always entails the (supplemental) risk of becoming a total or pure war. In pure or total war the war-machine's power of metamorphosis returns as a perverse monstrosity; an overwhelming urge to radical abolition of self and others which co-opts the state and sets it upon an apocalyptically suicidal trajectory: the unlimited essence of war (as an act of force) that Clausewitz identified is now given free rein (Reid 2006: 294).

When Deleuze asks, 'why is the [creative] line of flight a war one risks coming back from defeated, destroyed, after having destroyed everything one could', he is not using war simply as a 'metaphor' (Deleuze 2002: 140–41). Rather Deleuze and Guattari argue that a suicidal pure war is a danger integral to any deterritorialisation. Whilst we must deterritorialise or smooth space to create (and thus build war-machines), that movement, at its logical limit, potentially results in the suicidal dissolution of self (which reflects the surrender of the war-machine to its anti-productive supplement): 'War is like the fall or failure of mutation, the only object left for the war-machine after it has lost its power to change' (Deleuze and Guattari 2004b: 253). Suicide is the supplement that may be built on any line of flight given the correct (unlimited) conditions, such as, but not limited to, the short-circuiting of a war-machine by a state apparatus.

Just as molarity carries with it the risk of instituting state-totalitarian or despotic social arrangements and molecularity carries with it the risk of forming little black holes of microfascist certainty, all lines of flight open to suicidal excess (Deleuze 2002: 140–41). This is a crucial point, clarifying that both paranoiac and schizophrenic processes have integral risks or dangers. At the state level the danger on the third line manifests in the catastrophic charge released when a state apparatus is captured by its war-machine and set to pure war, but Deleuze and Guattari develop, in *A Thousand Plateaus*, numerous examples of the integral association between art's attempts to build smooth space and the tragic ends to which artists are often inexorably drawn (Deleuze 2002: 61; Deleuze and Guattari 2004b: 208, 220, 227, 330). Their point is not that war-machines are suicidal *rather than* productive, but that the productivity of war-machines (in building and occupying smooth space) carries with it a suicidal danger that resides on *all* lines of flight (just as a 'totalitarian danger' resides on all molar lines and a 'microfascist danger' resides on all molecular lines).

All lines of flight or deterritorialisation conceal suicide as 'a danger which is proper to them', and this danger manifests itself in a variety of ways (Deleuze 2002: 140–41).[1] For Deleuze and Guattari there are suicidal lines of flight in political assemblages which are not fascist (at the level of the individual, aesthetic and evolutionary/organic as well as social). The broader significance of this argument for Deleuze and Guattari's general thesis on politics and creativity/deterritorialisation in *A Thousand Plateaus* cannot be sufficiently engaged here; constraints on space insist that the argument remain tightly focused on the sustainability of their theory of fascism. Nonetheless, there is no doubt that it is the broader political consequences of Deleuze and Guattari's claim that schizophrenia has an integral danger which have called up such widespread antipathy to the idea of a third fascist line, as the following section will outline.

Regarding fascism, Deleuze and Guattari's point seems clear: beyond assembling the dangers on the molar and the molecular into a resonating paranoiac machine, Nazism built a line of flight into suicidal pure war. Fascism as a general category, for Deleuze and Guattari, is defined by the realisation of the dangers on *all three lines* of the political real – molar, molecular and flight. What gives fascism its *difference* (from totalitarianism) is the third line, which ensures that it always establishes suicidal states.

Fascist suicide

> Long live death!
>
> (Deleuze and Guattari 2004b: 254)

No longer is it sufficient to worry about paranoiac desire desiring its own repression and becoming closed down in black holes, succumbing to the temptations of identity, self-certainty, truth and presence. *A Thousand Plateaus* posits a danger inherent to creative schizophrenisation: that an abstract machine of mutation, in the form of a war-machine turned to pure war, takes itself as its object and embraces a strategy of radical self-abolition. This seems an astonishing theoretical move, one that makes the political schizophrenisation that is lauded in *Anti-Oedipus* a seriously risky business. Indeed, as Protevi points out, 'recognising these dangers' results in a 'caution' that appears throughout *A Thousand Plateaus* (Protevi 2000: 168). Such caution does not fit easily into the dualistic framework of *Anti-Oedipus*. Indeed, Protevi suggests that accepting the categorical nature of a disjunction between the texts is a precondition for any correct reading (see also Protevi 2000; Holland 2008).

For Nick Land (1993), this disjunction between the texts represents a fatal problem for the mobilisation of their thought. The idea of a line of flight 'gone wrong' seems to betray the anti-paranoiac spirit of the earlier text. The schizoanalysis of *Anti-Oedipus*, Land argues, was fundamentally a call to 'always decode ... and extinguish all nostalgia for belonging'. As such, 'schizoanalysis shares in the delicious [antihumanist] irresponsibility of everything anarchic, inundating, and harshly impersonal, seeks a fringe of experimentation that knows no bounds, pushing to the edge of capitalism (which is itself a schizophrenizing tendency), it is a dissolution of identity' (Land 1993: 67).

For Land, the job of Schizoanalysis is unpicking the ways in which all social forms (but capitalism in particular) refuse their own immanent processes of revolutionary schizophrenisation. The, admittedly 'crude', force of the earlier account lies precisely in its dichotomy between molecular, revolutionary, schizophrenic and creative and molar, reactionary, paranoid or fascistic: In sum, 'between the dissolution and reinstitution of the social order'(Land 1993). *Anti-Oedipus* simply *is* the challenge of the paranoiac and repressive with the schizophrenic and creative (Land 1993: 70). Abandoning the rigid exclusions of this dichotomy, for Land, implodes the entire Deleuzoguattarian project.

It seems clear that this is an overreaction. The theoretical developments of *A Thousand Plateaus* must be understood in terms of the evolutionary trajectory of Deleuze and Guattari's political theory. Indeed, an auto-problematisation of conceptual dichotomies which they construct forms an essential machine part of the very fabric of *Capitalism and Schizophrenia* as a rhizomic rather than arborescent text (as a processor of difference in repetition). Paraphrasing Deleuze, the concept of the 'suicidal line of flight into pure war' is designed precisely to disrupt the Anti-Oedipal 'dualism' of paranoia and schizophrenia (or molar and molecular), not simply by adding a 'new term', but by adding a new 'dimension' which cannot be contained in the dualism but rather re-inflects it with difference (Deleuze 2002: 132).

This is explicitly illuminated in *A Thousand Plateaus* by way of the Nazi example, inasmuch as a suicidal line of flight is seen to have inhabited the molar-molecular dynamics of Nazism from the beginning. Nazism, as we already know, was more than a totalitarian state-apparatus: its genesis certainly cannot be reduced to a military coup. Rather, Nazism was constructed when a microfascist movement took over the state. Deleuze and Guattari argue that to do so, the microfascist or segmentary resonance machine adopted the characteristics of a war-machine, building within the assemblage the (palingenic) line of flight that was to give National Socialism is characteristic mass appeal. Resonating within the social body, this schizophrenic war-machine always exceeded the totalitarian apparatus that later sought to harness its resonance to a paranoiac function.

> Unlike the totalitarian state, which does its utmost to seal all possible lines of flight, fascism is constructed on an intense line of flight, which it transforms into a line of pure destruction and abolition. It is curious that from the very beginning the Nazis announced to Germany what they were bringing: at once wedding bells and death, including their own death, and the death of the Germans, they thought they would perish but that their undertaking would be resumed, all across Europe, all over the world, throughout the solar system. And the people cheered, not because they did not understand, but because they wanted that death through the death of others ... One can always say that this is just a matter of foggy talk and ideology. But that is not true. The insufficiency of economic and political definitions of fascism does not imply a need to tack on vague, so-called ideological determinations. We prefer to follow ... the precise formation of Nazi statements, which are just as much in evidence in politics and economics as in the most absurd of conversations. They always contain the 'stupid and repugnant cry', Long live death!
>
> (Deleuze and Guattari 2004b: 254)

Deleuze and Guattari are clear that what they refer to in this passage is more than simply the work of an over-coding totalitarian ideology.[2] Rather, the war-machine that was established within the resonating microfascist segmentarity of German society carried within it an unlimited potentiality which was *only to be fully released* with the onset of total war but clearly pre-existed it. That frenzied line of flight manifested in a suicidalism both at the political and 'at the economic level, where arms expansion replaces growth in consumption and where investment veers from the means of production towards the means of pure destruction' (Deleuze and Guattari 2004b: 254). The 'paradox' of fascism is that it was defined, from the start, not by its totalitarianism, but by a 'reversion of the line of flight into a line of destruction' that always animated its foundational molecular segmentarity (Deleuze and Guattari 2004b: 253, 255).

To contain its mutant flows, the Nazi regime had sought to stabilise its war-machine within the resonant void of the totalitarian state, trapping a *mutation machine* within a militaristic narrative of national rebirth. By attempting to harness this schizo-function to a paranoiac order, a short-circuited or cancerous line of flight is set up (militarised *re*-birth as a corruption of the mutational impetus). By the 1940s, following this line, the Nazi state had been entirely set to total war, now explicitly pursuing the radical politics of abolition which proceeds from the paranoiac attempt to over-code the war-machine with its anti-productive supplement.

By short-circuiting a line of flight through a molecular segmentarity and a molar centrality, Nazism built a fully '*suicidal-state*'. Hitler's telegram 71, which declaimed 'If the war is lost, may the nation perish', was the 'normal outcome' of this particular assemblage of the lines. Turned to total war, the Nazi state apparatus became little more than an appendage of its suicidal war-machine (Deleuze and Guattari 2004b: 253).

> Paul Virilio's analysis strikes us as entirely correct in defining fascism not by the notion of the totalitarian state but by the notion of the suicidal state: so-called total war seems less a state undertaking than an under-taking of a war-machine that appropriates the State and channels into it a flow of absolute war whose only possible outcome is the suicide of the state itself ... It was this reversion of the line of flight into a line of destruction that already animated the molecular focuses of fascism, and made them interact in a war-machine instead of resonating in a state apparatus. A war-machine that no longer had anything but war as its object and would rather annihilate its own servants than stop the destruction. All the dangers of the other lines pale by comparison.
>
> (Deleuze and Guattari 2004b: 255)

The state apparatus became a machine-part of a society transformed into a massive engine for the production of pure war: the pursuit of collective rebirth through fire and bloodshed generating a politics which had no horizon but destruction. The Nazi pursuit of palingenic total war, as a perverse state mili-tarisation of the molecular dynamics of desiring mutation, was a line of flight into abolition (Deleuze and Guattari 2004b). This is what determined the fascistic (as opposed to simply totalitarian) character of Nazism for Deleuze and Guattari. It nurtured a suicidally schizophrenic war-machine at its heart.

This characterisation of Nazism as distinguished by quanta of deterritor-ialisation, a suicidal line of flight, strikes Nick Land as having only a tenuous link to the paranoiac realities of Nazism. Land argues that it is simply bizarre to claim that the Nazis had anything to do with war-machinic schizophrenisa-tion (Land 1993: 76). Nazis were the very opposite of an excessive release of desiring flows. If you schizophrenise, you 'let go'. If you let go, as Land puts it, 'you might end up fucking with a Jew, or producing something degenerate like a work of art'. To the contrary, Nazism is about 'Conspiracy, Lucidity, and malice', the proliferation of enemies and paranoid subjectivities, gloom, oppression, the love of obedience, leadership and symbols, 'the icons of molar identity' (Land 1993). To be a fascist is to pursue 'nostalgia for what is maxi-mally bovine, inflexible, and stagnant: a line of racially pure peasants digging the same patch of earth for eternity [and] above all, resent everything impet-uous and irresponsible ... to eliminate the disorder of uncontrolled flows, and persecute all minorities exhibiting a nomadic tendency' (Land 1993: 75). In short, Land argues, being a Nazi historically had nothing to do with 'letting go' or taking flight (Land 1993).

Whilst Deleuze and Guattari do identify the risks of an unrestrained deterritorialisation with the suicidal thrust of Nazism, their point clearly is not, by extension, that all deterritorialisation straightforwardly risks Nazism or fascism; this would certainly threaten to 'domesticate' their thesis (Land 1993). The Nazi suicide state is rather understood as having been assembled in a very specific 'set of conditions'; explicitly, the short-circuiting of a war-machine through molar-molecular totalitarianism (Deleuze and Guattari 2004b: 466).[3] The 'fascist line of flight' thus *in no way* detracts from the fact that Nazism was an assemblage with *paranoiac* molar and molecular lines.

Like Nick Land, Eugene Holland argues that Deleuze and Guattari's account of 'fascist suicide' makes for a misunderstanding of the regime's central character. He points out that 'what the fascist movement offered Germans was first and foremost renewed hope and confidence in the German nation, not the prospect of suicide' (Holland 2008: 79). Deleuze and Guattari, Holland argues, make the catastrophic error of following Virilio (1998) in misinterpreting Hitler's telegram 71 'as the interpretative key to the fascist movement and regime as a whole' (Holland 2008: 79). It seems clear to Holland that an 'apocalyptic moment of Hitler's sheds little or no light on the emergence of the fascist movement that depended for part of its support on rapid acceleration of the development of productive forces and on the massive integration of unemployed and underemployed populations into the workforce' (Holland 2008: 79).

For Holland, the Nazi regime pursued the mobilisation of the entire economy to war precisely in extension of its original promise to restore self-confidence in the German nation: 'What had not been possible to maintain (or attain quickly enough) through the development of productive force alone increasingly required the pursuit of power and domination (scapegoating at home and conquest abroad) to achieve' (Holland 2008: 83). Holland concludes that we have no reason to assume there was anything 'intrinsically "suicidal" about historical fascism ... rather, the Nazi State turned to total war and then pure destruction for contingent historical reasons' (Holland 2008). Whilst it is 'apparent from th[e] telegram that the fascist regime eventually reached a point at which Hitler could see its imminent demise and would have preferred its total destruction to defeat', given the peculiarity of this process to the idiosyncrasies of the Nazi event, the third line must be stipulated as irrelevant to any project seeking to chart the resurgence of fascism today (Holland 2008).

If Deleuze and Guattari's third fascist line were simply a theoretical extension from the Nazi case, and specifically Hitler's telegram 71, to fascism in general, it would certainly indicate a lazy reduction and the concept could be easily discarded in the way Holland (2008) suggests. The problem with such a reading is that quite apart from simply extending their theory of fascism from Virilio's reading of telegram 71, Deleuze and Guattari are absolutely clear

that they consent to the notion of the 'suicidal state' only because they understand suicide as a 'normal outcome' of fascism as a particular, and absolutely
contingent, machinic assemblage of desire. Fascism is defined as the assemblage of three lines, combining *both* reterritorialising and deterritorialising
desiring processes. In this context, Holland's dichotomisation of palingenesis
(rebirth) and suicidalism makes limited sense. What Deleuze and Guattari are
attempting to capture with the concept of the third line is the dangerously
uncontrollable excess of desire that defined the palingenic urge of Nazi fascism *alongside* the heavy centralisation of its totalitarian ideal. They suggest
that it was the perverse and proliferating over-capacity of desire within the
resonating molar-molecular apparatus which drove the Nazism project inexorably towards destructive abolition (of self and others).

The cartography of the lines of the Nazi assemblage reveals how the forces
of desiring production within German society (which drove towards the establishment of the Nazi totalitarian state apparatus) were *assembled with* the
molecular and molar paranoiac lines to foster a suicide machine. Far from trapping
or plugging the flow of deterritorialisation, that molar/molecular 'short-circuiting'
released suicidalism as a danger already latent in Nazism's unlimited project
of national palingenesis. The line of flight into abolition was released in the
attempt to trap a war-machine under the totem of a national re-birth (promising,
as Holland points out, 'renewed hope and confidence'), which was militarily
over-coded from its beginnings (as directed against the injustice of Versailles),
and thereby collapsed instantly into the pursuit of pure-war.

Holland's most incisive critique is in challenging Deleuze and Guattari's
claim that Nazism became suicidal as a consequence of some ontological predetermination rather than particular historical circumstances (Holland 2008:
79). The idea that Nazism was suicidal 'from the very beginning' certainly
seems problematic (Holland 2008: 79). An intrinsically suicidal valence seems
to challenge Deleuze and Guattari's claim to be doing cartography rather than
definitional taxonomy. Whilst the suicidal valence of Nazi statements 'from
the very beginning' is only noted as *a curiosity* by Deleuze and Guattari, it
risks inflecting their theory of fascism with an essentialist tone (Deleuze and
Guattari 2004b: 254).

As noted above, for Deleuze and Guattari, quanta of deterritorialisation
always contain a *potentially* (though not necessarily) unlimited trajectory which
is the danger 'proper' to them (the central point here is that creation is always
indissociable from auto-dissolution: i.e. *de*-territorialisation). This universal
danger does not, however, fully explicate Deleuze and Guattari's precise intent
in terming Nazism suicidal 'from the very beginning'. They explicitly argue that
the lines of flight or quanta emissions that crossed the Nazi social-movement and
built its popular appeal in the promise of palingenesis had to skirt excess so as
to allow them to 'interact in a war-machine instead of resonating in a state
apparatus'. It was, therefore, for Deleuze and Guattari, precisely the already
schizo-excessive chapter of Nazi desire that distinguished the movement from
other totalitarianisms, which generally tend towards conservative paranoiac

formations. In other words, though viewing its project in terms of *re*-birth, Nazi enunciations always had an extravagance or overcapacity that refused to be fully striated; the secret of fascism's unique horror was the paradoxically unlimited, even globalising, scope of its palingenic project.

This excessive, schizophrenic dimension is central to what distinguishes Nazism as a fascist movement from the totalitarian politics of paranoia for Deleuze and Guattari. The excessive and morbid formation of Nazi statements *from the start* was suggestive of, or opened into, the regime's eventual trajectory, but did not necessarily structurally pre-determine it.[4] As such, Nazism's eventually suicidal trajectory was only *materially* actualised with the machinic assemblage of all three lines during the Second World War (Deleuze and Guattari 2004b: 254). This broadly incorporates Holland's (2008) critique.

For the Deleuzoguattarian concept of fascism (as an assemblage of *three* lines) to be deemed valid, however, Holland (2008) is absolutely right to insist that it cannot simply be seen as a function of the specificities of Nazi ideology, or of Hitler's individual psychosis. Holland implies that Deleuze and Guattari's cartographic schema must stand or fall on its ability to provide a functional toolbox for mapping fascist events other than the German case. We do not, however, need to concur with Holland that Nazism was the *only* historical derivation of the machinic dynamics of fascist state suicide, and that Deleuze and Guattari's third line must therefore be ejected from a general theory of fascism. By demonstrating the utility of Deleuzoguattarian cartography for charting the quite different dynamics of the Meiji suicidal state, Deleuze and Guattari's theory of fascism (as the assemblage of all three lines) can be defended from the charge that it reduces all fascisms to Hitler's 'apocalyptic moment'. As a consequence, Deleuze and Guattari's third fascist line must be re-integrated into any programme for the analysis of twenty-first-century fascisms.

The fascist lines of the tokkōtai

Like Nazi Germany, Meiji Japan set out on 'a road that finally brought the country to self-destruction on a colossal scale in World War II' (Ohnuki-Tierney 2002: 61). Its development, during the latter stages of war in the Pacific, of the tokkōtai or 'special attack corps' under the direction of a war-machine set on total war, seems iconically to signify the emergence of a Japanese 'suicidal state' that conjugated *all three* lines of Deleuze and Guattari's schema of fascism. In this section the unique dynamics by which the Meiji state built its politics of self-abolition will be articulated through Deleuzoguattarian cartography, drawing on Ohnuki-Tierney's (2002) ground-breaking sociological analysis. Whilst provisional, this account will demonstrate how Deleuze and Guattari's schema of three lines is a useful conceptual tool for mapping fascisms beyond the German case, thus countering Holland's critical charge of their reduction of fascism to the idiosyncrasies of the National Socialist event, and reopening their concepts to think about fascisms today.

The molar line

The Meiji regime clearly involved the establishment of a totalitarian state apparatus. A molar line was drawn around the despotic figure of the emperor, who was framed in messianic terms as the representative of a national rebirth. This palingenic project may be dated from the forcible opening of Japan to external influences by Commodore Perry, which brought about the end of the much more supple and segmented Shogunate system in 1854. Following this catastrophic event, a wholesale remodelling of the Japanese internal order was pursued under the guidance of powerful domestic elites, with the explicit aim being to construct a strong centralised and nationalised state that would be able to resist such foreign incursions in the future.

The Meiji constitution was the key event in the codification of this nationalist project, establishing the imperial apparatus which rapidly initiated a state-led programme of interventions at the social, cultural and institutional levels. These reforms sought to Westernise the Japanese social order, and set up a European-style state bureaucracy. Supposedly 'useless' Japanese traditions were discarded under central direction, and a wide range of new institutions were put in place 'affecting all aspects of the daily life of the Japanese' (Ohnuki-Tierney 2002: 63).

Simultaneously the traditional Shinto folk religion was steadily over-coded by a molar segment. Local rituals were coordinated through imperial control of local shrines to develop a 'national Shintoism' under state direction: 'Imperial rituals were synchronised with newly instituted rituals in villages, schools, organisations and national shrines.' Ensuring there was a centrally coordinated shrine for each village meant that purely through continuing traditional worship, normal Japanese 'became willing participants in the governmental program on religion' (Ohnuki-Tierney 2002: 90). Shintoism was thereby increasingly over-coded by a molar-totalitarian function. Meanwhile, ethnic minorities, such as the Ainu, were marked through various strategies as genetically different from 'authentic' Japanese.

Victories in the Sino–Japanese (1894–95) and Japanese–Russian (1904–05) wars were an important catalyst for this molar over-coding. The celebration of these victories helped to solidify and confirm the molar national formation, giving birth to the militaristic colonial project that drew Japan into the Second World War (Ohnuki-Tierney 2002: 95).

The Meiji state apparatus was established gradually, over a far more extended historical period than the corresponding institutional formation in Nazi Germany. It was founded by a relatively small group of oligarchs rather than the up-swell of a microfascist social movement. Similarly, the institutional format and content of Meiji totalitarianism was clearly unique to its particular historical and cultural milieu, and notable for its exceptional focus on the quasi-deified figure of the emperor. Yet its palingenic project similarly entailed the *molar over-coding* of social, cultural and religious practices, institutional and military structures, and ethnic/religious identity. The Meiji assemblage was characterised by a massive molarisation which reached its zenith in the 1930s and 1940s.

The molecular line

Like Nazi Germany, and indeed all totalitarianisms, the molar line alone is insufficient to capture the dynamics of Meiji. Ohnuki-Tierney (2002) charts how, continuous to and resonating with the rise of a molar totalitarian apparatus, a molecular political aesthetic was constructed around the 'cherry blossom' imagery. This aesthetic brought into play a supple segmentarity to build a dynamic and supportive resonance machine within the closed vessel of the totalitarian state.

The 'cherry blossom' long had been associated closely with Japanese cultural identity; indeed, initially, following the fall of feudalism, there was some call for all the trees to be cut down, since they were identified with the now moribund regime (Ohnuki-Tierney 2002). The rising totalitarian state realised early on the potency of the symbol for social engineering. From the Meiji constitution onwards, Ohnuki-Tierney traces how 'successive state machineries deployed cherry blossoms', until it became the 'dominant political and military symbol' (Ohnuki-Tierney 2002: 102). Successive regimes engaged in the systematic planting of cherry trees, especially in castle grounds, as part of a symbolic marking of the departure *from* feudalism (Ohnuki-Tierney 2002: 121). The cherry blossom increasingly was characterised as a uniquely Japanese tree, superior to any found in China, Korea, or elsewhere. It became, in state-national discourse, an identifier of the particular Japanese essence or 'soul'. This was gradually incorporated into the discourse of colonial expansion: foreign territories were now claimed for Japan on the grounds that the Cherry Tree had been found there. In colonised spaces, the cherry tree was exported to 'symbolically stamp areas as spaces for imperial Japan' (Ohnuki-Tierney 2002: 122).

It might seem easy to argue that this simply reflected a *molar* ideological strategy, but Ohnuki-Tierney makes clear that the cherry blossom aesthetic always entailed a complex dynamism that frustrates any such reduction. The cherry blossom aesthetic long had been associated with a wide milieu of significations within Japanese culture, constituting a supple marker of self-hood. The cherry blossom as a cultural symbol was implicated not in a single set of meanings, but in a complex of *relationships*. Its anthropological connotations incorporated life and death, but also reproduction, fertility, time and norm-subversion (Ohnuki-Tierney 2002: 57). In this sense, the cherry blossom aesthetic from the very beginning incorporated multiple quanta of deterritorialisation, being defined by an abstract machine of mutation rather than over-coding. This dynamic interpretative mutability was fatally to limit the ability of the molar state to stabilise the aesthetic under the imperial referent.

As a consequence, to harness its deep cultural resonance, the cherry blossom was increasingly over-coded by the totalitarian state under a *military* connotation. Cherry blossom motifs were used to mark the new European style of Meiji army uniforms 'as Japanese' (Ohnuki-Tierney 2002). At first, military colonisation of the symbol focuses on the 'blooming life' of the soldier-as-cherry-blossom. Gradually, however, the flower comes to be over-coded with the idea of a 'beautiful' martial death for the emperor (*pro rege et patria mori*). During the Second World War, the Yasukuni Shrine was placed at the centre of this ideological strategy, aestheticising martial death 'for the emperor' through the narrative of heroic military dead being reborn at the shrine as 'falling cherry blossoms' (Ohnuki-Tierney 2002).

This military over-coding of the cherry blossom signifier increasingly was distributed throughout the capillaries of the Japanese social order. The '"stupid and repugnant cry", Long live death!' appeared now in school textbooks, songs and novels under a cherry blossom motif. We see traced, throughout the Japanese social order, a dispersed micro-repetition of state militarism, which was now bound into the much more supple register of patriotic sentiment associated with the cherry blossom as a uniquely Japanese flower (Ohnuki-Tierney 2002: 128). This seems to confirm Deleuze and Guattari's claim that 'the stronger the molar organization is, the more it induces a molecularization of its own elements' (Deleuze and Guattari, 2004b: 237). In Deleuze and Guattari's terms, this seems to mark the state-led development of a molecular cultural-resonance machine that bound Japanese society to the totalitarian project through an *aesthetic* militarism.

Coding the cherry blossom with an exclusively military connotation, however, meant that that aesthetic began to take on the characteristics of a war-machine over-coded with its supplement. The cherry blossom aesthetic, vibrating within the resonance chamber of the totalitarian state, builds 'a proliferation of molecular forces in interaction, which skip from point to point, before beginning to resonate together' under a purely destructive function (Deleuze and Guattari 2004b: 236). Clearly the molecularity associated with the cherry blossom aesthetic was different from the cancerous macrofascism that defined the Nazi event. No rise of a social movement preceded crystallisation into the Japanese totalitarian state. Yet the Meiji state establishes a no-less-cancerous resonance machine by harnessing the supple segmentations of the cultural-aesthetic milieu of the cherry blossom to its totalitarian militarism: building an aesthetic war-machine within the social body. In this way, the Meiji regime, like Nazi Germany, nurtured a war-machine at the heart of its resonant molar-molecular totalitarianism.

That this cancerous (aesthetic) molecularity was actively constructed through the Meiji totalitarian state's ideological strategy indicates that the historical assemblage of Japanese fascism ran a different course to the assemblage of Nazi fascism. Deleuze and Guattari are clear that the three lines may interact in multiple and dynamic ways. In its conjugation of the molar and molecular lines into a resonant war machine Meiji Japan was, however, like Germany under Nazism, to sow the seeds of a no less intense line of flight towards state suicide.

The suicidal line

Even before the molecular social dispersal of aesthetic militarism, the principle of death-before-capture had become a key trope of Japanese military discourse,

with the precise technique for 'honourable suicide' rather than surrender forming part of the training of every Japanese soldier (O'Neill 1981). There had already
been various practical military extensions of this principle of patriotic death.
Such acts as manned submarine collisions at Pearl Harbour and the so-called
Banzai charges, infamous in infantry engagements, all tapped into the aesthetic machine to structure and frame them as heroic and beautiful. It was
not until war in the Pacific approached its dénouement following a series of
catastrophic naval defeats that such methods were turned into a systematic
programme of military self-sacrifice.

At this point the tokkōtai, or special-attack corps, was established. These
pilots were trained to fly bomb-laden planes into enemy vessels. Suicidal attack
methods became an increasingly central element of the Japanese Pacific
strategy. Unsurprisingly, the cherry blossom was the 'exclusive visual symbol
for the tokkōtai operation' from the start (Ohnuki-Tierney 2002: 165). By the
end of the war Japan had expended thousands of its youth, often drawn from
the top universities, in such strikes. As the war approached it end, training for
the tokkōtai pilots shrank to an almost nominal length (ensuring that many
pilots simply missed their targets), yet the practice built in intensity as defeat
became ever more certain.

It is notable that the Meiji authorities took considerable convincing by the
strategy's advocates in the military hierarchy before suicidal-attack methods
were instituted as a *systematic* programme (Inoguchi and Nakajima 1978).
Despite the state's role in aestheticising military self-sacrifice, the system-
atisation of tokkōtai methods was perceived, initially, to be a bridge too far
by the central authorities. In turning the aesthetic resonance machine into a
cultural processor of martial death the state-apparatus had, however, by now
set up a suicidal trajectory on its own (molar and molecular) lines that reso-
nated powerfully with the suicidal tactics proposed by key elements of the
military hierarchy. In turning the aesthetic into a pillar of legitimation, the
totalitarian state had already synthesised the aesthetic with its military apparatus (with the cherry blossom literally marking the uniforms of soldiers and
sailors) and the very concept of martial death. Meiji could no more refuse the
logic of its actual suicidal extension than completely jettison its aesthetic
legitimation or resonance machine. As such, the Meiji state's eventual acquies-
cence to the tokkōtai strategy seemed almost inevitable. By this point the cherry
blossom aesthetic had more and more come to reflect the Deleuzoguattarian
account of a war-machine over-coded by its destructive supplement, to which
the state-apparatus itself had increasingly surrendered.

This process closely mapped with the dynamics outlined by Deleuze and
Guattari (2004b) in *The Nomadology*: a small group of military officers was
responsible for developing the strategy, and presented it to the state bureaucracy,
acting as representatives of a synthesised military-aesthetic war-machine staging a
take-over of the entire assemblage. This aesthetic war-machine now set out on
an unlimited line of flight into pure war (victory or death). The Meiji state apparatus became an appendage of its war-machine on a flight towards abolition.

Deleuze and Guattari point out that the 'reversion of the line of flight into a line of destruction ... already animated the molecular focuses of fascism' in the German case (Deleuze and Guattari 2004b: 255). Similarly, the birth of the tokkōtai cannot be understood without reference to the aesthetic war-machine that the totalitarian state had set to resonate within society. A Japanese line of abolition was built on the supple molecular character of the cherry blossom aesthetic (and its abstract machine of mutation), being turned to a line of destruction by the state-totalitarian apparatus, and therein building a war-machine over-coded by a line of destruction aimed at both the enemy and the self.

One certainly cannot overstate the psychological effect of the tokkōtai on their American adversaries (Hoyt 1983).[5] The practice seemed to spell out unequivocally the radical otherness and incomprehensibility of the enemy (Zeiler 2004: 109). Ivan Morris (1975: 168) argued that the special attack strategy 'produced indignation and rage out of all proportion to the tactical importance', and may well have contributed directly to the decision to drop the atomic bombs, inasmuch as it seemed to prove the likelihood of fanatical Japanese resistance to invasion. In this sense, the tokkōtai directly drove the very real possibility of collective abolition that faced Japan at the close of the Second World War (see also Rees 1997: 161; Zeiler 2004: 168). By the end of the war, it certainly seemed, at least to its adversaries, that Japan 'no longer had anything but war as its object and would rather annihilate its own servants than stop the destruction' (Deleuze and Guattari 2004b: 255). Yet, unlike Nazi Germany, at the very brink of abolition, following the atomic bombings of Hiroshima and Nagasaki, and the equally if not greater devastation wrought by strategic bombing, Japan's fascist state apparatus reasserted control over its war-machine and surrendered.

Virilio and Lotringer (1997: 212–13) argue that 'were it not for Hirohito, who was a fairly intelligent individual, the militarists would have carried out a national suicide: an entire country committing mass suicide'. Certainly, were it not for the emperor's decision to surrender, given the unlimited aestheticised trajectory of its line of flight there seems little doubt that much of the military establishment indeed would have fought to the last man, and insisted that the Japanese people join that aestheticised collective suicide. Some evidence of this possibility is to be found in the fact that many of the officers involved in the tokkōtai operations would commit suicide rather than surrender with their emperor. One officer central to its design, upon hearing of the emperor's decision to surrender, flew his plane into a mountain-side: surely the paradigmatic expression of a war-machine pursuing its line to its logical limit (Inoguchi and Nakajima 1978).

A Japanese state suicide, Virilio and Lotringer argue, would have been 'even more drastic' than that of the Nazis because it would have formed 'a collective pact' based on the cultural-aesthetic machine, rather than an individual injunction by the despot (Virilio and Lotringer 1997: 213).[6] The cherry blossom aesthetic certainly would have bound the population directly to any potential plunge into state suicide. Yet, the dynamics of this process are not as 'alien to our culture' as Virilio and Lotringer (1997: 213) imply. Whilst undoubtedly the supple segmentations of the cherry blossom aesthetic built on a uniquely Japanese cultural milieu, the construction of the Japanese suicide-state took place via an assemblage of the three lines which was clearly correspondent to Germany's. This suggests, from Deleuze and Guattari's point of view, a broader category of (fascist) assemblage.

Throughout the historiography of the Pacific War there has been a tendency to view the tokkōtai as indicative of some form of Japanese essence tied to Bushido Samurai traditions or a perverse cultural penchant for death (O'Neill 1981; Lamont-Brown 1997; Benedict 1967). Deleuzoguattarian cartography enjoins us to chart, in contrast to such a culturally essentialist reading, the machinic dynamics that conjugated the three lines to assemble its fascist politics of state suicide (when molar-totalitarianisms enter into resonance with a socially dispersed molecular segmentarity and pursue total war). The Japanese state militarised the cherry blossom aesthetic to build a resonance machine between the totalitarian state apparatus and the cultural segmentations of Japanese society. In turning that aesthetic to a purely military connotation, a line of abolition was constructed on its line of flight, which resulted in the liberation of a war-machine that dragged the entire state to the very brink of abolition.

There should be no doubt of the important differences that distinguish the fascist suicide states of Germany and Japan. Inasmuch as the Nazi totalitarian state was constructed by a war-machine (the National Socialist movement), which was then set to violent resonance within the state, it should be unsurprising that it was unable to pull back from the suicidal trajectory already inherent to its palingenic project. Meiji, realising that it must rein in its war-machine or follow its line of abolition, was able to return to its originary paranoiac foundations in the molar line (in the form of the emperor) to pull itself back from the brink of the abyss. Hitler, riding at the head of the war-machine, thrust on into utter desolation. This confirms that challenging paranoia with lines of flight is never sufficient. The suicidal danger that is proper to lines of flight is even more terrifying than the centralised power built on a conjugation of the molar and molecular, which was paradoxically, in the end, to *save* Japan from self-abolition.

Conclusion

> We cannot say that one of these three lines is bad and another good, by nature and necessarily. The study of the dangers of each line is the object of pragmatics or schizoanalysis, to the extent that it undertakes not to represent, interpret, or symbolize, but only to draw maps, marking their mixture as well as their distinctions.
>
> (Deleuze and Guattari 2004b: 250)

It should be clear from this chapter that mobilising Deleuze and Guattari's 'theory of fascism' need not be reduced to searching out events that directly repeat the Nazi rise to power. Rather, their cartographical schema enjoins us to map fascisms in terms of their contingent assemblage of the danger of all three lines of the political: molar, molecular and flight.

Holland argues that the rise of the Bush regime demonstrates that a late-modern capitalist *post-fascist regime* can collapse or regress into *fascism-proper*: 'Postfascism can in certain circumstances give way to a resurgence of something like old-fashioned fascism' (Holland 2008: 94). This argument is put to the service of a partisan politics, whereby Holland contrasts the 'old-fashioned fascism' of the Bush Republicans with the 'post-fascist' biopolitics of the Clinton Democrats. Indeed, he argues that the palingenic scapegoating of the Bush regime renders the subtler disciplinarity of post-fascism relatively preferable.

To some extent Holland is surely right to direct our attention to the paranoiac power of the religious-conservative resonance machine in the United States. Such totalitarian-religious political assemblages may conjugate their molar and molecular lines to build machines that seem to approach the status of fascist phenomena (as in Iran, for example), but to reduce, as Holland does, the third fascist line in Deleuze and Guattari's schema to a contingency of Nazism is to miss a crucial dimension of their political cartography of fascism as entailing *both* reterritorialisations and deterritorialisations. This has determinant significance if we are to extend their theory of fascism whilst remaining faithful to their brief comments in *A Thousand Plateaus* about the 'post-fascist' assemblage of *contemporary* politics.

Having disaggregated the suicidal line from the peculiarities of the Nazi fascist event by outlining its corresponding function in the Meiji fascist event, we must now set out to chart its evolutionary trajectory into the present day. Deleuze and Guattari directly followed their analysis of fascism with an account of the historical mutations which took place on its third line (pure war) after the end of the Second World War. They are explicit that fascist 'suicidal states' were 'the child precursors' of a *global politics of post-fascist suicide* that renders such territorial formations increasingly obsolete, initially, but not necessarily conclusively, through the terrifying pure-peace of nuclear deterrence. For Deleuze and Guattari, *state* fascism cannot simply be recapitulated because the suicidal line of flight serves new functions within the global assemblage. Deleuze and Guattari argued, following Virilio, that the bipolar war-machine of nuclear deterrence set up a suicidal global regime of 'pure-peace' that categorically displaces the suicidal national politics of fascistic 'total-war' (Deleuze and Guattari 2004b: 465, 516).

The terrifying cold peace of deterrence has now passed, but this certainly does not mean that the third line has *disappeared* from contemporary politics. It is rather conjugated anew. Deleuze and Guattari's statement that late-capitalist global order is 'post-fascist' is explicitly *not* positing the rise of a non-fascist order. Rather fascism continues directly into the post-fascist assemblage by way of global innovations of the suicidal line of flight. The fascist line of flight (as total war) mutates, via the Cold War, into what suggestively they term a 'new conception of security as materialised war, as organised insecurity or molecularized, distributed, programmed catastrophe', under which 'the enemy' is now defined precisely by its lack of specificity, as a register of disorder *per se* (Deleuze and Guattari 2004b: 516). Holland is ill-advised to search for the legacy of fascism only in its national repetition. He may well find here the echoes of the first two lines resonating, but they do so today within the framework of a global war-machine that has transformed state apparatus into cogs of its global bio-security mechanism (see Hardt and Negri 2000; Dillon and Reid 2009). Any contemporary fascism must be mapped in its relationship to this problematic.

This chapter has limited itself to elucidating and provisionally confirming the utility of Deleuze and Guattari's cartography of three fascist lines. By affirming the validity of the schema in its original format, against critiques such as Holland's (2008), it has re-opened the space for us to chart contemporary fascist re-assemblages of the three lines in Deleuze and Guattari's cartographic schema. Under the contemporary global regime of catastrophic bio-insecurity, territorial conjugations of the molar and molecular (in America and elsewhere) must be reinterpreted as moving parts in a global war-machine that over-determines them. If we wish to think about 'fascism today' with Deleuze and Guattari we cannot neglect its fundamental relationship to the protean *global politics of suicide* at work in this 'Anthropocene era' (Zizek 2010: 189). Without doubt, broader questions concerning the relationship between politics and suicide in the work of Deleuze and Guattari call for further *critical* elaboration, but if we are to mobilise their cartography in search of fascisms today the third suicidal line cannot be neglected.

Notes

1 Deleuze explicitly states, in his dialogue with Claire Parnet (2002), that suicidal lines of flight are not limited to the molar/molecular short-circuiting that assembles fascist suicide-*states*.
2 Though National Socialist state propaganda certainly deployed an ideology of 'glorious death for the fatherland', as exemplified in Munich's Tomb of the Martyrs.
3 On this note, Deleuze and Guattari argue that suicidal lines of flight emerge in various, non-fascist, assemblages.
4 What Deleuze would term a 'virtual' condition.
5 It is linked to a measurable rise in 'psychoneurotic illness' amongst the US troops at the time: R. O'Neill, *Suicide Squads: Axis and Allied Special Attack Weapons of World War II: Their Development and Their Missions* (Slamander Books Ltd, 1981).
6 Indeed, Virilio's claim that the Nazi suicide state is derivable solely from Hitler's telegram 71 suggests that Holland's charge of historical reductionism may well be more valid as a critique of Virilio than of Deleuze and Guattari.

References

Benedict, R. *The Chrysanthemum and the Sword* (New York: New American Library, 1967)
Deleuze, G. *Many Politics. Dialogues II*, ed. C. Parnet (Continuum, 2002)

Deleuze, G. and Guattari, F. *Anti-Oedipus* (London: Continuum, 2004a)

——*A Thousand Plateaus: Capitalism and Schizophrenia* (London: Continuum, 2004b)

Dillon, M. and Reid, J. *The Liberal Way of War: Killing to Make Life Live* (London and New York: Routledge, 2009)

Hardt, M. and Negri, A. *Empire* (Cambridge, Mass.: Harvard University Press, 2000)

Holland, E. 'Schizoanalysis, Nomadology, Fascism. Deleuze and Politics', in I. Buchanan and N. Thoburn (eds) *Deleuze & Politics* (Edinburgh: Edinburgh University Press, 2008)

Hoyt, E.P. *The Kamikazes* (Robert Hale Ltd, 1983)

Inoguchi, R. and Nakajima, T., with Pineau, R. *The Divine Wind: Japan's Kamikaze Force in World War II* (Toronto and London: Bantam, 1978)

Lamont-Brown, R. *Kamikaze: Japan's Suicide Samurai* (London: Arms and Armour Press, 1997)

Land, N. 'Making it with Death: Remarks on Thanatos and Desiring-production' (*Journal of the British Society of Phenomenology* Vol.24, No.1, 1993)

Morris, I. *The Nobility of Failure: Tragic Heroes in the History of Japan* (Secker and Warburg, 1975)

Ohnuki-Tierney, E. *Kamikaze, Cherry Blossoms and Nationalisms: The Militarisation of Aesthetics in Japanese History* (Chicago and London: University of Chicago Press, 2002)

O'Neill, R. *Suicide Squads: Axis and Allied Special Attack Weapons of World War II: Their Development and Their Missions* (Slamander Books Ltd, 1981)

Protevi, J. 'A Problem of Pure Matter: Fascist Nihilism in *A Thousand Plateaus*', in K.A. Pearson and D. Morgan (eds) *Nihilism Now! Monsters or Energy* (London and New York: Macmillan Press, 2000)

——'A Problem of Pure Matter: Fascist Nihilism', in K.A. Pearson and D. Morgan (eds) *A Thousand Plateaus. Nihilism! Monsters or Energy* (London and New York: Macmillan Press Ltd, 2001)

Rees, D. *The Defeat of Japan* (Praeger, 1997)

Reid, J. *The Biopolitics of the War on Terror: Life Struggles, Liberal Modernity and the Defence of Logistical Societies* (Manchester: Manchester University Press, 2006)

Theweleit, K. *Male Fantasies* (Cambridge: Polity, 1987)

Thoburn, N. 'What is a Militant?' in I. Buchanan and N. Thoburn (eds) *Deleuze and Politics* (Edinburgh: Edinburgh University Press, 2008)

Virilio, P. *The Suicidal State. The Virilio Reader*, ed. J. DerDerian (Oxford: Blackwell, 1998)

Virilio, P. and Lotringer, S. *Pure War* (New York: Semiotext(e), 1997)

Zeiler, T.W. *Unconditional Defeat: Japan, America and the End of World War II* (Scholarly Resources In, 2004)

Zizek, S. *Living in the End Times* (London: Verso, 2010)

9   Fascism, France and film

Ruth Kitchen

This chapter examines the questions of fascist violence and aesthetics in French cultural memory through the lens of post-war French film. It interrogates the problem of 'agent-less' violence and the lack of affect at work in fascist discourses. In *Cinema 2*, Gilles Deleuze argues for the potential of 'free indirect vision' in post-war cinema in which the confrontation between the sound image and the visual image allows the direct time-image to speak itself. This brings alongside the creation of an event by the sound image through the act of myth making or storytelling with the burial of that event in the 'any-space whatever' of the visual image (Deleuze 1989: 153, 183, 279) and liberates an affirmatory politics of the sound and the visual image which 'connects them to each other in the incommensurable relation of an irrational cut, the right side and its obverse, the outside and inside' (Deleuze 1989: 279). Although Deleuze's reading of the time-image in post-war cinema offers resistance to fascist tendencies, the cinematic image also has the potential for presenting, mediating and enacting further fascist violence.

In *A Thousand Plateaus*, Deleuze and Guattari identify four vectors or 'dangers' that give rise to and are identifiable in fascism: 'Fear then Clarity, then Power and finally the great Disgust, the longing to kill and die, the Passion for abolition' (Deleuze and Guattari 2004: 250). These vectors of fascism will be examined through the analysis of two French films, *Le Corbeau* (1943), in English *The Raven*, and *Caché* (2005), in English *Hidden*.[1]

Although they issue from different times and political circumstances, both films reveal the bleak trajectories of fascist violence. The fascist violence operating in Occupied France is tacitly alluded to in *Le Corbeau* and the memory of France's brutal oppression of those supporting and fighting for Algerian liberation is implicitly referred to in *Hidden*. These narratives and periods in French political and cultural history are connected by a cinematic aesthetic that chimes with the four 'dangers' of fascism described by Deleuze and Guattari. Although pertaining to different historical moments and political struggles, the *microfascisms* that become visible through the narrative and cinematic techniques employed by both films, invoke the spirals of shame and entrapment that reveal resonances between the vectors of current and future fascism and those of the past. The chapter will explore how the concepts of being on the inside, an 'insider', and being excluded, or an 'outsider' (*étranger*) are fusional components of fascist discourses visible in contemporary constructions of political identity and are also intimately connected with past cultural history and questions of agency and complicity.

The propensity for fascism lies in us all. In *The War: A Memoir*, a fictional journal documenting the real-life return of Duras's husband Robert Antelme from Dachau concentration camp, French writer Marguerite Duras writes that Europeans belong both to the race of Nazi perpetrators and to their Jewish, political and ethnic victims. In response to Duras's statement, French literary critic Martin Crowley observes: 'One can hardly be comfortable ... with the notion that a torturer's denial of his victim's humanity in fact affirms this humanity as shared' (Crowley 2000: 169). This implies that in the post-war world, any definition of human responsibility must include the characteristic features of Nazism because while fascist ideology sought to deny humanity, the acts of inhumanity it carried out were inscribed within the sphere of humanity. Duras's narrator is therefore proposing a shared responsibility for the crimes of National Socialism that forecloses the question of agency.[2] The issue of agency is central to the legacy and aesthetics of fascist violence. Questions of agency and responsibility for such acts can therefore only be addressed when the tendency to deny a common bond of humanity is considered part of the human condition. In *Cinema 2*, Deleuze argues that in the post-war period, cinema changes from being a cohesive representation of the world, 'the whole was the open', to a fragmented presentation of unconnected images the mediation of which the filmmaker no longer controls: 'the whole is the outside' (Deleuze 1989: 179).

> The author expresses himself through the intercession of an autonomous, independent character other than the author or any role fixed by the author, or the character acts and speaks himself as if his own gestures and words were already reported by a third party.
>
> (Deleuze 1989: 183)

For Deleuze, this shift has the effect of liberating cinematic aesthetics. However, this change in post-war aesthetics also mirrors a post-Fascist problem of 'agent-less' violence and lack of affect. In *A Thousand Plateaus*, Deleuze and Guattari assert that the potential towards fascism in the form of *microfascisms* can spring up indiscriminately regardless of religion, cultural background or nationality.[3] For France, the fascist violence experienced as a result of the German Occupation during the Second World War had a lasting cultural effect leaving traces in both thought and aesthetics. These memories returned powerfully during France's war in Algeria, when France, a nation formerly subjugated to German fascism, became the brutal suppressor of Algerian liberty. In April 1961 De Gaulle invoked Article 16 to declare a state of emergency in response to the increasingly aggravated outbreaks of violence caused by opposition to the war (Agamben 2005: 14). In his theory of multidirectional cultural discourses of aesthetics, Michael Rothberg writes that the use of torture in Algeria re-awoke memories and echoes of the acts of inhumanity committed by the Germans during the Occupation among former members of the Resistance and, perhaps more surprisingly, state officials:

> in submitting his resignation in 1957, the secretary general of the police in Algiers, Paul Teitgen, a former deportee, wrote that he recognized in Algeria 'profound traces ... of the torture that fourteen years ago I personally suffered in the basements of the Gestapo in Nancy'.
>
> (Rothberg 2009: 193)

There is a cultural resonance between the scars of witness, exposure to or involvement in acts of fascist violence during the German Occupation and those of colonial torture and oppression during the Algerian War, as French cultural critic Max Silverman points out:

> the interconnections between fascism and colonialism and between anti-semitism and colonial racism perceived by post-war theorists of racialized violence have for long fascinated a number of writers, filmmakers and other creative artists in post-war France, yet their works are not often received from this point of view, Alain Resnais' classic early film on the camps, *Nuit et brouillard* (1955), is both an evocation of the radical nature of horror and a parable for the war in Algeria. In the same year, Driss Charibi's novel *Les Boucs*, one of the first post-war novels treating anti-Arab racism alongside the horrors of the war (in the figure of Isabelle).
>
> (Silverman 2008: 418–19)

More recently, in 2002, the success of Jean-Marie Le Pen's National Front (FN) party in the first round of the French elections revealed the weighty support behind the far right in France. On the subject of fascism in France, Robert Paxton, the American historian known for his influential work on Vichy France, contrasts French support for the FN with the British National Party (BNP) (Paxton 2004).[4] Paxton observes that the aggressive and transparent model of fascism presented by the BNP has hindered the party's success, whereas in France, as in the Netherlands, far-right parties have sought to become palatable to the public and have consequently won popularity. Further debate about the undercurrent of fascism and implicit political injustice inherent in the French state was raised by the 2005 riots, when youths in the suburbs rioted, clashing with police and setting cars on fire, following the death of three youths of French-Algerian descent who died from electrocution on an electric fence as the result of a police chase (Emery 2010; Murphy 2011). In his exploration of different manifestations of French fascism throughout the twentieth century, Brian Jenkins observes that fascism is amorphous and multifaceted:

> Fascism comes in different national guises, changes shape and it moves through the phases of ideology-movement-regime, interacts with other movements, adapts to shifting conjuncture.
>
> (Jenkins 2005: 209)

Discourses of present-day fascist violence and its resonances with past fascism are a recurring theme in French cultural production to the present day (Sansal 2008; Littell 2006; Miller 2007; Paquet-Brenner 2010).

Fear

Deleuze and Guattari write that the first danger of fascism is fear: fear of the loss of security or stability (Deleuze and Guattari 2004: 250). Fear becomes visible in both films through the existence of a perceived threat to security and the culture of suspicion and surveillance that sparks further fear in turn. The corrosive cycle of fear and surveillance is endemic to and a product of fascist ideology. It feeds the steadily growing sense of strained anxiety that personal, social and state security is somehow being eroded. Deleuze and Guattari cite Daniel Guérin who claims that Hitler was able to seize power because the micro-organizations created by his followers presented him with 'an unequalled, irreplaceable ability to penetrate every cell of society' (Deleuze and Guattari 2004: 236). This claim conversely brings alongside the notion of the ever-watchful eye of the authoritarian state, famously theorized by Foucault in the Panopticon, with the idea that somebody may be watching not to enforce the law but to infringe it. In *Cinema 2*, Deleuze observes that the difference between pre- and post-war cinema is the 'rise of situations to which one can no longer react'. This leads to the seer, *voyant*, replacing the agent, *actant* (Deleuze 1989: 272). In *The Raven*, the scene in which Dr Germain, the town newcomer and main protagonist, receives his first letter is shot through the keyhole from the perspective of Rolande, a snooping teenage girl. Effectively, the spying camera eye captures and enables a sliding axis of active and passive witness that creates the atmosphere of secrecy and surveillance, which permeates the action. The letters of denunciation issue from a mysterious figure, The Raven, who is at once considered an outsider to the community and yet holds detailed insider knowledge of seemingly everyone's affairs. It transpires that all of the letters contain at least a grain of truth. The fear created by this unnameable insider 'other' creates guilt and secrecy and closes down communication, generating further suspicion. Vorzet, the flamboyant psychiatrist and husband of Laura, the woman with whom the letters accuse the protagonist, town newcomer Doctor Germain, of having an affair, advises Germain not to trust anyone. Not only does the oppressive silence of the population communicate suspicion, but it also suggests there are unspoken secrets to hide. In the letters, The Raven claims that he is purging society of its moral debauchery. However, the effect of the poison-pen revelations is progressively to unravel the social fabric of rural St Robin by revealing that a vast swath of its inhabitants from the highest to the lowest echelons of society are involved in socially, ethically, politically and legally compromising activities. Although The Raven is a self-appointed champion of moral virtue, he is acting outside the jurisdiction of the law. He is perceived therefore as an *insider-other*, a rogue element, which has penetrated the town's defences and must be flushed out.

Hidden opens with a static shot of the rue d'Iris looking towards a classic Parisian apartment building in the tranquil and affluent thirteenth district of the city. The rumble of distant traffic and early morning birdsong are broken only by the occasional cyclist, pedestrian, or passing car. However, as the minutes pass the stasis and banality of this scene becomes increasingly unsettling. French cultural critic Libby Saxton observes: 'we wonder who else, besides us, might be looking, and why' (Saxton 2007: 7). Our belief that we are watching the opening scene of the film is shattered by the discovery that we, like Georges and Anne, the film's protagonists, are watching a filmed recording of the outside of their apartment. The blurring of film and reality is achieved by Haneke's election to shoot the film on high-definition video making the tapes indistinct from real cinematic time. This 'framing' technique continues throughout the film. The seamless splicing of surveillance video footage into the film causes the viewer to begin to mistrust and interrogate the image. As in *The Raven*, there is a disturbing instability and lack of security conveyed by the uncertain temporal and spatial positioning of both protagonists and viewers. In *Hidden* this feeds a sense of growing paranoia about who is watching and who is being watched. The viewer is placed on the inside, and becomes conscious that he or she is not only subject but also an object of the gaze. The camera eye rigidly limits the field of vision, forbidding off-screen sight and increasing the sense of impossibility of escape from the controlling eye and delimiting the possibility of accessing the 'bigger picture' to contextualize the meaning of minutiae. The camera's oppressive gaze composes an incomplete picture that is both suspicious and disconcerting. In agreement with Saxton's reference to the 'out-of-field' vision in *Caché*,[5] French cultural critic Max Silverman adds that the image is only readable through a reconnection with the 'hors-champ':

> Those who have acquired a way of reading the image will realise that far from the ending withholding its hidden secret, it actually makes it readable, not in the sense of solving the whodunit (that is neither here nor there), but in terms of the transformation of the image from a screen to a Benjaminian constellation composed of complex interconnections between the visible and the 'hors champ' and between present and past.
>
> (Silverman 2010: 63)

Although both Saxton and Silverman refer to the 'hors-champ' as a stabilizing resource that has the potential to 're'-frame the present in light of the past, Deleuze asserts that in post-war cinema, 'there is no out-of-field to inhabit' (Deleuze 1989: 278). Contextualization or mediation in this sense is therefore prohibited. The cinematic trick of the camera eye that delimits space and, by implication, time (that is, the connection between past and present), causes the audience to reassess their position in relation to the image. No longer an agent, 'actant' in control of the image but instead a seer, 'voyant', a simultaneously active *and* passive witness of the film, the viewer becomes increasingly aware of his or her complicity in the action being played out on the screen.

Clarity

The movement of clarity is the second vector of fascism. Deleuze and Guattari observe that through vision and sounds we begin to perceive spaces or holes permeating structures that previously appeared solid:

> That is precisely what clarity is: the distinctions that appear in what used to seem full, the holes in what used to be compact; and conversely, where just before we saw end points of clear-cut segments, now there are indistinct fringes, encroachments, overlappings, migrations, acts of segmentation that no longer coincide with the rigid segmentarity. Everything now appears supple, with holes in fullness, nebulas in forms and flutter in lines. Everything has the clarity of a microscope. We think we have understood everything, and draw conclusions.
>
> (Deleuze and Guattari 2004: 251)

With clarity comes the realization that there are breaches in personal and societal structures results in the deterioration of shared common values and sense of community. The loss of belief in the transparency and integrity of the law translates into the breakdown of law and objective morality. We are both agents *and* objects enmeshed in and directed by quantum flows. In his theory of the effects and management of violence in ancient societies, the French cultural anthropologist, René Girard, uses the term 'sacrificial crisis' to signal a period of chaos, violence and revenge brought about by a lack of difference between the 'pure' and the 'impure', or 'good' and 'evil'. As these spaces or holes erase the distinctions between individuals, mediation fails. There is no one to act as mediator. This heralds the onset of Agamben's 'state of exception'. Agamben asserts that the situation of 'iustitium' in Roman law is aligned with the 'state of exception' or emergency.

> a citizen who acts during *iustitium* neither executes nor transgresses a law but *inexecutes* [insegue] it. His actions, in this sense, are mere facts, the appraisal of which, once the *iustitium* is expired, will depend on the circumstances. But as long as the *iustitium* lasts, they will be absolutely undecidable, and the definition of their nature – whether executive or transgressive, and, in the extreme case, whether human or bestial, or divine – will lie beyond the sphere of the law.
>
> (Agamben 2005: 50)

By exploring the shift in the etymology of 'iustitium', which changes from designating a 'state of exception' to the public mourning over the death of the sovereign, Agamben locates the state of exception, lawlessness or 'anomie', in the sovereign or legal body, 'nomos'.

> If the sovereign is a living nomos, and if, for this reason anomie and nomos perfectly coincide in his person, then anarchy (which threatens to loose itself in the city upon the sovereign's death, which is to say, when the nexus that joins it to the law is severed) must be ritualized and controlled, transforming the state of exception into public mourning and mourning into *iustitium*.
>
> (Agamben 2005: 70)

The result of the loss of the sovereign results in 'charivari', the suspension of normal legal and social structures and hierarchies that accompanies upheavals in political or social order. This is sometimes celebrated by publicly performed parodies of law and justice. This moment brings about the blurring of all differences already observed by Deleuze and Guattari and Girard. In *The Raven*, law and order is effectively erased by the growing frenzy for denunciation as no one is shown to be above suspicion. The town's authority figures and care givers are slandered. The mayor is accused of corruption and the chief doctor of the hospital and the hospital nurse are accused of malpractice. The post office is inundated with letters addressed in Raven-style handwriting, leading a post room worker to comment that 'everyone is at it'. In *Hidden*, although initially portrayed as victimized subject of surveillance, Georges, quickly becomes a suspect. His dismissal of the first tape as a teenage prank, his refusal of Anne's suggestion that they call the police, and later, the muted intimation that he may know the provenance of the tapes and the violent child-like pictures that accompany them suggest that he is hiding something. Similarly, other characters, Anne, Pierrot, Majid and Majid's son, flatly deny accusations made against them but also refuse to answer probing questions or to provide evidence to the contrary. In *The Raven* and *Hidden* cracks appear in familial and social units. Isolation reigns. The 'clarity' created by the blurring of differences is a challenge to the established ethical order. The characters' motivations and integrity come under scrutiny, intensifying the discourse surrounding belonging and 'otherness' as it becomes increasingly unclear who is on the inside 'in the know', and who remains outside 'in the dark'. The permeation and fluidity of these boundaries unleashes a sense of unbounded threat and terror and engenders violence. In Deleuze and Guattari's depiction of 'clarity' chaos reigns and anyone can be a policeman or an SS.

> Instead of the great paranoid fear, we are trapped in a thousand little monomanias, self-evident truth and clarities that gush from very black hole and no longer form a system but are only rumble and buzz, blinding light giving any and everybody the mission of self-appointed judge,

dispenser of justice, policeman, neighborhood SS man. We have overcome fear, we have sailed from the shores of security, only to enter a system
that is no less concentricized, no less organized: the system of petty insecurities that leads everyone to their own black hole in which to turn
dangerous, possessing a clarity on their situation, role, and mission even
more disturbing than the certitudes of the first line.

(Deleuze and Guattari 2004: 251)

Clarity, as a fascist line of flight, can therefore be seen to permeate the fixed
social boundaries of home, work and the 'outside'. The eradication of difference
uproots former solidarities and undermines social and legal infrastructures
challenging their ethical precepts and asserting the need for radical action
through the personal dispensation of justice. Paxton observes that fascism seeks
to eradicate all borders between the public and the private (Paxton 2004). In
Hidden, the borders between personal and private spaces are persistently trans-
gressed. After Georges tracks down and threatens Majid and his unnamed son
in their home, Majid's son intercepts Georges at his workplace and confronts
him about his harassment of their family. Later, when Pierrot, Georges's son
disappears, Georges leads the police to Majid's flat in Romainville, where the
police roughly apprehend Majid and his son. French cultural critic, Jefferson
Kline observes:

Haneke seems to bring the film's fictional events into interpretative arrangement not only with the long tradition of the Franco-Arab conflict, but
also with the current dynamics of the 'war on terror'.

(Kline 2010: 588)

The analogy of contagion used in both films is suggestive of the germinant
potential of microfascisms to permeate all strata and perceived 'boundaries'
of society. Contagion appears in the form of information. In *The Raven*, the
'information' contained in the letters literally 'informs on' other members of
the community and instigates further acts of community-orchestrated 'agent-
less' violence. Vorzet plots the town's frenzy for denunciation on a chart likening
the spikes and falls in letter sending to the temperature of a feverish patient.
In *Hidden*, 'information' takes the form of visual media – the videotapes,
cinema and television – during Georges and Anne's anxious discussion about
their son Pierrot's failure to return home, the television news, in the background,
flashes images into the family home of the war in Iraq, torture in Abu Ghraib
and the Asian bird flu epidemic. The television screen is framed by the ceiling-
to-floor bookshelves that decorate the dining room, mirroring the set of the
literary TV show that Georges presents. It is in the report on the threat of a
global bird flu pandemic that the word *caché* (hidden), the film's title, is blurted
into the couple's dining room. Here fascist lines of flight permeate the 'inside-
outside' boundaries of the family's social, cultural and personal space spreading
contagion or virus. As Deleuze and Guattari point out, 'What makes fascism

dangerous is its molecular or micropolitical power, for it is a mass movement: a cancerous body rather than a totalitarian organism' (Deleuze and Guattari 2004: 236). This plague-like power of fascism is vividly evoked by the last lines of Albert Camus's *The Plague*, where Dr Rieux observes the town's people's jubilation that the plague, widely considered to stand as an allegory for Nazi oppression, has ended. Rieux observes that the plague can never be truly expelled but instead lies dormant within the fabric of society.[6] The cultural implications of Western microfascist complicity in the occupation of Iraq, acts of torture carried out by American soldiers and the endemic nature of a potential global pandemic resonate powerfully with Georges and Anne's feeling of fearful impotence at their son's potential abduction by their stalker. However, in both films the superfluity of information in text and image suggests not only the impossibility of holing up the spaces and fluidity of the structures underpinning individual and societal relations by revealing that the perceived dividing lines between the inner worlds and the world outside are organic and permeable, but also reveals the emptiness of the information that informs us of this. In *Cinema 2*, Deleuze observes that the 'nullity of information must be overturned in order to defeat Hitler' (Deleuze 1989: 269). 'Information' in neither film is in fact the creator of chaos but rather a conduit that reveals the porous and open boundaries within individual, social and cultural identities and societal structures. However, the becoming viral of information releases its potential as object *and* vehicle of fascist violence.

Power

'Power', the third danger identified by Deleuze and Guattari, relates to the questions of agency, complicity and impotence. Deleuze and Guattari observe that power and impotence are alternating currents that run between and connect the poles of power.

> Every man of power jumps from one line to the other alternating between a petty and grandiloquent style, drugstore demagoguery and the imperialism of the high-ranking government man. But this whole chain and web of power is immersed in a world of mutant flows that eludes them. It is precisely its impotence that makes power so dangerous.
>
> (Deleuze and Guattari 2004: 252)

In the films, the notion of power is related to both personal and cultural history. Past power dynamics determine present behaviours and choices. This bears loaded implications for the future. In *The Raven*, rather than revealing the secret 'true morality' of the heavily stereotyped characters, Clouzot fills in the caricatures bringing them to life. It transpires that Germain, the morally conservative scientist, is concealing his former identity as a famous brain surgeon, following the tragic and traumatic death of both his wife and first child in childbirth. As a result, he demonstrates immense difficulty in forming emotional attachments, declaring at one point that he has 'neither friends nor enemies'. It turns out that Denise, the vampish femme fatale, has conducted numerous love affairs in an attempt to allay feelings of ugliness and bitterness about her ugly, deformed clubfoot, which is the result of a childhood accident. Marie Corbin, the spinster nurse, who is initially suspicious of Germain's intentions towards her sister Laura and of Laura's responsiveness to his advances, is revealed to harbour real feelings of jealousy towards her sister, who has married Vorzet, Marie's former fiancé. The characters' present actions are therefore determined by their pasts. These histories are concealed, however, because their revelation could potentially sow seeds of suspicion about whether the motivating force behind the malicious letter writing may be the settling of old scores. The characters are rendered impotent and mute by past events over which they have no power. It is notable that the film's frame of reference extends beyond the screen to Occupied France, where the political choices of the film's audience were also being stifled and suppressed by Raven-like Nazi control. The film is further steeped in questions about complicity and power as Henri-Georges Clouzot, the director, was working for Continental Films, an allegedly French company, which employed French actors and directors and produced French-language films, but was in fact financially supported by Goebbels's propaganda ministry.[7] At the time of the film's release, despite being a huge success with audiences, *The Raven* was criticized by Vichy, the Resistance and the Germans.

> This was not a picture of healthy provincial life as Vichy conceived it, and it is not surprising that the film was criticized by the Vichy press for traducing all the icons of the National Revolution. Nor was the film ever released in Germany: it was judged to be morbid, and the authorities could not approve a film that implicitly criticized delation. But criticisms in the Resistance press were no less strident: it vilified the film for portraying such a debased image of France.
>
> (Jackson 2001: 325)[8]

The film, then, as a cultural object presents us with a complex web of power as it tells of the ethical uncertainty and feelings of impotence and complicity provoked by the presence of fascism.

In *Hidden*, Georges links the surveillance tapes and the disturbing child-like drawings of a child vomiting blood and a decapitated cockerel to his childhood. Georges's family took in a young Algerian boy called Majid after his parents, workers on the family estate, disappeared in the FLN pro-Algerian independence protest in Paris on 17 October 1961. It is inferred that Georges, then a jealous six-year-old unwilling to share his home, contrived to and succeeded in getting rid of Majid by telling his parents that Majid was vomiting blood and that he had threatened Georges with an axe. The suspected return of this past locks Georges into a disturbed but determined silence about this memory, which is indeed also silenced in the film, where it is only alluded to through flashbacks and in Georges's nightmares. The bigger 'story', relating to the historical and cultural backdrop of France's war against Algeria, the torture of insurgents by the French military and the bloody suppression of the 17 October pro-FLN demonstration by the Paris police is also left unspoken.[9] It is these events that are alluded to and concealed by the film's title, *Hidden*, *Caché*. Thus while they are implicitly gestured to through the unfolding of the narrative, they are left unexplored. However, the splicing of dissonant and unrelated images of the past into the contemporary present of the film establishes connections between them. In *Cinema 2*, Deleuze observes, 'cuts or breaks in cinema have always formed the power of the continuous' (Deleuze 1989: 181). The film in fact mirrors how this event was suppressed in French cultural memory by the government, media and historians until the 1980s.[10]

Deleuze and Guattari write: 'it's too easy to be anti-fascist on the molar-level and not even see the fascist inside you' (Deleuze and Guattari 2004: 237). The eye of the film camera and the unseen observer or surveillance camera places the viewer under scrutiny as it also catches us in the act of looking. Saxton observes that the viewer's previously unquestioned sense of justice and moral authority is compromised by becoming aware of being seen watching. This predicament 'confronts us with uncomfortable questions about spectatorial complicity and agency' (Saxton 2007: 13). This makes the viewer not only ashamed and paranoid in the way described by Jean-Paul Sartre in his theory of the gaze, but also complicit in and impotent witness to acts of fascist violence and power (Sartre 1943: 275). Social theorist Martin Alonso cites humiliation as a social differentiator in movements of mass destruction, such as totalitarianism, colonialism and ethno-nationalism describing it as 'an emblem of asymmetry inherent to any form of domination for it entails the deepest treatment of dispossession and plundering, the one entailing dignity and honour' (Alonso 2011: 11). However, I would argue that it is in fact shame that provides this function by placing the witness in a position of active disempowerment. This aporia evokes the way in which the witness is simultaneously caught, compromised by and made complicit with the narrative structures and/or the acts of perpetrators. In his thesis on witness and the archive, Agamben notes that shame involves the subject being forced to bear witness to his or her own desubjectification:

> To be ashamed means to be consigned to something that cannot be assumed. But what cannot be assumed is not something external. Rather, it originates in our own intimacy; it is what is most intimate in us (for example our own psychological life). Here the 'I' is thus overcome by its own passivity, its ownmost sensibility; yet this expropriation and desubjectification is also an extreme and irreducible presence of the 'I' to itself. It is as if our consciousness collapsed and seeking to flee in all directions, were simultaneously summoned by an irrefutable order to be present at its own defacement, at the expropriation of what is most its own. In shame, the subject thus has no other content than its own desubjectification; it becomes witness

to its own disorder, its own oblivion as a subject. This double movement, which is both subjectification and desubjectification, is shame.

(Agamben 1999: 106)

It is this deep complicity forcing the witnessing of inhumanity in humanity that resonates with the idea of responsibility divorced from agency raised at the beginning of the chapter in relation to the writing of Marguerite Duras. Both films demonstrate the disturbing effects of fascist power on the characters in *The Raven* and *Hidden*, who are rendered impotent by the pervasive presence of the insider-outsider who enmeshes them in a network connecting an over-determined present with an inescapable past. Viewers are similarly compromised by and complicit in the fascist power dynamic of the camera and cinematography which renders them insider-outsiders in the filmic power discourse. Deleuze and Guattari write:

Only microfascism provides an answer to the global question: Why does desire desire its own repression, how can it desire its own repression? The masses certainly do not passively submit to power; nor do they 'want' to be repressed, in a kind of melancholic hysteria; nor are they pricked by an ideological lure. Desire is never separable from complex assemblages that necessarily tie into molecular levels, from microformations already shaping postures, attitudes, perceptions, expectations, semiotic systems, etc. Desire is never an undifferentiated instinctual energy, but itself results from a highly developed, engineered setup rich in interactions: a whole supple segmentarity that processes molecular energies and potentially gives a fascist determination.

(Deleuze and Guattari 2004: 236–37)

In both films, the desire for totalitarian-type oppression is borne out of the inextricable complicity of discovering oneself as an historical cog in the machine. Thus the dream of absolute disempowerment, which desires the negation of responsibility, emerges with the awareness of the potential revolutionary power of one's acts. The characters experience feelings of impotence and victimization as they become further enmeshed in the politics of power through acts of fascist violence. Here, we see the organic evolution of the fascist power dialectic. The suppression of the past and the violent mobilization of powerlessness as justification for current actions is evidence of this tendency. This vector makes victims into perpetrators and vice versa. Alonso illustrates the way in which the claim to collective victimhood promotes and excuses acts of violence in programs like *Lebensraum*, the *manifest destiny, la mission civilisatrice*, the *Full Spectrum Dominance* of the American neoconservative PNAC (Plan for a New American Century), *Greater Serbia, Eretz Israel*, to cite a few examples, 'sufferings real or perceived, have more power than joy to compact individuals into social blocks, on the one side, and to the comparative advantage of negative emotions on the other', thus 'the group provides a context that renders aggressive behaviour socially acceptable and normatively appropriate' (Alonso 2011: 15). In both films, characters attempt to renegotiate and seize power by reterritorializing fascist lines of flight through the persecution of scapegoats. In *The Raven*, realizing that they are failing in flushing out the letter writer, the town's people begin to pursue instead the main targets of The Raven's allegations. Thus nurse Marie Corbin is sacked and pursued from the hospital to her ransacked house by a jeering, violent mob, at which point she is apprehended and imprisoned. Similarly, the town council try to oust Dr Germain by attempting to trick him into performing an illegal abortion, a crime of which the letters accuse him. Finally, in an act of vengeance, the mother of a cancer patient who committed suicide after receiving a letter confirming his condition was terminal, murders Vorzet believing him to be The Raven. In *Hidden*, Georges determines that Majid is the source of the videotapes and pictures and embarks on a campaign of terror by tracking down and threatening both him and his son. Saxton observes:

> Ironically it is in the course of attempting to establish his innocence that Georges inadvertently reveals his guilt, and begins to merit punishment. The videotapes start to catch him out, capturing his contemptuous treatment of Majid and exposing his denials and protestations of ignorance as half-truths or, on occasion, barefaced lies. At stake here are not the falsehoods of a selfish six-year-old but an adult's refusal to confront and acknowledge responsibility for the consequences of his past actions.
>
> (Saxton 2007: 10)

These reterritorializing acts chime with René Girard's concept of the 'surrogate victim'. The 'surrogate victim' is an outsider already shunned, excluded, or in some way condemned by the community. The expulsion of the 'surrogate victim' offers a potential solution to the fear about the 'breach' of security by *microfascist* 'elements' and the porous boundaries and holes that have appeared in societal structures as a result. Individuals previously scattered by isolation, paranoia, aggressive protectionism and violence are united by the shared assault on a named individual who then assumes the status of a common enemy. In her work on genocide and collectively approved violence, Helen Fein coins the term 'universe of obligation' to designate those to whom we have commitments and for whom we feel responsible (Fein 1979). In this case, the 'surrogate victim' would not be included 'in' this universe. For Agamben, the state of exception 'iustitium', which suspends the law, creates a vacuum of power. It is in the struggle and search for the 'auctoritas'[11] that the persecution of the 'surrogate victim' occurs.

> It is as if the suspension of the law freed a force or a mystical element, a sort of legal *mana* (this expression is used by Wagenvoort to describe the Roman *auctoritas*) that both the ruling power and its adversaries, the constituted power as well as the constituent power, seek to appropriate.

Force of law that is separate from the law, floating *imperium* being-in-force [vigenza] without application, and more generally, the idea of a sort of 'degree zero' of the law – all these are fictions through which law attempts to encompass it own absence and appropriate the state of exception, or at least to assure itself a relation with it.

(Agamben 2005: 50)

In the state of lawlessness, 'inexecution' of the law against the 'surrogate victim' takes place (Agamben 2005: 50). The void that opens up within the law and political power also opens up the space of powerlessness to think that Deleuze, in *Cinema 2*, recognizes in Artaud (Deleuze 1989: 166). At this moment of 'inexecution' and 'powerlessness', we find the agent-less violence of victimization of the surrogate. In *The Raven*, the individuals selected are social outsider Marie Corbin, the stranger to the town Dr Germain, and finally Vorzet, the flamboyant and eccentric psychiatrist whose extreme relativism makes him an ethical outsider to the town's conservative way of life. In *Hidden*, Georges selects Majid, a cultural outsider, a first-generation, low-waged Arab-Algerian immigrant. The 'surrogate victim' becomes both the damned and the saviour of the persecutor(s). The punishment and expulsion of the surrogate unites and empowers the persecutor's enabling 're'-securitization through establishment of division and boundaries. The ejection of the allegedly pernicious but ultimately redemptive influence of the surrogate victim restores peace by (re)asserting societal and legal order. In other words, the selection and punishment of the surrogate victim enacts the unthought of thought, articulated by Deleuze in Artaud's reading of the 'powerless' subject of cinema.

Artaud never understood powerlessness to think as a simple inferiority which would strike us in relation to thought. It is part of thought, so that we should make our way of thinking from it, without claiming to be restoring an all-powerful thought. We should rather make use of this powerlessness to believe in life, and to discover the identity of thought and life.

(Deleuze 1989: 170)

However, in the case of these films, this does not reconnect us to thought but instead bears witness to and is complicit in 'agent-less' violence, to the very thing which Deleuze identifies in Artaud's celebration of cinema's rendering of the powerlessness to think: 'this central inhibition, of this internal collapse and formalization, of this "theft of thoughts" of which thought is a constant agent and victim' (Deleuze 1989: 166). Thus the community offsets the problem of real thought, which would force questions of agency and collective responsibility by designating and expelling or 'outing' the 'surrogate victim'. This collective externalization of the problem as a 'necessary evil' removes agency and the process of self-reflection and critical inquiry that would lead to the discovery that we are all located on the sliding axis that runs between surrogate victimhood and the perpetration of violent persecution.[12]

Lines of flight/lines of destruction

For Deleuze and Guattari the difference between totalitarianism and fascism lies on the line between orthodoxy and radicalism. 'Totalitarianism is quintessentially conservative. Fascism, on the other hand, involves a war machine' (Deleuze and Guattari 2004: 254). In other words, totalitarianism seeks to establish and preserve boundaries whereas fascism is dynamic and revolutionary, a plague-like power that can potentially infect anyone. Agamben cites Carl Schmitt, who claims that Hitler and Mussolini were 'quasi-dictators' as they allowed the legal framework of former governance to subsist alongside a constitution that was not legally formalized (Agamben 2005: 48). In other words, they were not dictators of the totalitarian model but rather fascist 'auctoritas' figures who brought stability to the 'iustitium' state of exception by re-appropriating the systems in place for their purposes. Although totalitarianism is perhaps desirable because it distances the question of personal responsibility, as we have already seen in the section on 'Power' and in the metaphor of contagion, fascism is instead pervasive. It creatively exploits the desire for reterritorialization by redrawing boundaries and difference for new political purpose. Paxton observes that 'Fascism in action looks much more like a network of relationships than a fixed essence' (Paxton 2004: 207). This active selection and practice of a code of extreme ethics plots leads us to Deleuze and Guattari's final danger: the line of flight that plots a trajectory of pure destruction. The fascist line of flight ends in annihilation of both the self and of others. Deleuze and Guattari write:

> The line of flight crossing the wall, getting out of the black holes, but instead of connecting with other lines and each time augmenting its valence, *turning to destruction, abolition pure and simple, the passion of abolition.*
> (Deleuze and Guattari 2004: 253)

They recall the Nazi announcement that the Socialist movement would bring wedding bells and death to Germany. The lines of flight that mobilize *microfascisms* are simultaneously the stirrers of mass movements and revolution. Elsewhere Deleuze and Guattari describe the transformational movement of a line of flight as a war machine. Only when the line turns to war as end does it take on a fascist nihilism thus losing all creative power and becoming bent purely on destruction.

> war is like the fall or failure of mutation, the only object left for the war machine after it has lost its power to change. War, it must be said, is only the abominable residue of the war machine, either after it has allowed itself to be appropriated by the State apparatus, or even worse, has constructed itself a State apparatus capable only of destruction. When this happens, the war machine no longer draws mutant line of flight, but a pure, cold line of abolition.
> (Deleuze and Guattari 2004: 253)

A permanent state of war is therefore both the end and necessary condition of fascism. Deleuze and Guattari observe the desolation and desperation generated by fascist movements: 'They themselves emanate a strange despair, like an odor of death and immolation, a state of war from which one returns broken' (Deleuze and Guattari 2004: 252).

This theme of destructive violence is borne out in *The Raven* by the earlier-mentioned suicide of one of the hospital patients after a letter from The Raven informs him that he has terminal cancer. This act bears the hallmark of despair and impotent resignation and submission to a greater force. In *Hidden*, Georges reacts to the horror of witnessing Majid slit his own throat by seeking out the dark, escapist sanctuary of the cinema. The security of filmic fiction literally screens Georges from reality. It satisfies a conservative orthodoxy providing a distance from the question of Georges's agency and complicity in Majid's death. However, *Hidden* does not provide such a distance. Cinema and digital culture are shown here to act against Deleuze's reading of Artaud. The unthinkingness of the characters' engagements with these media breeds affect-less microfascist tendencies. Once at home, Georges takes sleeping tablets, *cachets*, a further homonym of the film's title, in an attempt to distance consciousness of reality and conscience. Majid's suicide is shocking not only because the graphic throat-slitting scene is totally unanticipated but also because of the violence that emanates from this act. Previously we described Majid as a scapegoat, a victim of an *iustitium*, a state of exception that has wreaked chaos in Georges's world or a surrogate victim, to use Giraud's phrase, of Georges's microfascist tendencies. Yet, there is a further level to this act. Majid's suicide is borne out of desperation at the violent persecution to which Georges has subjected him as a cultural outsider both during their childhood and now again in their adult lives. In this sense, the nihilism that emanates from Majid's act aims at forcing Georges to face the consequences of his own campaign of terror through further horror. Majid's suicide plots a *microfascist* trajectory as it allows him to seize agency reterritorializing the *microfascism* demonstrated by Georges's acts by transforming it into his own deterritorializing fascist line. This movement coincides with Deleuze and Guattari's observation that, 'Suicide is presented not as a punishment but as the crowning glory of the death of others' (Deleuze and Guattari 2004: 254). It is pertinent to this argument that the viewer is also forced to witness the act of suicide as Majid gives no intimation of his intentions, thus there is no 'look away now' prelude to the act. As a consequence, like Georges, the audience is also forced into a shocked complicit collusion in Majid's suffering and death. In *The Raven*, the slitting of Vorzet's throat by the mother of the suicide victim in vengeance for her son's suicide must also be considered a fascist line of flight. While this act ends the film and Dr Germain declares that it solves the mystery, in fact it leaves a number of questions unanswered. Earlier in the film, Vorzet points out that it is highly unlikely that the 850 letters received during the two-month spate of denunciation were the work of just one person. Both Denise and Laura separately admit to writing letters and, at the height of the letter-writing frenzy, a post office worker observes that 'everyone is at it'. Although Vorzet dies at his desk writing a Raven-style letter declaring that the town's curse has been lifted, rather than an end to violence, I would suggest that this act symbolizes a mutation of the vector of microfascist violence. It perpetuates the cycle of violence by jumping the strain spiralling and transforming victim into perpetrator. It thus bears a latent, threatening legacy for the future. *The Raven* concludes with an over-the-shoulder shot of Dr Germain looking out from the window over Vorzet's desk, where the psychiatrist lies in a pool of blood, watching the suspected killer, the mother of the cancer patient, make her way down the sunny street. This open ending suggests a kind of 'going underground', which is, as we have observed, a germinant trait of *microfascisms*.

Fascist lines foster new violence and seed new *microfascisms*. Slavoj Zizek postures that the war on terror is not perhaps after all targeted at terrorists but at tacitly reterritorializing and consolidating the precepts of Western democracy and identity among Westerners by inflecting the rise of the anti-globalist movement with fears over security and power (Zizek 2004). Perhaps this is not even a distraction. By indulging in the bloody horror and the full and raw exposure of the Western masses to the 'deterritorializing' dissension and instability of the Middle East, the war on terror and now the Arab Spring make us treasure our own increasingly restricted freedoms and accept as a necessity the tightening control of their borders. In this vein, it is interesting to reflect on how the subversive and persistent deterritorializations and *micro-fascisms* of Occupied France implicitly illustrated in *The Raven* return in a different guise relating to the colonial and post-colonial debates of the 1960s and as part of a twenty-first-century discourse on cultural integration and Arab-Islamist terrorism in *Hidden*. This evolution of *microfascisms* resonates against the reterritorializations of French politico-cultural history by French historians such as Robert Aron (1958). However, the cultural inheritance of fascist complicities is clearly not limited to France alone. Paxton affirms that fascism exists within all democratic countries.

> 'Giving up free institutions,' especially the freedoms of unpopular groups, is recurrently attractive to citizens of Western democracies, including some Americans. We know from tracing its path that fascism does not require a spectacular 'march' on some capital to take root; seemingly anodyne decisions to tolerate lawless treatment of national 'enemies' is enough.
>
> (Paxton 2004: 220)

Hidden also provides insight into and critical commentary of other national histories and cultural memories beyond France, as Silverman observes:

> Haneke has argued that *Caché* works just as effectively as an indictment of other cultural heritages: 'I don't want my film to be seen as specifically about a French problem. It seems to me that, in every country, there are dark corners – dark stains where questions of collective guilt become

important. I'm sure in the United States there are other parallel examples
of dark stains on the collective unconscious.'

(Silverman 2010: 63, note 4)

Haneke's 2010 film *The White Ribbon* implicitly explores the reasons behind the
rise of Nazism in Germany though the lens of a series of violent events in a small
village at the eve of the First World War that appear to have been orchestrated by
the local children. Similarly, Haneke observes that this film is not simply an
indictment of Germany's past but also serves as an allegory for harrowing and
shameful events and periods in other countries' pasts (Cinefilms 2010).

So far, in this analysis of Deleuze and Guattari's four dangers of fascism we
have followed lines that lead to destruction. In concluding, I would like to
consider the potential for creative and revolutionary lines of flight within the
fascist discourse of *The Raven* and *Hidden*. Children appear in the final scenes
of both films. In *The Raven*, the mother of the suicide victim passes children
playing as she walks down the street and away from the murder scene. French
cultural critic Chris Lloyd proffers that these children convey a sense of hope-
fulness for the future (Lloyd 2007: 52). *Hidden* ends with a seemingly innocuous
long shot of the steps of (Georges's son) Pierrot's high school. However,
careful viewing reveals Pierrot sitting on the steps in conversation with Majid's
son. There has been no previous intimation that the boys know each other. The
ambiguity of this scene is much debated. I would suggest that both film endings
could augur positively or negatively for the future. However what is interesting
about the ending of both films is the subtle interjection of chance into narratives
that appear cripplingly over-determined by microfascist lines. In *The Raven*, the
children in the street are playing dice. In *Hidden*, the boys are sitting on the steps
of the Stéphane Mallarmé high school. Both references bring to mind Mallarmé's
influential experimental poem *A Throw of the Dice Never Eliminates Chance*.
In *Difference and Repetition*, Deleuze alludes to this poem when he describes
how the divine game of chance (re)opens the possibility of freedom:

> First, there is no pre-existent rule, since the game includes its own rules.
> As a result, every time, the whole of chance is affirmed in a necessarily
> winning throw. Nothing is exempt from the game: consequences are not
> subtracted from chance by connecting them with a hypothetical necessity
> which would tie them to a determinate fragment; on the contrary, they
> are adequate to the whole of chance, which retains and subdivides all
> possible consequences ... This is the point at which the ultimate origin is
> overturned into an absence of origin (in the always displaced circle of the
> eternal return). An aleatory point is displaced through all the points on
> the dice, as though one time for all times. These different throws which
> invent their own rules and compose the unique throw with multiple forms
> and within the eternal return are so many imperative questions subtended
> by a single response which leaves them open and never closes them.

(Deleuze 2001: 353–54)

The revolutionary dice roll describes the trajectory of a war machine and line of flight that is creative rather than nihilistic. Badiou describes this movement as 'an ethic of truths' using the illustration of cultural renaissance.[13] The films reveal how past fascist and microfascist complicity contrives to shame and terrorize us, engraining fascist violence deeper into our cultural inheritance. This either silences our voices making us 'outsiders' or the 'guilty' scapegoats of contemporary political discourse, or we in turn become 'insiders' the new terrorists of nihilism. The aesthetics of microfascism revealed in *The Raven* and *Hidden* engender distrust, discord, disempowerment and destruction foreclosing hope.[14] Yet, as Deleuze and Guattari point out, *microfascisms* originate from transformative lines of creative resistance and revolution. Their trajectory is not pre-determined. The films remind us that the violence of the past cannot be undone or erased. However, resistance to fascism means the refusal of subjugation to or seduction by fascist power. In the final scenes of *The Raven*, Dr Germain and Denise recognize and celebrate the transformational power of new love; where both had previously considered their outlooks doomed and hopeless, they now look forward to becoming parents and a new life together. In *Hidden*, the implied friendship between the sons of Georges and Majid suggests a transformation of the former colonial and cultural divide. By presenting viewers with the legacy of the agent-less spiral of microfascist violence, the films warn of the vectors of past and indeed future microfascist trajectories within historical and contemporary political discourse. However, they also communicate the potential for a new throw of the dice to make an affirmative break with the past and realize the hope of fostering future freedoms.

Notes

1 *The Raven*, directed by Henri-Georges Clouzot and released in 1943, is a classic film of the Occupation era. It caused controversy across the political spectrum both at the time of its release and after the Liberation and has continued to provoke debate up to the present day. In the film, a spate of poison-pen letter writing creates social divisions in a provincial town. The letters, which sow fear and suspicion, fraying the social fabric of the town and bringing all the members of the municipality into conflict, are all signed 'The Raven'. The film bears loaded, although, of course, prohibited cultural references to the practice of denunciation encouraged by the Nazis. During the Occupation, three million letters of denunciation were received by the German authorities (Halimi 1989).

   Michael Haneke's *Caché* gained considerable critical acclaim for its implicit cultural reference to France's troubled colonial relationship to Algeria and the war of independence. Set in the present day, the presenter of a literary television programme and his family begin to receive videotapes that contain surveillance footage of their house recorded on a hidden camera. The tapes are accompanied by a number of childish violent drawings. The family's sense of security is eroded as the ominous threats create a volatile atmosphere of unpredictability and violence. While the film gained special renown for its shocking depiction of suicide, *Caché* interrogates the effect of past political and cultural violence on present-day life in France. The film makes reference not only to the bloody state-sanctioned suppression of the peaceful demonstration by the FLN, pro-Algerian liberation protestors, by the French police on 17 October 1961, but also to the torture of prisoners at Abu Ghraib by American soldiers and, implicitly, to anti-Arab/Muslim socio-political discourses in France. Haneke's oeuvre is well known for its portrayal of extreme physical and psychological violence. His recent film, *Das Weisse Band* (*The White Ribbon*, 2010), set on the eve of the First World War, explored the generational tension between parents and children in a German village. The film tacitly explores the complex forces that motivated the younger generation towards the fascism of National Socialism. Although *The White Ribbon* provides engaging material for the analysis of fascist aesthetics, this chapter chooses to focus on fascism within the French context as the experience of Nazism in France, invasion and ensuing occupation and collaboration, poses different questions from those that arise from the situation in Germany.

2   Crowley observes: 'Conventional thinking about responsibility – in which responsibility divorced from agency makes no sense – cannot apply, for Duras, after the traumatic event. The delimitation of implication produced by such conventional responsibility in the face of historical trauma (largely along the lines of national identity, as signalled by Duras's confrontational reference to "l'idée d'égalité, de fraternité") is simply inadmissible to Duras as a response to the Holocaust, which must, she insists, be understood at the level of our concept of what it means to be human' (Crowley 2000: 163).

3   'Fascism is inseparable from a proliferation of molecular focuses in interaction, which skip from point to point, before beginning to resonate together in the National Socialist State. Rural fascism and city or neighbourhood fascism, youth fascism and war veteran's fascism, fascism of the Left and fascism of the Right, fascism of the couple, family, school, and office: every fascism is defined by a micro-black hole that stands on its own and communicates with the others, before resonating in a great, generalized central black hole' (Deleuze and Guattari 2004: 236).

4   Paxton's first book, *Vichy France: Old Guard, New Order 1940–1944*, shed new light on the extent of French involvement in the implementation of Nazi policy in France.

5   'The rich and varied repertoire of off-screen spaces constructed by the film opens out in all directions onto unchartered territory which, like the "anti-classical" *hors-champ* analysed by Bonitzer and Deleuze's "radical Elsewhere", is heterogeneous to the space we see, a repository of latent meaning that transcends homogenous space and time' (Saxton 2007: 15).

6   'And, indeed, as he listened to the cries of joy rising from the town, Rieux remembered that such joy is always imperiled. He knew what those jubilant crowds did not know but could have learned from books: that the plague bacillus never dies or disappears for good; that it can lie dormant for years and years in furniture and linen chests; that it bides its time in bedrooms, cellars, trunks, and bookshelves; and that perhaps the day would come when, for the bane and the enlightening of men, it would rouse up its rats again and send them forth to die in a happy city' (Camus 1948: 285).

7   *The Raven* was one of thirty feature films produced between 1941 and 1944 that were financed by Continental Films, a Paris-based collaborationist film production company. The company was directed by Alfred Greven and affiliated to Goebbels's propaganda ministry. It employed French directors and the viewing public were generally unaware that, although legally French, production was controlled and financed by the Germans. Continental Films' counterpart in the unoccupied zone was the Comité d'organisation de l'industrie cinématographique (COIC). Continental had an advantage over the COIC because it was controlled by the Germans and consequently was not subject to the more rigorous censorship of film production operating under Vichy. During his time at Continental, Clouzot wrote the screenplays for the 1941 films *Le Dernier des six* and *Les Inconnus dans la maison*, and directed two films, *L'Assassin habite au 21* (1942) and *Le Corbeau* (1943).

8 *The Raven* received its most virulent attack in a 1944 clandestine Resistance article where critics Georges Adam and Pierre Blanchard compared the film unfavourably with Jean Grimillon's 1944 *Le Ciel est à vous*. They criticized *The Raven* for its negative portrayal of the French populace as petty-minded and backstabbing and for pedalling the implicit message that the values of French society had rotted under the Occupation. They read the film as anti-nationalist propaganda. Julian Jackson observes: 'While *Le Ciel à vous* showed the Resistance and Vichy to be competing up to a point for shared ground, *Le Corbeau*, (*The Raven*), simultaneously disapproved of by the Resistance, Vichy, and the Germans, was disconcerting because it offered no simple answers' (Jackson 2001: 326). Adam and Blanchard's hugely influential article contributed to the film being banned as pro-collaboration propaganda after the Liberation in August 1944 and to Clouzot being suspended from working as a director until 1947. There is still controversy as to whether the film is simply a representation of fascist tendencies during the Occupation or rather a subtle piece of resistance warning against the pervasive dangers of fascism.

9 In French, the word 'histoire' means both history and story.

10 Didier Daeninckx's novel *Meutres pour mémoire*, published in 1985, is widely credited with bringing the memory of this event back into the public domain after over twenty years of cultural repression. The plot revolves around the connection between contemporary politics, the events of 17 October 1961, and the Occupation. D. Daeninckx, *Meurtres pour mémoire* (Paris: Gallimard, 1984).

11 Through the introduction of the 'auctoritas', a Duce or Führer figure who is anomic and metajuridical, who is directly opposed to the normative juridical identity of the 'potestas', and who brings together anomie and nomos, Agamben claims that 'the system transforms itself into a killing machine' – that is to say, a fully fascist operation (Agamben 2005: 86).

12 The claims of Colonel Gaddafi that the 'rebels' involved in the Libyan uprising were either mentally ill or 'foreign elements' under foreign influence offer a recent illustration of this microfascist tendency.

13 'It is only by declaring that we want what conservatism decrees to be impossible, and by affirming truths against the desire for nothingness, that we tear ourselves away from nihilism. The possibility of the impossible, which is exposed by every loving encounter, every scientific re-foundation, every artistic invention and every sequence of emancipatory politics, is the sole principal – against the ethics of living-well whose real content is the deciding of death – of an ethic of truths' (Badiou 2002: 38–39).

14 Deleuze and Guattari quote Fitzgerald: 'I had a feeling that I was standing at twilight on a deserted range, with an empty rifle in my hands and the targets down. No problem set – simply a silence with only the sound of my own breathing ... My self-immolation was something sodden-dark' (Fitzgerald, quoted in Deleuze and Guattari 2004: 253).

References

Agamben, G. *Remnants of Auschwitz: The Witness and the Archive* (New York: Zone, 1999)
——*State of Exception* (Chicago, Ill.: Chicago University Press, 2005)
Alonso, M. 'Collective Identity as a Rhetorical Device' (*Synthesis Philosophica* No.51, 2011, 7–24)
Aron, R. *The Vichy Regime: 1940–1944*, trans. Humphrey Hare (London: Putnam, 1958)
Badiou, A. *Ethics* (London, Brooklyn: Verso, 2002)
Bouchareb, R. (dir.) *Days of Glory* (TFI, 2006)

Camus, A. (1948) *The Plague* (London: Hamish Hamilton).

Cinefilms, 'Michael Haneke on Violence', YouTube. 2010, www.youtube.com/watch?v=VOx3rpkMtY8.

Clouzot, H.-G. (dir.) *Le corbeau* (Optimum Releasing Ltd, 2005)

Crowley, M. *Duras, Writing and the Ethical: Making the Broken Whole* (Oxford: Clarendon Press, 2000)

Deleuze, G. *Cinema 2* (London: The Athlone Press, 1989)

——*Difference and Repetition* (New York: Continuum, 2001)

Deleuze, G. and Guattari, F. *A Thousand Plateaus: Capitalism and Schizophrenia* (London: Continuum, 2004)

Emery, M. 'Europe, Immigration and the Sarkozian Concept of Fraternité' (*French Cultural Studies*, No.21, 2010, 115–29)

Fein, H. *Accounting for Genocide: National Response and Jewish Victimization During the Holocaust* (New York: The Free Press, 1979)

Halimi, A. *La délation sous l'Occupation* (Paris: Éditions 1, 1989)

Haneke, M. (dir.) *Caché* (France: Artificial Eye Sony Pictures Classics, 2005)

——*The White Ribbon* (Artificial Eye, 2010)

Jackson, J. *France: The Dark Years 1940–44* (Oxford: Oxford University Press, 2001)

Jenkins, B. (ed.) *France in the Era of Fascism: Essays on the French Authoritarian Right* (Ottawa: Berghahn Books, 2005)

Kline, T.J. 'The Intertextual and Discursive Origins of Terror in Michael Haneke's Caché', in R. Grundmann (ed.) *A Companion to Michael Haneke* (Malden, MA, and Oxford: Wiley-Blackwell, 2010)

Littell, J. *Les Bienveillantes* (Paris: Gallimard, 2006)

Lloyd, C. *Henri-Georges Clouzot* (Manchester: Manchester University Press, 2007)

Miller, C. (dir.) *Un Secret* [A Secret] (Paris: UCG, 2007)

Murphy, J.P. 'Baguettes, Berets and Burning Cars: The 2005 Riots and the Question of Race in Contemporary France' (*French Cultural Studies* No.22, 2011, 33–49)

Paquet-Brenner, G. (dir.) *Sarah's Key* (Hugo Productions, 2010)

Paxton, R.O. *The Anatomy of Fascism* (London: Penguin Books, 2004)

Rothberg, M. *Multidirectional Memory* (Stanford: Stanford University Press, 2009)

Sansal, B. *Le Village de l'Allemand ou le journal des frères Schiller* (Paris: Gallimard, 2008)

Sartre, J.-P. *L'etre et le néant* (Paris: Gallimard, 1943)

Saxton, L. 'Secrets and Revelations: Off-screen Space in Michael Haneke's Caché (2005)' (*Studies in French Cinema* No.7, 2007, 5–17)

Silverman, M. 'Interconnected Histories: Holocaust and Empire in the Cultural Imaginary' (*French Studies*, lxii, 2008, 417–28)

——'The Violence of the Cut: Michael Haneke and Cultural Memory' (*French Cultural Studies* No.21, 2010, 57–65)

Zizek, S. 'The Ongoing "Soft Revolution"' (*Critical Inquiry* No.30, 2004, 292–332)

Index

200   *Index*

suicide 170, 171; modern political cinema 78, 84–6, 91, 93; molar/molecular dimensions 153; political theatre 85, 92; political theology 60; politics of the novel 37; politics of paranoia 153, 157; politics of technology 60–1; *Waltz with Bashir* 99, 100, 114–18, 120 (protopolitics 100, 106, 110, 113, 117); *see also* biopolitics; cinema and political aesthetics; macropolitics; micropolitics; politics of lines

politics of lines 10–11, 126–47, 148, 149–71; fascism 11, 126, 127, 132, 133, 157, 162; governance 128, 130, 132, 133; lines of creation 126, 127, 130; lines of destruction 126, 127; macro-fascism 127, 132; macropolitics 129, 131; micro-fascism 127, 132; micropolitics 129, 131; molar line 129, 130, 132, 133, 148, 150–5, 157, 164, 165; molecular line 129–30, 131, 148, 150–5, 159, 165–6, 169; movement 126, 127, 129–30, 133, 134, 139–40; political *problematique* 126, 127, 128, 133; security *dispositif* 128, 134, 135–6, 139; segmentarity 129–30, 132, 133; Spinozan ethico-politics of bodies 11, 126, 128, 143–5; suicidal line 11, 132–3, 134, 146, 148, 155–7, 158–9, 161–2, 166–9, 171; *A Thousand Plateaus* 126–7, 128–9, 134, 148; three lines schema 126, 127, 128–34, 148, 149–71; uncertainty 128, 133, 139; unpredictability 126, 127, 137; *see also* governance; lines of flight; milieu; movement

power 181–6; bio-politics 47; fascism and desire of 1, 4, 19; fascism as system of power relations 1, 2, 3, 5, 187; knowledge/power relation 22; 'the power of the false' 10, 97–8, 121; liberal power relations 4; resistance to 47, 127, 145

practice 13–14, 20–6; definition 20, 22; desire/practice relation 23–4, 25–6; fascist practices 8, 21–2, 24–6; Foucault, Michel 13, 22; ideology/practice relation 23–5; knowledge 22–3, 24; normative governance 20–1; norms/fascism relation 22; religious and economic practices 24–5; social nature of 21; volitional and epistemic elements 20, 23–6

pre-emption 9; global triage 69–70, 72, 75; legitimacy 69–70; operating system 70

propaganda: National Socialism 171; propaganda film 30, 182, 192, 193

Protevi, John 149, 150, 158

psychoanalysis 21–2, 46

racism 7, 64, 91, 117, 175; racial supremacy 52

Rancière, Jacques 30, 32, 37, 85

The Raven (*Le Corbeau*) 11–12, 173, 191, 192; clarity 179–80; Clouzot, Henri-Georges 181, 182, 191, 192, 193; Continental Films 182, 192; creative and revolutionary lines of flight 190–1; criticism 182, 193; denunciation 176–7, 179, 180, 188–9, 191; fascist violence 173, 174, 184, 191; fear 176–7; information 180–1; 'insider'/'outsider' dualism 176–7, 184; Nazi Occupation 12, 173, 182, 189, 191; power 181–2, 184–6; suicidal line 188–9; 'surrogate victim' 186; surveillance 176, 177, 179, 182; *see also* France; *A Thousand Plateaus*

Ravetto, Kriss 6, 7, 30, 37

Reich, Wilhelm 13, 42, 43, 73

Reid, Julian 1–12, 78–95; *The Liberal Way of War* 57, 128, 138, 140, 142, 171; logistical life 69

Resnais, Alain 175

responsibility 124, 174, 185, 192; 'agent-less' violence 173, 174, 180, 184; responsibility to protect 49–50; *Waltz with Bashir* 113, 116–19, 123–4, 125

revolution 5, 16, 74, 93, 125; fascism 15, 187; lines of flight 190–1

Riefenstahl, Leni 122; *The Triumph of the Will* 28, 33

Rokeach, Milton 40

Rothberg, Michael 175

Rousseau, Jean-Jacques 14

Sabra and Shatila massacre 97, 112, 114–15, 120, 123; Sharon, Ariel 125; *see also Waltz with Bashir*

Sartre, Jean-Paul 183

Saxton, Libby 177, 183, 185, 192

schizophrenia 157, 158, 160; deterritorialisation 149, 155; Nazism 160, 162; paranoia/schizophrenia dualism 149, 155, 157, 158; schizoanalysis 15, 158, 169;

CPSIA information can be obtained
at www.ICGtesting.com
Printed in the USA
LVHW031549250919
632254LV00006B/438/P

9 781138 840485